INTERNATIONAL STUDIES

of the
Committee on International Relations
University of Notre Dame

INTERNATIONAL STUDIES

WHAT AMERICA STANDS FOR

WHAT AMERICA STANDS FOR

edited by
STEPHEN D. KERTESZ
M. A. FITZSIMONS

UNIVERSITY OF NOTRE DAME PRESS

1959

Library of Congress Catalog Card Number 59-10415

© 1959 University of Notre Dame Press

Notre Dame, Indiana

PREFACE

THE CHAPTERS of this volume were presented and discussed in meetings held at Notre Dame on March 29–30, November 8, 1957, and March 24, 1958. The essays provide only major examples of the values and practices of American politics, culture, and society. The discussions made it clear that many important questions, such as the special role of labor unions or businessmen on the American scene, or the vast social legislation programs, should have been included in this symposium. But the editors also recognized that "What America Stands For" cannot be stated completely, and decided to publish only the topics discussed at the two meetings.

Four of the essays were published in *The Review of Politics:* Professor Johnson's "Freedom, Equality, and Segregation," Vol. XX (April, 1958); Professor Hardin's "American Agriculture," *ibid.;* Dean Burchard's "The Meaning of Architecture," Vol. XX (July, 1958); and Professor Abell's "The Religious Aspect of American Life," Vol. XXI (January, 1959). Professor Fitzsimons' "American Civilization: The Universal and the Unique," has been published in abbreviated form in *Worldview,* Vol. I (January, 1958), and in *Dokumente* (April, 1958).

The editors extend their warm thanks and appreciation to all contributors, whose spirit of cooperation made the symposium possible and the task of the editors enjoyable. We are grateful to Quentin L. Quade, research assistant to the Committee on International Relations, for his resourcefulness and valuable service rendered during the preparation of the symposium.

The Editors

vii

40963

CONTENTS

chapter 1

The Objectives of the Symposium

Stephen D. Kertesz
University of Notre Dame

THE WORK of the Committee on International Relations is concentrated on problems of foreign policy. Our publications and symposia from 1949 to the present have examined primarily major ideological and political forces which influence foreign political trends in the contemporary world. Since in our era domestic political considerations have a significant impact on foreign policy, in the course of our search we have been necessarily confronted with fundamental problems of domestic societies. The right solution of these basic questions means victory or defeat for the democracies in their struggle with totalitarian states, and for this reason our Committee has published several volumes dealing with political problems of democratic governments.

In the broad field of international relations our current concern is the study of the dilemmas which confront all liberal, democratic governments in the process of making and executing foreign policy. In the course of this research and study, we have seen with growing clarity and a sense of urgency that a primary criterion of a successful foreign policy for the United States is the awareness at home and abroad of the meaning of basic American ideas and purposes in the contemporary world.

This problem is of particular importance today when the democratic governments are confronted with truly formidable totalitarian states. While the Soviet world usually appears as a monolithic unity, betraying only occasional cracks in its red walls, the natural by-product of freedom is diversity, diversity filled with real or apparent contradictions. Although in the long run the democratic system of government is more flexible than the totalitarian state, the latter can more easily concentrate efforts in certain specific directions. For example, the Soviet states have placed military power ahead of improving living standards. The successful use of this miltary power can be further enhanced by a surprise factor, since in dictatorships the really important policy decisions are seldom preceded by public discussions or announcements. This difference in procedure between democracies and dictatorships may be of vital significance. Our allies and especially the non-committed world consider developments in the United States and the Soviet Union as a supreme competition which may decisively influence their fate. Soviet success in the field of intercontinental missiles and the launching of two earth satellites caused genuine consternation and bewilderment among our friends on both sides of the Iron Curtain. They felt that we had let them down in a race which they cannot basically influence, but on which their future depends.

Fear of communist expansion has not been without foundation. The declared objective of communism has always been global conquest, and since the second World War the Soviet Union has realized some of its most cherished territorial ambitions. The power situation in Europe and Asia has undergone fundamental transformations, and today communist regimes dominate over 900 million people; that is, more than one-third of the world's population. Furthermore, in four decades an efficient system of general education has attacked with success illiteracy in the Soviet Union, and the U.S.S.R. has become one of the two strongest industrial and military powers. This is an impressive performance. On the other hand, the method of communist expansion, the inhuman cruelty of the system, and the human costs involved in communist achievements are not so generally known. Thus, the achievements encourage the underprivileged to seek answers to their problems in the doctrines of communism and not knowing the price of Soviet progress, there is nothing to discourage them from following Marxist-Leninist-Stalinist dogmas as the truth that will set them free from oppression and poverty. For some unbalanced intellectuals communist doctrines may have the same attraction.

Because of the communist threat, we have been inclined to see the contemporary crisis almost exclusively in the context of the struggle between the Soviet and non-Soviet worlds. This perspective has neglected rampant global nationalism and some of the new social forces reshaping all of human society, thus indirectly strengthening the appeal of communism to anti-colonial movements in Asia and Africa.

While opposition to communism is necessary, opposition in itself is a negative attitude. The great strength of communist ideology and propaganda consists in affirmative answers for all problems. These answers usually contain falsehoods, but they are answers, and the underprivileged peoples on all continents, that is, the great majority of the human race, are eager for a positive answer to their problems.

Soviet success in the field of military technology and sciences have added new elements to the unfavorable picture of the *homo Americanus* in many countries. Americans are characterized and sometimes caricatured as a comfort-loving people whose greatest ambition in life is to have bigger and better cars, color-television sets, deepfreezers, and so on. Our friends are afraid that the American people, amidst the legitimate enjoyment of the highest living standard on the globe, may refuse to make sacrifices which involve a temporary lowering of this standard. Such a state of mind was the overture to doom for several empires in the past and similar attitudes significantly weakened the British and French power position in the 1930's. There is no reason to believe that this will be the case in America. The American system is resilient enough to answer in time the Soviet challenge, and American citizens are farsighted enough to make necessary sacrifices if they are called upon to do so.

Although communist ideology has lost its original impetus and strength, the worldwide communist movement remains a formidable enemy for two reasons. First, it is still supported, directed, and used by one of the two superpowers. Second, even without Russian power and political support it might yet thrive in the Free World as a parasite on the weaknesses of Western civilization and on the political shortcomings of the democracies and of Western statesmanship.

However, at the present stage of human affairs, the attack on the bankrupt communist ideology is not an answer to the problems of the world. Events in Poland and the Hungarian Revolution exploded many aspects of the communist myth. Today the crucial question in man's struggle against misery, ignorance, and oppression is no longer the attraction of communist doctrine but the discovery of and attack on the social, political, and economic problems of the contemporary world. The human race has reached a crossroads. For all its apparent success, the Soviet system has failed in some fundamentals of human relationships but the unsolved problems remain for mankind.

Although the American system is sometimes put forward as a general panacea, it is obvious that American political institutions cannot be transplanted to countries with entirely different political traditions and with greatly differing social-economic conditions. But the American experience, American ideals, and practices can provide some useful examples for all freedom-seeking nations.

In the last two centuries, no other human experience has been so revealing and attractive to liberty-seeking people as the American experiment, called, not without warrant, "the permanent revolution." From the first years of the Republic, many thousands of people of different nationality, faith, and background have been streaming to the American shores. The political system of this country has made possible the fusion of a heterogeneous multitude into the American nation—a republic which has become a symbol of a better future for men everywhere. In the early years of the American Republic Thomas Paine stated with prophetic vision:

> So deeply rooted were all the governments of the old world, and so effectually had the tyranny and the antiquity of habit established itself over the mind, that no beginning could be made in Asia, Africa, or Europe, to reform the political condition of man. Freedom had been hunted round the globe; reason was considered as rebellion; and the slavery of fear had made men afraid to think.
>
> But such is the irresistible nature of truth, that all it asks, and all it wants, is the liberty of appearing. The sun needs no inscription to distinguish him from darkness; and no sooner did the American governments display themselves to the world, than despotism felt a shock, and man began to contemplate redress.

Thomas Paine's 170-year-old words were never more true than in our time when the whole of human society has been threatened by a new, totalitarian form of tyranny.

In this era of dynamic changes in human society we may be justly proud of the living standard of the American people, and of the fact that in America, seven per cent of the world's population is producing about half of the vital world production in goods and services. All these are gratifying circumstances, but it is incomparably more important to carry high the beacon of world leadership in ideas. The United States has been a champion of liberty by tradition and conviction. The Declaration of Independence, the American Constitution, and many pages of American history seem to establish a claim for American leadership not only in material fields but even in basic freedoms and general moral objectives.

The message of the American Revolution was liberty: freedom of thought, expression, worship, and inquiry, and free communication with other peoples. The proclamation of liberty, however, was followed by the acceptance of a well organized authority and order under the new Constitution. Freedoms restricted by constitutional authority and the rule of law made possible a prodigious technical progress and an ever rising living standard. Difficulties experienced in some of the new states established since the second World War demonstrate that freedom alone is not enough but must be supplemented with the safeguards of a well-established constitutional authority.

The freedoms and privileges of an orderly life guaranteed to Americans by a Bill of Rights are cherished aspirations for millions of oppressed human beings to whom a knock on the door may mean a concentration camp or worse. The combination of political freedom, high living standards, and social dynamism in the United States may serve as a practical demonstration to the common man all over the world that he may secure in a democratic constitutional system, the economic and social advantages and cultural progress advertised by the communists, without giving up his liberty and human dignity.

On the other hand, forceful American opposition to communism has created the false impression abroad that contemporary Americanism is essentially a self-defensive attitude of a selfish and highly materialistic society. Nothing could be further from the truth. Few men despise well-being, physical comfort, and other material advantages of life, but the basic characteristic of American society is not materialism. Americans feel deeply the

situation of others, are not indifferent to human suffering anywhere on the globe and respond generously to the outcry of those
in distress. Between 1921 and 1923 the United States organized a
large-scale famine relief in the Soviet Union although not even
diplomatic relations existed between the two countries. Secretary
of Commerce Herbert Hoover, in charge of this most efficient
operation, was strongly anti-Bolshevik. When the relief terminated, the Soviet Government gave a great banquet in the
Kremlin for him and his staff. In their speeches the Russian
leaders said that the American relief saved seventeen to twenty
million lives. On a previous occasion, during the great famine
of 1891–1892, the American people sent five ship-loads of grain
and other gifts to Russia. Similar American relief operations saved
the lives of uncounted millions in the Far East, especially in
China and in other parts of the world. Not selfishness, but humanitarian action and the principle of helping one's fellow man,
particularly the underdog, are characteristic features of the American society. No people in the course of history has ever been
so willing to help and rehabilitate the economies of foreign
nations, including former enemies, as liberally as the North American Republic. Since, however, not all poor nations can be helped
equally, in matters of foreign aid considerations of national policy
play a role in determining allocation.

It is impossible, however, to measure the relative proportions
of materialism and idealism in a society—except in times of
major crisis. It is more important that the American nation has
and has always had a positive message for the world. This
message is not an ideology or coherent doctrine but a continuous
striving for a better life, a process which has lasted since the
establishment of this country. The new nations of the world find
here an example of how to achieve national independence and
economic growth without the loss of freedom and human dignity
which has characterized totalitarian dictatorships.

In order to appraise the situation, we have to realize, first of
all, what the mid-twentieth century is all about and what our
role in it is. We must become accustomed to quick and sometimes
whimsical changes. Break-throughs, short cuts, and concentrations
in certain branches of military technology may change from time
to time the relative strength of the competing political systems.

Military strength is a momentous factor because competition between the Soviet and non-Soviet systems will remain peaceful as long as the Free World is stronger. Military superiority, however, only provides a respite to prepare answers to the fundamental challenges of our age.

Since liberation of the captive nations by military means is not included in the program of the democratic countries, and since it is impossible to convince the communist leaders of the validity of our system, it is necessary to concentrate on problems which can be solved outside the Soviet orbit. Thus the principal American task remains to provide guidance and assistance for the new nations of Asia and Africa without abandoning the old countries of Europe and neglecting the sister republics in Latin America. Success in this effort will not fail to have its impact on developments in communist states. The unity and strength of the Free World thus augmented should work toward the liberation of captive nations and support whatever liberalizing tendencies exist in the Soviet Union and China.

This is a supreme objective. But for cooperation we need mutual understanding. Often enough not only Asia and Africa, but even the Europeans and Latin Americans have difficulties in understanding developments in the United States. In recent years many of the social and economic changes occurring in America have been fundamental, and it is almost miraculous how successfully traditional American concepts have been applied to the rapidly changing conditions of contemporary life. Profound transformations in American society, however, are hardly noticeable in countries where political and social changes usually are carried out through more spectacular, if not violent means. The common roots of civilization and yet the differences in operation of political institutions, which seek similar objectives through different methods, are added sources of misunderstanding between the United States, Europe, and Latin America.

Although diversity is the direct consequence of free development, citizens of leading Western European countries and Americans are often inclined to think of the cultural and political pattern of their own states as the model for other democracies, and often expect to find approaches and conditions elsewhere which are similar to their own. Western Europeans are inclined to judge foreign countries according to their own standards, and Americans usually look at the outside world through American eyes. Thus, the international application of national outlooks becomes a kind of blinkers which often causes much confusion.

Another source of misunderstanding is the temptation to compare American attitudes with policies of other leading powers, particularly with British policies in by-gone decades. It is often overlooked that Great Britain ruled the waves and many shores in an infinitely less complicated world where the leading powers were guided by similar basic values and recognized common standards. In that past period of history totalitarian ideologies had not yet entered upon the scene of world affairs; atomic weapons for mass destruction did not exist and wars were fought for limited objectives.

The United States was suddenly catapulted into a leading position as one of the two superpowers on the ruins of what was known as the Western state system. It is a truism that the United States was unprepared for world leadership. But it is equally true that, in view of the radically changed world conditions and the suddenly unbalanced power situation, no nation was prepared. Some former world powers have perhaps had more experience and professional skill in diplomacy, but their historical traditions and the resulting rigidity of concepts are not always an asset in quickly changing situations. However it may be, American attitudes are scrutinized, criticized, or praised, but more often misunderstood than appreciated, in all corners of the globe.

A leading Italian journalist, Luigi Barzini, Jr., in *Americans Are Alone in the World*, commenting on Western European opinion of the United States, noted:

> Western Europeans do not know the United States. They think it is a country like their own, to be judged according to the same principles. They do not know the great American contradictions, the fatal choice between a noble crusade or utter indifference, the eternal struggle toward completing the forefathers' dream, the refusal to accept the world as it has always been, history as the ancients had known it, human nature as Christ Himself had recognized it. In comparison with the United States, where apparently anything can happen at any moment, Russia sometimes looks like a familiar monster, a huge heartless bureaucratic tyranny, which usually behaves according to its own rules, whose moves can be reasonably predicted. (Pp. 137–138)

Barzini's view, which presents the Soviet Union as a predictable evil and the United States as an unpredictable factor in world politics, is shared by many. For a superficial observer, this view is not without foundation. It is not always easy to grasp the American system, which is not dominated by an over-all ideology. The dynamism of the pluralistic American society operates in a pragmatic way. Although this approach does not lend itself to easy definition, American purposes and the general framework of the American *modus operandi,* with all its virtues and short-comings, can be and should be explained to foreign nations. It is well to keep in mind that despite many transformations on the American scene since the foundation of the Republic, today only the Vatican's and Great Britain's political systems are older than the American Constitution. Among the written constitutions, the American is the oldest. Although American values originate in Western European civilization, there is a distinct American way of life, there are specific American aspirations and ideals.

This means that the United States has a relatively long continuous history, an old and generally respected political system, and well-established values on the basis of which it is possible to clarify, coordinate, and possibly define basic spiritual, political, social, and economic objectives. The Committee on International Relations decided to participate in this important task with the organization of the symposium, *What America Stands For.*

Foreigners and even many Americans are ignorant of the great explosion of growth and of the fundamental social changes which have taken place in the United States particularly since the second World War. Although there are still large areas where improvements could and should be made, it is a fact that the vast majority of American wage-earners actually enjoy the material well-being that Marxist theory promises but communist governments do not deliver to the workers. A wide distribution of national income and of political power has made more workers the effective possessors of private property than in any other social system known to history. This appears clearly from the comparison of real wages earned by workers in the United States and in foreign countries. Thus the picture of the United States promoted in some foreign countries as an anachronistic survival of nineteenth-century capitalism, is entirely erroneous. On the other hand, the high American living standard is well-known on both sides of the Iron Curtain and understandably enough, often becomes a source of envy. At the same time it generates a feeling of satisfaction if not superiority in many Americans. Sometimes the success of American ways inspires a missionary zeal and even attitudes reflecting a superiority complex which, in turn, causes adverse reactions in foreign countries.

The objective of this symposium is to give a significant response to the urgently felt need of presenting major American values and practices and the meaning of contemporary America in political, social, and cultural fields, without at the same time omitting the shortcomings of the American system. It is our earnest hope that this critical appraisal of the United States will be a further step on the difficult road to the evolution of a truly cooperative society of states. This task involves an insight into, and a clarification of American traditions, ideas, and resources, and ultimately the projection of the image of the many sides of America, free from propagandistic slogans, to the world. Since in this period of great change and opportunity most of the nations do not have a satisfactory answer for their own problems, a clear presentation of American ideas, institutions, purposes, and practices would seem to be a brotherly service to the commonwealth of man. Although essays included in this volume have covered a wide variety of areas, certain points are common to all the contributors and we may note some of them.

Several contributors emphasize and illustrate that in this changing world the American Constitution as well as the federal and municipal administrations have responded adequately to the challenges of our time and we may have a reasonable hope that American governmental institutions will be flexible enough for adaptation to future changes. Another reassuring phenomenon is that despite the world-wide trend toward centralization, American self-government and individual freedom are as viable as ever. In this connection we may note that although the requirements of our scientific age have increased the influence of scientists in American government, technocracy does not threaten the United States. The behavior of American scientists is in harmony with the American tradition, and the American political parties through congressional committees and other means give them a political forum.

As diversity and pragmatism permeate the American political scene they characterize the American educational system also. Indeed, the dynamism and growth which all European observers notice in American educational institutions provide another demonstration of the American attitude toward the rapidly changing problems of our age as well as a demonstration of the attempt to seek solutions through the pragmatic approach in the context of the diverse American way of life. Although the American educational system has very serious weaknesses, it not only affords greater scope for creative minds, but gives youth a far wider range of choice than is made available in the more rigid educational systems of the Old World.

The important role of organized religion on the American scene corresponds to the moral seriousness of American society which receives expression in American literature as well. Both religious concepts and letters reveal that Americans take their ideals, principles, and responsibilities seriously.

It is clear that the changing American scene is not without stable values and ideals, such as belief in the American brand of democracy. Most of the papers unfold an optimistic view of the future and an unshaken belief in the American way of life and in the American solutions of contemporary difficulties. The optimism with which even difficult issues are presented expresses confidence in the future of America and mankind as a whole. The inclination to anticipate a favorable outcome of events is a healthy approach; it is a manifestation of a positive attitude without which no nation can survive and no goals can be achieved. This does not mean, however, that the contributors to this volume are unaware of the shortcomings of the American system, the necessity of reforms, and the staggering problems that confront our generation.

They recognize that in the contemporary world an unusual burden falls to the United States. The burden may be defined as follows: we must become clearer about America's impact on the world, and accept a considerable measure of responsibility for that impact. On the one hand, that is particularly difficult for us to do, because since the establishment of the Republic Americans have been primarily preoccupied with domestic affairs. But a large part of American influence abroad comes directly from our domestic life, the American standard of living, which American wealth and dynamism, advertisements, movies, gigantic cars —all completely unofficial and sometimes untoward exports— have presented to foreign nations. On the other hand, it is clear that in spite of our domestic preoccupations, a powerful American tradition, extending from the Declaration of Independence to our own time, proclaims universal political affirmations. The American creed is a belief in the fundamental rights and liberties of all men, in the equality of all men, and in spite of glaring difficulties, in the universal validity of democracy, in the principle that people can rule themselves. Abraham Lincoln stated: "Our Declaration of Independence meant liberty not alone for the people of this country but hope for all the world for all future time. It means in due course the weight should be lifted from the shoulders of all men."

This universal character of the American creed does not imply a determination to impose American standards and values on other nations—whatever the attractions of the American way of life and the potentials inherent in the American system may be. Conditions of life, natural resources, historical and social background are very different in the various parts of the globe. American economic and industrial methods and the American form of social justice cannot be transplanted in their totality into other parts of the world. We should reconcile ourselves to the fact that many undeveloped countries will always be poor for want of natural resources, due to climatic and other causes, and that even those with resources may progress haltingly. To be sure, these countries can and should be taught to benefit from our technological experience. But they must be taught realistically; the less fortunate nations cannot be expected to follow the same path we have pursued; rather they must follow the path marked by their tradition, incorporating into this tradition new features which will substantially benefit their societies.

Although the American nation in its unsought position of world leadership is deeply concerned with fostering peace and stability, it is also a source of global restlessness and confusion. On account of the uncertainties and imprecision of American political thought —a by-product of pragmatism—our friends abroad often do not understand American attitudes and sometimes think that the United States is marking time in a period of great opportunity.

An additional difficulty is that the American Constitution established an unusually complicated system of formulating foreign policy, mainly because of the important no-man's land between presidential and congressional powers and because of the many congressional powers without corresponding responsibilities.

Proclaimed principles which are not followed up by purposeful political actions, and policies the likely results of which are not thought through, may become particularly harmful. Foreign policies initiated under the impact of domestic considerations may create lasting trouble and may even cause havoc in international relations.

Here, the moral imperative of accepting responsibility for officially declared principles and for American policies, and the calculation of interest coincide to suggest that we must in some measure try to guide the effects of America's impact on the world. Sometimes moderation in words, and serenity in policies, are the better part of wisdom, if not an imperative necessity for a world power.

Above all, we must strengthen the universally attractive characteristics of American life with spiritual depth. This is all-important, for the price we have had to pay for abundance and astonishing mobility and adaptability to changes is a curious rootlessness and restlessness. The consequence of this has been a tendency to become superficial and in some measure irresponsible in our social and foreign relations.

In discussing American ideas, traditions, and resources, we should look at our own system with a critical attitude and humility. We have to recognize the necessity of compromises with the rest of mankind and we should be filled with understanding and charity when assessing the virtues and shortcomings of other nations. Although most of our contributors are inspired by an optimistic outlook and vigorously express their belief in American institutions and practices, this symposium is in part an exercise in self-criticism. Optimism for the final outcome of human issues, faith in the success of the American struggle for a better world, and a realistic self-criticism, are all necessary for the preservation of the intrinsic values of the American political system and way of life.

part I

POLITICS

chapter II

The Living Constitution

Jerome G. Kerwin
University of Chicago

THE MOST optimistic member of the Constitutional Convention of 1789, Gouverneur Morris, predicted that the new constitution would last about seventy-five years. We have no record of the opinion of the most pessimistic member. Some members, we are told, went forth in disgust before the Convention adjourned, and breaking the rule of secrecy, began an energetic campaign against the adoption of the proposed fundamental law. Undoubtedly there were a few members of the Convention who would have been glad to have seen the new constitution go down to defeat. "Nor can it be decided," writes Professor Homer C. Hockett, "whether the people at large favored or opposed the Constitution. Since the ballot was so restricted, any attempt to arrive at popular opinion is almost pure conjecture." [1]

To many it was an unsatisfactory bundle of compromises, "extorted," as John Quincy Adams later said, "from the grinding necessity of a reluctant nation." [2] If Patrick Henry, in refusing to serve as a member of the Convention smelt a rat, others with a less keen sense of smell found the list of delegates chosen to serve worthy of little confidence. One contemporary wrote: "I do not wish to detract from their merits, but I will venture to affirm that twenty assemblies of equal number might be collected, equally acceptable both in point of view of ability, integrity, and patriotism. Some of the characters which compose it I revere: others I consider of small consequence, and a number are suspected of being great defaulters, and to have been guilty of

1 *Constitutional History of the United States* (New York, 1939), p. 220.
2 *Jubilee of the Constitution* (New York, 1839), p. 55.

17

notorious peculation and fraud, with regard to public property in the hour of our distress." [3] One can only surmise what this contemporary would have said if he had wished "to detract from their merits." With the source of the document suspected by many, with indifference toward the work of the convention fairly prevalent, and with the feeling among defenders of the document that something less than a satisfactory piece of work had been accomplished, it may confidently be asserted that the adoption of the Constitution of the United States was one of the major miracles of the eighteenth century.

The finished document as presented to the states, if prosaic, nevertheless was practical. Like many a practical performance it did not arouse enthusiasm. What orderly arrangement it possessed was due to the labors of James Wilson and Gouverneur Morris who took a "hodgepodge of resolutions" and formed them into a presentable proposal. In substance it showed that experience was the mother of its invention. During the Convention one delegate had warned: "Experience must be our only guide. Reason may mislead us." It is no wonder that Professor Farrand could write: "No document originating as this had and developed as this had been developed could be logical and even consistent. That is why every attempted analysis of the Constitution has been doomed to failure. From the very nature of its construction the Constitution defies analysis upon a logical basis." [4] Considering the fate of the numerous constitutions of France promulgated during and following the French Revolution—documents drawn up with the utmost respect for reason and logic—we may be thankful that the framers of our own Constitution displayed that measure of practical wisdom which Aristotle had warned lies at the base of all politics. The framers did not regard it as a model document. "This paper (the Constitution)," wrote Robert Morris to a friend, "has been the subject of infinite investigation, disputation, and declamation. While some have boasted it as a work of Heaven, others have given it a less righteous origin. I have many reasons to believe that it is the work of plain honest men, and such, I think, it will appear."

3 P. L. Ford, *Pamphlets on the Constitution of the United States* (Brooklyn, N.Y., 1888), p. 115.
4 Max Farrand, *Framing of the Constitution* (New Haven, 1913), p. 201.

How could this document, unsatisfactory but acceptable to Washington and Hamilton, much less satisfactory to Jefferson, completely unsatisfactory to some heroes of the Revolution, and as it would have been to some of our friends today because it does not mention God, find acceptance among the thirteen states? It was largely a case of take it now and change it later. Washington put it in these words: "As a constitutional door is open for amendment hereafter, the adoption (of the Constitution) under the present circumstances of the Union, is in my opinion desirable." Or again: "The people . . . can . . . decide with as much propriety on the alterations and amendments which are necessary, as ourselves. I do not think we are more unified, have more wisdom, or possess more virtue, than those who will come after us." Hamilton, while favoring the new Constitution, agreed with many who did not like particular provisions. In the *Federalist* (No. 83) he wrote: ". . . particular provisions, though not altogether useless, have far less virtue and efficacy than are commonly ascribed to them." The framers were well aware, too, that instruments of reform in one age may be sources of political evil in another.

The agonizing experience of the states under the Articles of Confederation constituted a second good reason for the adoption of the new Constitution. As Washington exclaimed during those days of political and economic chaos: "Who but a Tory could have predicted this?" If the new document but remedied the defects of the Articles, many argued, it would be worth a trial.

A third reason for the acceptance of the new form of government was the silence of the fundamental law on some controversial questions such as national suffrage, and the generality of the provisions. Strong government advocates such as Hamilton were convinced that generality meant growth and the necessary flexibility to meet changing conditions. Many generations later Woodrow Wilson was able to say: "The Constitution of the United States is not a mere lawyer's document, it is a vehicle of life, and its spirit is always the spirit of the age."

It is in this sense that I speak of the living Constitution. Had flexibility not been inherent in the Constitution it is questionable whether Gouverneur Morris' estimate of a life span of seventy-five years would have been realized. There is no "magic in the written word, apart from the situations of which it is a part," wrote the late Professor Charles E. Merriam. And he continued: "Words it is true, have their own peculiar symbolic power which must not be underestimated, but the symbolism itself is of little value if it is not representative of what is socially living and active. There is nothing so dead as a dead symbol." [5] Chief Justice Waite put it another way in 1877 in the *Pensacola Telegraph Case,* in speaking of the Commerce clause:

> The powers thus granted are not confined to the instrumentalities of commerce, or the postal system known or in use when the Constitution was adopted but they keep pace with the progress of the country, and adapt themselves to the new developments of times and circumstances. They extend from the horse with its rider to the stagecoach, from the sailing vessel to the steamboat, from the coach, and the steamboat to the railroad, from the railroad to the telegraph, as these new agencies are successively brought into use to meet the demands of increasing population and wealth. They are intended for the government of the business to which they relate, at all times and under all circumstances. (96 U.S. 1)

In other words the generalities of law like the principles of ethics are objectively conceived but must be subjectively applied if they are to subserve human needs and ends. I do not mean to say that the stretching of meaning may not reach the breaking point; in the last analysis the genius of a people for self-government and the preservation of their liberties must be the bulwark against irrational action. If the ability to apply wisely the written word to changing circumstances is lacking in a state, no written constitution can last through the storms that periodically break in the affairs of men and nations. In the 1830's De Tocqueville wrote:

> In examining the Constitution of the United States, which is the most perfect federal constitution that ever existed, one is startled by the variety of information and the amount of discernment that it presupposes in the people whom it is meant to govern. The government of the Union depends almost entirely on legal fictions; the Union is an ideal nation, which exists so to speak, only in the mind, and whose limit and extent can only be discerned by the understanding.[6]

5 Charles E. Merriam, *The Written Constitution and the Unwritten Attitude* (New York, 1931), p. 12.
6 *Democracy in America* (Henry Reeve Text—revised, New York, Alfred A. Knopf, 1953), I, pp. 166–167.

Judges, legislatures, executives, and electorate have through the years discerned the limitations and the possibilities of the federal fundamental law. Throughout the years of the life of the Republic some have felt we have sacrificed stability for mobility, others have felt that this process has been reversed. But after a hundred and sixty-eight years, the Constitution of the United States stands as the oldest of written documents governing the destiny of a free people. From a hodgepodge of ill-assorted resolutions, cleverly but not logically pieced together, it has become a *living* symbol of free government.

How interesting it is to trace the evolution of our fundamental law! In the first days of the Republic Congress set up a national bank otherwise not provided in the Constitution, and the Supreme Court, watchdog of the document, approved and set its seal of approval upon a doctrine of broad, implied powers. Jefferson, defender of strict interpretation, wrestled with the problem of acquiring new territory—nowhere mentioned in the Constitution, but in the purchase of the Louisiana territory he decided to "do sub-silentio what shall be found necessary." Monroe to the disgust of an insistent Congress vetoed a bill for the expenditures of federal funds for internal improvements on constitutional grounds which his successors approved without question. Until Jackson's time the presidential veto was used against Congressional acts of doubtful constitutionality but Jackson informed the country he would wield the veto on legislation he considered unwise. Yet even with all the cries of dictatorship in Jackson's time De Tocqueville wrote "that when he (the President) is at the head of the government, he has but little powers, little wealth, and little glory to share among his friends." [7] But the same author foresees the circumstances of the growth of executive power:

> It is chiefly in its foreign relations that the executive power of a nation finds occasion to exert its skill and strength. If the existence of the Union were perpetually threatened, if its chief intents were in daily connection with those of other powerful nations, the executive government would assume an increased importance in proportion to the measures expected of it and to those which it would execute.[8]

7 *Ibid.*, p. 129.
8 *Ibid.*, p. 126.

And this we have seen come to pass. But executive power has been strengthened by internal crises as well. Facing Civil War Abraham Lincoln declared that if necessary he would break the Constitution to save the nation's life. And within the memory of many are the drastic measures of the New Deal, with all the executive power therein incorporated, adopted to save the nation from economic collapse. Expansion of federal powers moved slowly but none the less surely in the second half of the nineteenth century with the control of business and commerce and in the promotion of railroad building. Yet the movement was not all in one direction, for seventy years ago when Texas was suffering from severe drought Congress appropriated funds to help several stricken counties. President Cleveland vetoed the measure with these words: "I can find no warrant for such an appropriation in the Constitution. . . . Federal aid in such cases encourages the expectation of parental care on the part of the government and weakens the sturdiness of our national character." Were it today we might ask: "Does severe and continued drought strengthen the national character?" In passing we might note that in that same drought-afflicted area of the present day we have spent 550 million dollars of federal money.

In Theodore Roosevelt's time came the empiric theory of constitutional interpretation. According to this theory Congress should not debate endlessly about the constitutionality of any legislation. If the need existed for this legislation, the Supreme Court could attend to the question of constitutionality. Theodore Roosevelt declared that as executive he would take any action in any specific case if the Constitution did not specifically deny him the power. A twilight zone existed, he held, between the power granted to the states and that granted to the federal government; in such a zone the federal government could act. This the Supreme Court refused to accept. He did, however, find enough power in the Constitution for federal control of our natural resources to an extent that the framers had not even dreamed of.

Woodrow Wilson further extended federal control over the banking system and over business for the protection of the people. The country for the first time experienced to the full extent the power of a president in emergency and war. The federal controls over labor and social relations, business, and the farmer under the New Deal and Fair Deal are of too recent history to recite. While Franklin Roosevelt and Truman fought for and established the principle of welfare democracy, Eisenhower, it is said, has made this principle respectable in his theory of "Modern Republicanism." And in the field of foreign relations no president has insisted upon a more liberal interpretation of the power of the executive in foreign affairs than the present Chief Executive.

The Constitution has grown by judicial interpretation, by legislation, and by extension of executive power, especially during emergencies. Its greatness lies not alone in its distinct and definite provisions, but in those parts which may be applied to changing conditions and times. One cannot get all the answers to constitutional questions from the constitution itself or by reference to the intention of the framers. The framers in some cases did not have the same intention supporting the same articles. Professor William Anderson has said:

> In the very first national administration and in the first Congress serious questions arose for which the Constitution had no obvious answer. Has the President alone the power to remove officers whom he has appointed with Senate consent? May he declare the nation's neutrality in a foreign war, when the United States has a treaty of mutual assistance and defense with one of the belligerents? May Congress charter a United States bank, levy a protective tariff, or provide for national assumption of state debts? Has the Supreme Court the power to pass on the constitutionality of acts of Congress?
>
> To none of these or various other questions that arose did the Constitution or the utterances of the framers provide any clear and specific answer (and most of the framers were still living). As each issue arose the Congress and the President at the time had to work out their own answers. In this they, and the Supreme Court, too, soon became participants in the continuous process of making and remaking the Constitution to meet the needs of the time. This is a process that goes on today and will continue in the future.[9]

True, some things can be learned from the intention of the framers, but where in these there is vagueness and the letter of the law lacks clarity, the wisdom of each generation must make its own prudential decision. The Americans had inherited from their English forebears a tradition of "the inevitability of grad-

9 W. Anderson, *The Nation and the States, Rivals or Partners?* (Minneapolis, 1955), p. 66.

ualness" in matters governmental. They believed in the value of traditional concepts applied with common sense to immediate problems. Government was to protect and promote the temporal welfare of living beings. They would agree with Plato that the state was a nest and not a cage. Government was not conceived by them as a strait-jacket that would break with each strain, but a flexible instrument of growth which would meet the urgent needs of an expanding social order.

While the Civil War put an end to the idea of the sovereign states, the dispute goes on as to the place of the states in the Union. No one now argues that the United States is a loose confederation of states with a right existing in each state to withdraw from the Union. Academicians may argue over the question of whether a constitutional amendment depriving the state of its equal representation in the Senate, would not break the compact of union, but no one else worries about what in the long foreseeable future may never happen. We are hearing of a doctrine of interposition (first proclaimed in New England during the War of 1812) according to which a state may refuse to enforce within its borders a federal law or a decision of the Supreme Court. While not proclaimed as a doctrine some states to all intents and purposes followed this line during prohibition days. But like the poor, the cry of states' rights is destined to be always with us. In this connection it is of interest to note what Hamilton thought would be the cost of running a state government. Writing in *The Federalist* (No. 34) he said: ". . . in a short course of time the wants of the States will reduce themselves within a very narrow compass . . . the only revenue of any consequence, which the State governments will continue to experience will be for the mere support of their respective civil lists; to which if we add all contingencies, the total amount in every State ought to fall considerably short of two hundred thousand pounds." In terms of today's value of the pound this would be about $4,300,000 for each of the states. The budget of the State of New York in 1957 was about one billion three hundred and fifty million dollars. This would not indicate certainly that the states were losing many governmental functions. James Madison referred to the states as "subordinately useful." As a matter of simple fact with the growth of all governmental power the states are more powerful today than they have ever been. The size of state budgets should be convincing evidence of this. In no federal union are the individual units or states as powerful as the states in the American union. Yet the power of the federal government has grown, sometimes at the expense of the states, through the recognition of national problems that can only be dealt with on a national basis, or, if statements at a recent conference of governors may be believed, because of the regrettable inefficiency of state governments. Nor do the same people always fall on the same side in this dispute over state versus federal power. Not so many years ago representatives of large corporations seriously considered making the federal government the collector of taxes in order to avoid the chaos of differing taxing systems. These same people, however, would have spurned federal control in other spheres.

When problems press upon people or communities they will normally seek help where they can find it. To look to a central source for help, a source up and beyond the local community is common throughout the land. This will often involve an appeal from the city to the county or to the state, or even to the Federal Government. Urgent problems are more real to people than long-established theories.

Some years ago in the region about Chicago, the popularly elected members of the Board of Trustees of the Sanitary District went to Washington to petition for permission to increase the flow of water from Lake Michigan through the Chicago River. Involving navigable waters of the United States and in addition a treaty between our government and the government of Canada, this was a federal question. The trustees, spurning the shorter route to Washington, decided to go by way of New York. The stop-over in New York afforded an excellent opportunity for a large, prolonged, and boisterous party at the Waldorf-Astoria. The interest of the trustees, at least, for the moment, was not in the flow of water. The noisy party was held at the tax-payers' expense. At once a clamor arose among the voters of the Sanitary District to change the method of choice of the trustees from popular election to appointment by the Governor. In other words, many of the voters were willing to trade local autonomy for supposedly disinterested selection by the state executive.

I do not mean to say that an action of this kind is always un-
justified. Often the people of a community do not have the
necessary power to remedy a local evil. Recently it has been
recommended that an office of local government of full cabinet
rank be set up within the Federal Government with various
powers over municipal affairs. Why does this cry arise in a country
which prides itself on the vitality of its local governments? The
cities of our country, particularly the large urban areas, are
plagued with problems of finance, police, planning, drainage,
water supply, transportation, and housing. The state legislatures,
for the most part rurally controlled, have neglected to aid in the
solution of these pressing problems even when they have had
the means to do so. Matters of this kind involve the health and
welfare of millions of people. The metropolitan communities are
also plagued by the jealousies and obstructive tactics of surround-
ing suburban towns. Without the power or the financial resources
to solve their difficulties, the large cities are looking to the Federal Government for help. Already large grants of federal money
have been given them for housing and the more recent demand
is for assistance in solving the transportation problem. Some authorities on local government have long advocated the creation
of new states of the Union out of these large metropolitan areas.
It is a problem that may not be ignored and the failure of state
governments to deal with it will increase the pressure for federal
action. Where the relief is, there the people will go.

It is always well to remember that no strict, distinct line between state and central government can be drawn today—if it
ever could have been drawn. It was Madison who wrote in *The
Federalist* (No. 46):

> The federal and state governments are in fact but different agents and
> trustees of the people, constituted with different powers and designed for
> different purposes. The adversaries of the Constitution seem to have lost
> sight of the people altogether in their reasonings on this subject; and to
> have viewed these different establishments, not only as mutual rivals and
> enemies, but as uncontrolled by any common superior in their efforts to
> usurp the authorities of each other. These gentlemen must here be re-
> minded of their error. They must be told that the ultimate authority,
> wherever the derivation may be found, resides in the people alone, and
> that it will not depend merely on comparative ambition or address of the
> different governments, whether either or which of them, will be able to

enlarge its sphere of jurisdiction at the expense of the other. Truth no less than decency requires that the event in any case should be supposed to depend on the sentiments or sanctions of their common constituents.

The trend toward greater central control has been a world-wide phenomenon for the past seventy-five years in all countries. This movement has been inevitable. Rapid means of communication have tied distant parts of all countries more closely together. It is no longer, as it was in 1776, a journey of three days from New York to Washington. It is now only a matter of hours from one end of this country to the other. In the early days of this country a New England town supplied most of the necessities of life for the people living therein. Today every community depends in large part upon commerce from distant parts of the Union to keep it alive. Economically the United States is one. Important general concerns of the public cannot wait upon the decisions of all fifty states. The noteworthy thing still remains, however, that in this country more local self-government remains—dynamic and effective—than in any other civilized power on the face of the globe. A defensible case could be made for the person who looking at the distribution of powers in our federal union would marvel not at extent of federal power but at the restrictions still imposed, respected, and observed in federal action. When Madison in *The Federalist* wrote that too many opponents thought of the different levels of government as rivals rather than partners responsible to the same superior, he gave the key to the underlying element in many of the disputes that rage today over the respective spheres of national government and the states. As a matter of fact many functions, and perhaps there will be an increasing number, are performed in partnership. Despite contrary views members of Congress represent states or districts and are in no hurry to hand over their constituencies lock, stock, and barrel to the federal government. On the contrary, a more critical view of our Congress represents it as composed of members who are too local-minded as against the demands of the national interest. In the recent dispute on the off-shore oil fields, nothing that was said in favor of aiding education, or observing party platforms, or reasoning of the Supreme Court could drag the representatives from the off-shore oil states away from protection of their local bailiwicks. It should also be remembered that every attempt to bring about a greater degree of party discipline and party regularity in the Congress runs right up against the prevailing sentiment of responsibility to the local constituency. In truth, for that reason it cannot be said that we have national political parties in the United States. We have a loose federation of regional and local political groups under two different national labels. A program for any situation that means the surrender of local power or local control must have behind it a strong national backing promoted by an overriding necessity. Looking back over the history of the United States I am impressed not by our profligacy in the surrender of local power but by our shrewd maintenance of a balance of power between the two spheres of government. Especially with the events of recent years am I impressed, for we live in a time when one is sorely put to it to think of any problem of government that does not have national implications.

An editorial in *The New Republic* (September 30, 1957) explains inter-governmental relations in the United States as follows:

> Our government, to be sure, consists of discrete institutions—States and the Union, the Executive, Congress, the Judiciary. But all effectiveness depends upon their involvement with each other, their intimacy, even if it is sometimes the intimacy of creatures locked in battle. For they are revolutionary institutions, invented by men whose stance was one of protest and wariness of power, and they were each equipped intentionally with serious infirmities. It may be safely posited that none is by *itself* capable of attempting any purpose that may lie within its own formally prescribed area of competence. Singly they may always be frustrated. And so it was meant to be. Therein is the safeguard. But effective operation requires working together.

We have big business, we have big labor, we have big cities, we have big domestic social problems, undeniably we have big problems of foreign relations—in fact we are not averse to boasting of our bigness. Yet the result inevitably follows that government, the supreme social institution, will reflect that character of the society in which it is established.

I am not insensible to the danger lurking in too much centralization nor ignorant of the principle of subsidiarity. In any new problem where centralization is called for, the burden of proof should be placed upon the advocates of centralization. The good citizen should be as vigilant in matters of this kind as in all matters of public concern. And while it has been said many times it bears repeating, that important questions in the sphere of government operation can not be settled on the basis of slogans—such as "states' rights," "bureaucracy," or "socialism." A calm and judicious application of theory to existing conditions rules out both the dreamer and the crusader in the solution to problems of this kind.

The price of union involves the sacrifice of local power and local interests. There is only *one* United States. But unfortunately the thinking of some people has not advanced beyond the era of the Articles of Confederation when state sovereignty almost wrecked our hardly won independence. A federal union supplanted the loose-jointed confederation and the founders of that union were prudent enough to draw no hard-set lines of distinction between state and federal spheres. True, the powers of the Federal Government are enumerated but for the most part along general lines as one look at the commerce clause will show. What they did not contrive in flexibility of provisions, an early Chief Justice of the United States, Marshall, added by judicial decision.

Whatever expansion in state-federal relations has taken place in our fundamental law, an equally great expansion has taken place in the understanding of and the exercise of the powers of the president. Professor Edward Corwin has said: "What the presidency is at any particular moment depends in important measure on who is President." [10] Of the thirty-three men who have been president, some have been mediocre, some have been made great by the responsibility of the office, some have been strong presidents, some have been great statesmen. In the 1880's Lord Bryce in *The American Commonwealth* devoted a chapter to the problem: "Why Great Men are not Chosen President." It is true that the mediocre men have outnumbered the great men. But no president has been guilty of that extreme corruption which has debased the heads of many countries throughout history. Yet if many have been mediocre, some have been in every sense of the term great and inspiring leaders. Even the mediocre have at times

10 E. S. Corwin and L. W. Koenig, *The Presidency Today* (New York, 1956), p. 28.

been made great by the very majesty of the office. The modern strong presidency as an office may be said to date from Theodore Roosevelt. The varying crises of war and depression have expanded greatly the power and prestige of the office during the present century. Most of the presidents of this era have fulfilled the prime qualities for a president which Hamilton listed in *The Federalist:* "energy . . . unity . . . decision . . . activity . . . secrecy, and despatch."

In no part of the Constitution can anyone find an adequate description of what the office means today. In broad general phrases the office is described; what is made of the office depends upon acts of Congress, time and circumstances, and the person who occupies it. Nothing in all history is more interesting than the problem of executive power. At all times men have realized the need of power and responsibility in the office and for a wide area of ill-defined action for the protection of the common good at home and the safety of the state abroad.

The political philosophy of the Middle Ages is replete with discussions of the power of the monarch. He is variously described as being "above the law of the State, the source of the law of the State as well as the fountainhead of all justice." He is sometimes described as partaking of the priesthood and Charlemagne has been pictured in the vestments of a priest. What of the checks that should be placed upon him? Because of the responsibilities that are his, the checks for the most part have had to be self-imposed. Commentators of the Middle Ages contended that he should observe the Divine and the Natural Laws and the customs of the realm, but that the restrictions should be self-imposed. As the structure of government developed, institutions and legal methods evolved imposing restrictions, but the heads of state to this day exercise great areas of power and in some degree remain judges of their own acts. Witness the unaccountability of our own president to the courts of the land while he remains in office.

In the United States the military, the diplomatic, and the economic problems which confront us now and in the future call for a most effective executive. The power he may exercise by personality alone far exceeds anything written in the law. Modern inventions have given him means of persuasion and control through radio and television and rapid means of travel such as the Founding Fathers never dreamed of. At any time of the day he may by modern means of communication come into our homes and inform, persuade, and warn. Contact with the head of the state is now more immediate than at any previous time.

There are dangers to this immediate influence of personality as Louis Koenig points out:

> The present-day setting of the Presidency invites a return of . . . mediocrity to the office. Television puts a new premium on affability. The winsome grin and mellifluous tonality do wonders for the presidential candidate. The uncertainties of our nuclear age bring new mass stirrings of the father complex which makes anxious people over-value the President as he appears and under-critical of him as he really is. These and other forces contribute to a major danger of the modern Presidency, that personality will become a substitute for policy.[11]

In the last analysis "the President," says Woodrow Wilson, "is at liberty both in law and in conscience to be as big a man as he can."

While the Congress, as already pointed out, serves local constituencies, the president has only one constituency—the whole people. He is the unifying force. Should he, however, fail to exercise strong leadership, the Congress becomes a parliament of competing blocs or submits to the dictates of an inner oligarchy. There are, to be sure, three major branches of government, but only the executive can furnish leadership. People will always complain of rubber-stamp Congresses and dictator presidents during the incumbency of strong executives but these same executives have educated the public, have led the public, have stirred the imagination of the public, and have rarely failed to secure the support of the public.

No country has found means of expressing itself to the world except through the executive office. In the United States it was early recognized that the only spokesman for the nation could be the president or his delegates. As the nation has assumed a greater role in world affairs the president has logically assumed or been delegated more power. The delicate and involved matters of foreign policy do not lend themselves on all occasions to prolonged debate and public discussion. At all times the president

11 L. W. Koenig, "The Man and the Institution," *Annals of the American Academy of Political and Social Science*, Vol. 307 (September, 1956), 13.

must have an area of maneuverability to meet the challenges of the country's foe. Especially is this true if complete secrecy shrouds the moves of our opponents. In the rapidly moving events of the present day, it is utterly impossible for the president to call for Congressional consent in every decision he makes. One member of Congress in commenting upon President Eisenhower's request for power to act in the Middle East called it a request for a delayed declaration of war. And some have complained that the power already inherently existed in the presidential office and that the President was simply asking Congress to shoulder a responsibility which was primarily his. No president will lightly throw the country into war these days. Congress is bound to watch and to criticise, but the final responsibility is the president's. In every case of public policy—foreign and domestic—the last word is with the president. This whole ideal was succinctly and aptly expressed by the sign on former President Truman's desk: "The buck stops here."

The growth of the presidency as an institution is amply indicated by the rise of the presidential staff. Since the creation of the Bureau of the Budget in 1921 through the rise of the National Security Council, the Council of Economic Advisers, and the Office of Defense Mobilization the presidential staff has grown to over 1200 people. "They exist," says Professor Koenig, "solely to serve the President, to see that he is adequately and currently informed, to assist him in foreseeing problems and planning future programs and to ensure that matters for his decision reach his desk promptly and in condition to be settled intelligently and without delay." [12]

America may not boast of great political philosophers. Some have even contended that there is no political philosophy that is distinctly American. In the strict sense the framers of the Constitution were not political philosophers. Unlike the people who approved the Declaration of Independence who appealed to a law of nature above the law of man to justify rejection of one political authority, the framers of the Constitution were called upon to construct a framework of government. Certainly principles of political philosophy are found in the Constitution, such as the separation of powers (not exactly stated as such), the due

12 *Ibid.,* 14.

process clauses, and the various protective measures for the citizens. During periods of great revolutionary upheaval people turn more for defense of their causes to eternal values. But the Revolution had already won America its independence when the Constitution was written, and a job of construction was now imperative. From the day-to-day experience which most of the framers had had as state officials, they drew the plans for the new government. They took the traditional philosophy for granted even though the Age of the Enlightenment and the confused philosophy of John Locke had in some measure corrupted it. The Constitution itself describes a free, popularly responsible commonwealth. To the framers it may have meant a republic. To Jackson it meant a representative democracy. Harsh critics said the two Roosevelts claimed it as a personal fief. In modern times it is frequently described as a welfare democracy. But the Constitution itself gives it no name except a union. Some years ago the late Charles E. Merriam gave a series of lectures entitled: "The Written Constitution and the Unwritten Attitude." In lively style he compared the written document with the development in interpretation and application of the text. His main thesis is put in these words: "Each generation makes a new spirit, a new constitution, a new way of doing things political, a new set of understandings as to what should be done for the common good by the government." And this has been the cause of our political success. Before this Republic had reached its twenty-fifth birthday the industrial revolution had begun to change the economic and social life of the western world. In no country was the advance of industrialization more rapid than in the United States. So common had change and movement become, that people came to think of change in all things as the order of the day. A man born in 1820 and living his three score years and ten would have seen more change in the material ways of living and in the rapid flow of inventions than any man living a like span of life ever would have seen in any previous period of history. Until 1900 only fifteen amendments had been added to the Constitution and ten of these were almost concurrent with the adoption of the Constitution itself. The turbulent twentieth century has brought seven more—two of these deal with prohibition, its enactment and repeal. To me this cautious pace in the change of the fundamental law has been due to the flexibility of the original document and to the prudence of a mature citizenry. While a watchful guard must always be kept over the American charter, I see no present reason for the alarm of some people fearing as they do that we are about to or already have torn the Constitution to bits.

The times ahead bristle with challenges. The problems appear overwhelming. The problems raised by mass education, urbanism, science, automation, and world-wide instability seem staggering. As the Constitution has stood the rapid changes of the past, I feel sure that it will be wisely adapted to fit the changes of the future. Change to us is less a phenomenon than it was to the generations before World War I. We take a more sober view of the innovations which science has brought into our lives. We know the blessings and the dangers that lurk in the discoveries of our day, for while we know the possibilities for a better life that lie within them we conceive of no future millennium. Events during and following World War II have led us to expect no transformation in the nature of man effected either by science or political institutions. A generation that thinks in this wise may be grave but it is not cynical. The tradition of a reasonably flexible charter of government will save us from hopelessness as the necessity of change confronts us. We may be thankful to the past leaders in our political life that they have handed down to us both a priceless heritage of lasting values and a living document of fundamental law.

chapter III

Freedom, Equality, and Segregation

Guy B. Johnson
University of North Carolina

▀▄

I

NINE-SCORE-AND-THREE years ago, as Abraham Lincoln would put it, "our fathers brought forth on this continent a new nation, conceived in liberty and dedicated to the proposition that all men are created equal." The ideas of liberty and equality, expressed so eloquently in the Declaration of Independence and the Constitution, are the very foundation stones of American citizenship.

In the American democratic creed, freedom and equality are inseparable. Freedom is like love—you *share* it without loss, and you realize its fullness only when you share it *equally* with someone else. The very essence of freedom is that the restraints which make it possible and the privileges which it confers must be applied equally to all citizens. When restraints are unequal, privileges are unequal, including the privilege of struggling for equality.

The main virtue of the American system of government is that it provides the machinery for the orderly and peaceful resolution of conflicts and adaptation to changing situations. With its popular suffrage, its representative congress, its division of functions, its amendable Constitution, and its Supreme Court, it is an admirable system which gives us about what we deserve. But it also has the defects and the risks of its virtues. Popular opinion may be prejudiced or unrealistic and may express itself in legislation or policies or judicial decisions which do great damage to the basic freedoms of certain persons or groups before the corrective processes of the system return us to our normal course. There is no foolproof way of dealing with popular hysteria, demagog-

35

uery, and powerful recalcitrant regional blocs. In the long run, the integrity of our government depends upon the devotion of the people to the ideals of freedom and equality.

Few will dispute the statement that the greatest strain upon the fabric of our political system, the greatest challenge to the consistency of our belief in freedom and equality, is the problem of the legal and social status of the Negro people. On this issue we have spent more time, more debate, more bitterness, and more blood than on any other single issue in our history. And even at this late date, 92 years after the emancipation of the slaves, we find a number of our Southern states shouting nullification of a ruling of the Supreme Court of the United States concerning the basic rights of the Negro as a citizen.

How have we come once more to this sort of crisis? How did it happen that in 1954 A.D., when the Supreme Court made its momentous decision against segregation in the public schools, seventeen of our states still had mandatory racial segregation by law in public schools and in other public facilities? How did we ever get started on the road of segregation? Why has segregation persisted? Is segregation compatible with freedom and equality? What good has it done? What harm has it done—to the Negro, the white man, the South, and the nation? How much desegregation has occurred? What are the consequences of desegregation? What is the outlook for the solution of this problem in our day?

II

First, let us examine the term segregation. It is often said that segregation is a perfectly normal social process. As a sociologist I would say that this is quite true. Consciousness of kind or group identification on the basis of race, religion, language, ethnic background, and the like, is indeed a natural and a universal phenomenon. This sort of voluntary separateness with respect to certain associations or institutions is not at all incompatible with our American democratic ideals. In fact, one of the virtues of democratic government is that it permits the harmonious integration of widely different groups by insuring all of them equal freedom to be different as long as they conform to certain common national values.

When powerful majority groups use their social and economic power so as not only to exclude certain groups from their social circles but to restrict their job opportunities, their places of residence, their schooling, their whole way of life, we have a different kind of segregation. This is the kind of segregation which is commonly found among the Negro people above the Mason-Dixon line. It is a combination of voluntary and involuntary forces, and it frequently produces a pattern of racial segregation which is structurally about as rigid as the Southern type. But, however reprehensible one might consider this kind of segregation to be, there is one thing that it is not: *it is not imposed by an act of government itself.* Furthermore, state government in the North is beginning to look for positive ways of trying to prevent discriminatory actions without infringing upon freedom of belief and opinion. There will be a good deal of discrimination in the North for a long time to come, and the role of law in preventing it will be limited, for the problem is basically moral and social rather than legal.

A third type of segregation is the type which is imposed by law. Of course, we have no federal segregation statutes, but all seventeen of our Southern and border states have required racial segregation by constitution or statute or both, on the presumption that our national Constitution *permits* them to do so. This mandatory legal segregation became the target of a great deal of litigation conducted by the National Association for the Advancement of Colored People in behalf of Negro plaintiffs, and the culmination was the Supreme Court decision of 1954 invalidating the school segregation laws. The result is well known. There is massive resistance, even defiance, of the edict of the Court, and we are now in the greatest constitutional crisis since the secession and Civil War.

It is this compulsory type of segregation which I wish to discuss in relation to the American ideals of freedom and equality. At this point I might as well state what my own sociological and ethical judgments are. I believe that compulsory legal segregation on the basis of race or color is an arbitrary restraint upon freedom and a denial of equality before the law. It is inconsistent with our national charter because it involves the government in the subversion of the very principles upon which it is founded.

III

If compulsory segregation has seemed so "right" to so many people for so long, it is good for us to take a brief excursion into our history and see "how we got that way." Most of us are either ignorant on this subject or are possessed with what may be worse, misinformation. One popular historical myth about legal segregation is that it is of ancient vintage, that it developed early during the slavery regime as a necessary means of controlling the slave. The truth is that while there were hundreds of laws concerning the status and conduct of the slaves and free Negroes, it was not considered necessary to provide legal sanctions for racial separation.

A corollary myth of history is that emancipation and reconstruction temporarily set aside the South's supposed long-standing system of segregation, but that when the Southern white people regained control of their state governments they angrily and immediately reconstituted the system of white supremacy and Negro subordination by passing the segregation laws. The truth is that for twenty-five to thirty years after the Southern white people had regained political control and long after all of the federal troops had gone from the South, they got along without the Jim Crow laws. This period, from about 1870 to 1895, was a fluid, unsettled period. There were alternatives—the South could recognize the Negro's rights as a citizen and go forward in a spirit of cooperation, or the South could stubbornly try to subordinate the Negro in every way—and the striking thing is that the South seemed committed to the first of these alternatives. Let me convey some of the flavor of that period by citing a few items from the stream of history.

> *Item 1.* The year is 1876. The Democrats in South Carolina, under the leadership of Wade Hampton, are trying to oust the Republican "carpet-bag" regime. They are trying to wean the Negro vote away from the opposition. Their platform declares "our acceptance, in perfect good faith, of the thirteenth, fourteenth, and fifteenth amendments to the Federal constitution." Hampton stumps the state, saying, "not one single right enjoyed by the colored people today shall be taken away from them. They shall be the equals, under the law, of any man in South Carolina." The Democrats take control of the state government.

Item 2. The year is 1878. The Democrats in South Carolina are again talking racial harmony. Negroes are still voting and holding office. A typical newspaper editorial says: "The color line has been obliterated, and we are all moving along together upon a higher and better platform of equal rights and equal justice to all. . . ." Another paper comments that it would like to see "every good Democrat put down the enunciation of race antagonism. . . . We want every good colored voter to join our party and help swell our majority in each county. The bugaboo of social equality has never disturbed our equipoise."

Item 3. The year is 1878. Col. Thomas W. Higginson, militant New England abolitionist who had led a regiment of Negro troops during the Civil War, visits the South, wondering if there is not "some covert plan for crushing or reenslaving the colored race." He admits that he finds no such indications. Comparing the acceptance of Negroes in the South at the polls, in public office, on trains and street cars, with their treatment in New England, he decides that the South is doing rather better than New England.

Item 4. The year is 1879. The British traveller, Sir George Campbell, is looking at conditions in the South. He reports: ". . . the humblest black rides with the proudest white on terms of perfect equality, and without the smallest symptom of malice or dislike on either side. I was, I confess, surprised to see how completely this is the case; even an English Radical is a little taken aback at first."

Item 5. The year is 1885. A Boston Negro journalist, T. M. Stewart, radical champion of racial equality, visits his native state of South Carolina. "I put a chip on my shoulder," he reports, "and inwardly dared any man to knock it off." He is literally looking for trouble, but he finds practically none. He reports to his paper: "Thus far I have found traveling [in Virginia and the Carolinas] . . . more pleasant than in some parts of New England." He observes the easy conversations of whites and Negroes and comments that "I think the whites of the South are really less afraid [of] contact with colored people than the whites of the North."

Item 6. The year is 1892. In Georgia the Populist party leader, Tom Watson, is saying that "the colored tenant . . . is in the same boat with the white tenant, the colored laborer with the white laborer," and that "the accident of color" makes no difference in their interests. He tells the Negroes that "if you stand shoulder to shoulder with us in this fight," the Populist party will "wipe out the color line and put every man on his citizenship irrespective of color."

Item 7. The year is 1897. The legislature of South Carolina is considering the passage of a Jim Crow law for railway trains. A Charleston editor, representative of the white "aristocracy," is opposing the bill. ". . . our opinion is that we have no more need for a Jim Crow system than we had last year, and a great deal less than we had twenty and thirty years ago." Such a law is "unnecessary and uncalled for" and it will be "a needless affront to our respectable and well behaved colored people. . . . The common sense and proper arrangement, in our opinion, is to provide first-class cars for first-class passengers, white and colored. . . . To speak plainly, we need, as everybody knows, separate cars or apartments for rowdy or drunken white passengers far more than Jim Crow cars for colored passengers."

Now, I would not have you believe that the South following the end of military reconstruction reached a golden age of inter-racial sweetness and harmony. Far from it, for there was plenty of hypocrisy, political opportunism, race hatred, lynching, and all the rest. Yet the clear fact remains that those who "redeemed" the South from the hated Republican reconstruction regimes were on the whole moderate in their views on Negro citizenship and did not rush headlong into a program of Jim Crowism. For a long time they followed a pattern which might well have become the way of the New South.

One of the saddest stories in our history is the story of the retreat from that era of moderation. In the 1890's and the early 1900's Jim Crow laws spread over the South like a relentless plague. What is the explanation? Historians still disagree over the details, but there is one important set of factors about which there is no disagreement. The common white people were looking for a place in the sun. They often despised and hated the Negroes, and they resented the smug and moderate manner of the old planter class in its dealings with the Negroes. A great farm depression was also sweeping the nation, and an agrarian reform movement complicated the conflict of the races.

At any rate, the Negro, profiting at first from the competition of the various factions for his vote, suddenly found himself the scapegoat. Having outdone one another in exploiting the Negro vote and using the rankest frauds at the polls, the white political factions began to work out compromises. The new line was, "We white people must stick together in one party, and for the sake of white supremacy and clean elections we must put the Negro down without any mercy." And so they let loose all of their frustration and pent-up hostility upon the helpless Negro. They raised the cry of "the Negro menace," they cheated, they intimidated, they lynched and murdered until they had the Negro at their mercy.

Then, as if to add insult to injury, they made disfranchisement "legal" and they wrote racial segregation into the constitutions and statutes of the Southern states.

Never during slavery had the ideology of white supremacy and Negro inferiority been given such complete expression. Never had the South been so solid. Gone was moderation, gone even the right of dissent. In their place was a rigid and uniform racial orthodoxy which has charted the thoughts and acts of Southerners from that day to this. Surely, this was the South at its worst. In 1911, the Reverend Edgar Gardner Murphy, one of the few Southerners in the first part of this century who might be called, even charitably, a liberal, looking back on this movement, said: "Its spirit is that of an all-absorbing autocracy of race, an animus of aggrandizement which makes, in the imagination of the white man, an absolute identification of the stronger race with the very being of the state."

The responsibility for this flight into racism and Jim Crowism does not rest upon the South alone. The North was guilty, too. It grew weary of the furor over reconstruction, wondered whether the war had been worth fighting, and acquiesced in the Southern "solution" of the problem of the Negro. The Negro was guilty because he tried to go farther and faster than his qualifications justified. The Congress was guilty because, having muddled the job of legislating the rights of the Negro under the Fourteenth Amendment, it gave up and completely abandoned the field. But if I had to nominate the real villain in this drama, I would point to the Supreme Court. This is a serious charge, and it bears some discussion.

Shortly after the Civil War three amendments were added to the national Constitution. The Thirteenth abolished slavery; the Fourteenth, among other things, conferred citizenship upon the Negro: and the Fifteenth specifically tried to protect his right of suffrage. The Fourteenth Amendment perhaps has been the subject of more controversy and litigation than any other provision in the Constitution. The crucial part of it, Section 1, reads as follows:

All persons born or naturalized in the United States, and subject to the jurisdiction thereof, are citizens of the United States and of the State wherein they reside. No State shall make or enforce any law which shall abridge the privileges or immunities of citizens of the United States, nor shall any State deprive any person of life, liberty, or property without due process of law, nor deny to any person within its jurisdiction the equal protection of the laws.

The Amendment ends with a section which says: "The Congress shall have the power to enforce by appropriate legislation the provisions of this article."

Congress, perhaps with more fervor than intelligence, did pass a good deal of legislation designed to insure the complete equality of the Negro. Although some of it obviously went beyond the intent of the Fourteenth Amendment, much of it seemed to be quite in harmony with the Amendment. But the Supreme Court was in a mood of compromise, appeasement, and retreat. In the famous *Slaughter House Cases* of 1873 and in *United States v. Reese* and *United States v. Cruikshank* in 1876, the Court whittled down the "privileges and immunities" which were considered to be under federal protection, and in the Civil Rights cases of 1883 it nullified virtually every section of the federal Civil Rights Acts. As the various states began to feel out the situation with segregation statutes, and as test cases went before the courts, the Supreme Court gave aid and comfort by ruling that segregation was a legitimate exercise of the "police powers" of the state and therefore did not make the state guilty of an act of discrimination. In *Hall v. DeCuir* (1877) the Court held that if a public carrier wanted to segregate its passengers, the state could not *prohibit* the practice, and by the time of *Plessy v. Ferguson* (1896) the Court was ready to say that the state could itself *require* segregation by public carriers. Mississippi's new legal devices, which had as their obvious purpose the disfranchisement of the Negro, came before the Court in *Williams v. Mississippi* in 1898, and the Court thought that they were not a violation of the Fourteenth or the Fifteenth Amendment. Thus during the very period when the South still had alternatives and was showing signs of going the way of moderation, the Supreme Court was virtually inviting the Southern extremists to go all-out for segregation.

One of the cases which I have mentioned, *Plessy v. Ferguson* (1896), stands out for two reasons. It crystallized the doctrines of separate-but-equal toward which the Court had been moving, and it symbolized dramatically the failure of the Court to come to grips with the real issue. Plessy, a colored man, had been

ejected from a Louisiana railway car reserved for whites and con-
victed for violating a state segregation law. He carried his case
to the Supreme Court, where he contended that the question of
whether the separate facilities were equal was wholly irrelevant.
His appeal brief argued:

> . . . it is not of the smallest consequence that the car or compartment
> set apart for the Colored is "equal" in those incidents which affect physical
> comfort to that set apart for the Whites. These might even be superior,
> without such consequences. Such considerations are not at all of the
> order of those now in question. Whatever legally disparages and what-
> ever is incident to legal disparagement is offensive to a properly constituted
> mind. The White man's wooden railway benches, if the case were such,
> would be preferred to any velvet cushions in the Colored car. If Mr. Plessy
> be colored and has tasted of the advantages of free American citizenship,
> and has responded to its inspirations, he abhorred the equal accommoda-
> tions of the car to which he was compulsorily assigned.

To this argument the Court turned a deaf ear. The Louisiana
law, it said, was a valid use of the state's police power. If Mr.
Plessy felt degraded or stigmatized by the separate car, it was
only because he chose to feel that way. Oh, how the South loved
the Supreme Court that day!

There is some irony in the fact that the lone dissent from this
doctrine was registered by the Southern member of the Court,
Mr. Justice Harlan of Kentucky. Some of his language is as follows:

> In my opinion, the judgment this day rendered will, in time prove to be
> quite as pernicious as the decision made by this tribunal in the Dred
> Scott case. . . . The arbitrary separation of citizens, on the basis of
> race, while they are on a public highway, is a badge of servitude wholly
> inconsistent with the civil freedom and the equality before the law estab-
> lished by the Constitution. It cannot be justified upon any legal grounds.
> . . . The thin disguise of "equal accommodations" . . . will not mislead
> anyone, nor atone for the wrong done this day.

Great indeed was the wrong done that day and other days
around the turn of the century by a Supreme Court which was
listening with the wrong ear and which was lacking in a fervent
faith in the American ideals of freedom and equality. Once the
Court has established a precedent, as it did in the case of *Plessy v.
Ferguson,* it does not easily depart from the precedent. It took
the Court nearly sixty years to rediscover the principle that equal-

ity is indivisible, that there is no such thing as some sort of middle ground in which we can have both equality and compulsory segregation. And so I submit the thought that the earlier Supreme Court, which fell short of the glory of the American Dream was the real villain in this drama. We have lost more than sixty years on a dead-end road, sanctioned as "the law of the land" by the Supreme Court of the United States, and every American who understands what America really stands for should thank God that on May 17, 1954, our Supreme Court unanimously and completely abandoned the idea that compulsory segregation is compatible with freedom and equality.

IV

The Supreme Court can change the validity of laws in the twinkling of an eye, but it cannot wipe out the consequences of a long-standing system of thought and action based upon those laws. The consequences of compulsory segregation in the South are very real, and we shall be paying them for a long time to come.

Let us look briefly at those consequences. First, are there any good consequences of compulsory segregation? The Southern ideology contends that segregation is a sort of benevolent and philanthropic institution which "protects" the interests of the Negro, which mediates to him the wisdom and virtues of white society, which gives him a chance to develop "in his own way" under his own leaders in his own institutions. And, of course, the Negro is "happy" this way, and it is only when he is stirred up by "outsiders," Communists, the N.A.A.C.P. or other "subversives" that he ever questions the rightness of things as they are. I have heard these arguments all of my life and I have thought about them a great deal, but I must confess that not even as a relatively hard-boiled sociologist can I see the "good" of legal segregation. I would concede that compulsory segregation is *one* possible way of structuring the relations between groups so as to hold overt conflict to a minimum, but it is not the *only* way, and the price it exacts is much too high. In short, I see no desirable consequence of compulsory segregation which could not also have been attained through the normal operation of the processes of group identification and voluntary social separation.

In assessing the evil results of compulsory segregation, it is admittedly hard to separate the consequences of Jim Crow as such from the consequences of the larger system of caste relations of which Jim Crow is but one part. However, there are certain things that we can say definitely about legally imposed segregation *per se*. Based as it is upon the authority of the state, it structures the relationships of white people and Negro people in a way which rules out the very possibility of certain kinds of contact between the two groups. Thus the processes of interaction, communication, competition, and the like, which are the very life blood of a dynamic society are inhibited to a serious extent. Furthermore, it imposes this structure on a uniform state-wide basis, so that no local community, no matter what its wishes or needs might be, has the right to experiment or deviate one whit from the law of segregation. Now, when we add to these basic qualities of legal segregation all of the ways in which it encourages and facilitates other bad consequences, we have a very gloomy picture indeed.

The effects of this system are all too obvious. The Negro is the main victim. The separate facility, the Jim Crow sign, has always been to him a hated symbol of second-class citizenship. At the very time when he needed most the tutelage of the more advanced race, the contact with models of culture which would enable him to complete his transition from Afro-American slave patterns to American patterns, he was suppressed and set into the strait jacket of compulsory segregation. He fell from high hope to black despair, and he has never got over the blow to his morale. He has sought the ways of least resistance, because to struggle, to aspire to something higher in life, seemed more punishing than rewarding. The system of caste and segregation works so thoroughly and automatically that it has tended to produce in the Negro masses a type of character which is painfully like the white man's stereotyped image of the Negro. It is a sorry spectacle indeed when the white man points to the results of this vicious circle as proof of the necessity for its continuation, but this is precisely what the Negro has been up against. Even under optimum conditions from here on out, it will be several generations before the Negro can overcome this damage to his morale and his motivation.

The Southern white man has also been damaged, although he is loath to admit it. He has been the victim of the fears and myths which he has created in order to justify the legal subordination of the Negro. In a real sense he has enslaved himself. He has dissipated much of his energy in the business of being on the defensive—explaining "The Southern viewpoint," asking for sympathy, crying that he is "misunderstood," contending that he is the Negro's "best friend," and so on and on. He has punished his liberals who dare to question the orthodox race credo, and he has rewarded his race-baiters and demagogues. I hate to use such a strong term as "brainwashed," but I suggest that basically what has happened to the South is that the generation which grew up after the coming of the Jim Crow system was so thoroughly "brainwashed" by its elders in the ideology of white supremacy and Negro inferiority that many of its members have never found their way back to the world of reality. Their behavior during the present battle over desegregation is eloquent testimony of their blind commitment to a course of action which can only be labelled for what it really is—subversion.

To trace the effects of the race-caste system on the development of the Southern region would take us far beyond the reaches of this paper. Let me merely make two points which will cover much of the ground. First, in spite of some rather remarkable social and economic progress in the South in the past quarter of a century, almost any tabulation of the ranking of the forty-eight states with respect to the usual indices of human well-being still shows most of the former Confederate states clustered at the bottom of the scale. Second, in its preoccupation with racial orthodoxy and one-party solidarity the South has forfeited its once outstanding position in national political leadership. Prior to 1868, we had seventeen presidents. Eleven of these were Southerners, and nine of the eleven were living in the South at the time of their election. Of the sixteen presidents since Andrew Johnson, only one, Woodrow Wilson, was even born in the South, and it is generally conceded that he would not have had a ghost of a chance, had he made his political career in the South.

The whole nation shares in the consequences of, and in the moral responsibility for, the perpetuation of compulsory racial segregation in the South. No aspect of our American life is better advertised or more skillfully exploited abroad by our enemies than the seamier side of our race relations. The tragic thing is that all too often they do not even have to exaggerate or fabricate, they merely spread the news. The bare fact that, with the exception of the Union of South Africa, we are the only civilized nation on earth which has maintained racial segregation by law into the second half of the twentieth century is a fact that we shall not live down for a long time to come. One good reason for implementing the 1954 decision of our Supreme Court is to redeem in some measure our moral leadership of the free world, but a still better reason is that we need to rescue our democracy from the strain of leading a double life.

V

Now, if I have given the impression that the South has completely stagnated and that there has been no progress in the relations of the races in the past fifty years, I want to correct that impression at once. The truth is that there has been a vast amount of progress by the Negro, by the whole region, and in the relations of the races. We are far enough away from the bitterness of the Civil War and the reconstruction period that many in the younger generation can look back upon them with considerable calmness. Two world wars and a great depression have taught us a great deal about our interdependence, and the great imponderable forces such as urbanization, industrialization, and mass education have broadened our horizons and enlarged the opportunities of both races in the South.

The Negro, through his own efforts, has done much to give the lie to that old notion of his racial inferiority. He has begun to produce a class of intellectuals, professionals, and business men who have won the admiration and respect of a large portion of white society. His progress during the 92 years since his emancipation is unparalleled in history, and while it might have been twice as great if he had had the rights of a first-class citizen, the fact remains that it is remarkable.

Let us take a brief look at the dimensions of the Negro's progress. He came out of slavery, five million strong, but owning very little of this world's goods. He was illiterate and he was almost completely dependent upon two lines of menial work, farm labor and domestic service. Today he is over seventeen million strong, his illiteracy is reaching the vanishing point, and his health and standard of living are immensely better than ever before. His occupational horizons have broadened, and while he is still concentrated in the less skilled jobs, he is represented in every category of technical and professional employment.

The following data recently made available by the United States Department of Labor illustrate the almost dramatic changes which have taken place since World War II. In the period, 1940 to 1957, the number of Negroes working as farm laborers decreased 44%, and the number employed in domestic service decreased 83%. At the same time Negro professional people were increasing 103%; operators and technicians, 181%; clerical and sales people, 223%; proprietors and managers, 131%. One-third of the Negroes in the United States now own their own homes, and the annual purchasing power of the Negro population is estimated to be about $17,500,000,000. In 1930 only 27,000 Negroes were enrolled in college. In 1956 the number was 196,000, an increase of 622%, which, by the way, was six times as high as the increase in white college enrollment.

The white people have played a crucial role in the changes in patterns of race relations. The demagogue and race-baiter are not, for all the notoriety they bring us, the true representatives of the South. The average Southerner respects the American creed of freedom and equality, and he feels the sting of his conscience because he knows deep down that what his forbears have done to the Negro is something which he would not want done to him. Perhaps this is why his private morality with regard to race is often so much better than his public actions. Certainly many white Southerners have maintained in their personal relations with certain Negroes a friendliness and helpfulness which has done much to mitigate the effects of Jim Crowism. There has even been a certain amount of honesty about the business of "separate-but-equal," for in the past fifteen years the white man has willingly seen hundreds of millions of dollars of public funds devoted to the equalization of Negro schools, hospitals, playgrounds, and the like. I am firmly convinced that there is a great reservoir of common sense and decency in the South which, when the nullifiers and resisters have shot their bolts, will take over and work out the problems of desegregation in a constructive way.

The role of the Christian churches in the South must not be overlooked. Even before the Supreme Court decision on school segregation many of the great religious bodies were formally questioning the morality of segregation, and since the Supreme Court decision most of them have issued further official statements endorsing the Court's ruling and calling for the acceptance of that ruling by the people of the South.

It is probably not generally known outside the South that segregation itself was beginning to give way for some years before the fateful decision of 1954. Partly through court action and partly through voluntary action, the Southern look was changing. For example, non-segregated travel in interstate coaches, pullmans, dining cars, and buses had become commonplace in most of the Southern states, and fifty or more public, private, and church-supported colleges and universities had opened their doors to Negroes for the first time.

The transition from segregated to desegregated higher education in the South is a dramatic example of the possibilities of peaceful social change in the relations of the races. Let me sketch the story briefly. Ten years ago the number of Southern white institutions which admitted Negroes could be counted on the fingers of two hands, and these schools were all in the border states. Under the impact of Supreme Court decisions, more public institutions opened their doors at the graduate and professional level, while additional church-supported colleges, not wishing to be outdone, began to admit Negroes. Then, when the Supreme Court made it clear that its 1954 decision would be applied across the board and that no public institution could deny admission to *any* qualified student at *any* level, there was a further increase in the ranks of integrated institutions. Here is the statistical picture at present (remembering, of course, these figures may already be out of date):

Type of Control	Total in South	No. Integrated	% Integrated
Public	206	110	52
Protestant	188	60	31
Roman Catholic	45	36	80
Private	114	30	26

Thus, out of a total of 553 "white" higher institutions in the South, 236, or nearly 45%, are now desegregated, and this in spite of the fact that five states—Alabama, Florida, Georgia, Mississippi, and South Carolina—have no desegregated public colleges. And let it be remembered that up to the time of the unfortunate mob violence in connection with the admission of Miss Autherine Lucy to the University of Alabama, nearly two hundred instances of integration had already occurred without a single serious incident of racial friction.

But what of the public schools? In view of the outcries of Southern politicians, the Southern "Manifesto," the talk of "massive resistance," and the newspaper headlines about mobs and dynamitings and federal troops, one might think that the South has put up a solid front against school desegregation. Not so, for the pattern of desegregated schooling is spreading slowly, and for the most part unspectacularly, across the map of the South. There are 2,985 school districts in the South known to have pupils of both races. As of last month, 751 of these, or one-fourth, had integrated their schools. Three states (West Virginia, Missouri, and Oklahoma) and the District of Columbia had almost complete integration of their public school systems. Four others (Delaware, Kentucky, Maryland, and Texas) were rather far advanced in desegregation, and three (Arkansas, North Carolina, and Tennessee) had begun in a few districts. The other seven states, all of them in the Deep South except Virginia, form the hard core of resistance to desegregation. How long they will hold out and how far they will go in making good their threats to abolish their public schools remains to be seen. But one thing is certain: there is no longer a solid South of segregation. The defiant states may hold out indefinitely, but they are going to be lonelier and lonelier.

To me it seems almost a miracle that three years after the Supreme Court decision, one-fourth of the school districts in the South have desegregated and that 95% of this desegregation has happened without serious friction. When agitators and hysterical parents lay off and let things take their natural course, the school children quickly settle down to the hum-drum business of going to school together.

The South is learning some simple lessons. It is learning that there is no mass migration of Negroes into desegregated facilities;

that the co-racial use of the same schools has little, if anything, to do with intermarriage, mongrelization, and private social worlds; and that all it is being asked to do is to do what the North and West have been doing for many years.

VI

If I have dwelt upon the issue of legal segregation as it has existed in the South, it is not that I consider the North and West to be models of fair play, but simply because I believe that this problem of *compulsory* racial segregation is the crucial moral issue of American government in the twentieth century. To resolve this issue in our day is to reunite the nation and to put it into a better position to grapple with the problems of human relations which lie ahead.

The net consequences of the abandonment of compulsory segregation are certain to be far short of what many white people *feared* they would be, and they are certain to be far short of what many Negro people *hoped* they would be. I suggest that the greatest positive consequences will be that the white man shall be rid of his false fears and of the stigma of unfair legal compulsion against the Negro, while the Negro shall be rid of a hated symbol of second-class citizenship and a handy alibi for second-rate achievement.

I foresee a New South and a new day, when no man will expect the state to legislate his superiority, when the demagogue will be shunned like poison, when the talents of Southern leaders shall again be channeled into statesmanship, and a Southerner can once more sit in the White House.

The battle over desegregation is very bitter right now, and it will get worse before things get better. Its worsening may be a good sign, a sign that the reactionary resisters realize that the jig is about up. To the extent that they go all-out for violence, they bring the timid moderates to their senses, and when this happens, the tide will have turned. Governor Orval Faubus, with quite reverse intentions, converted more people to a sober appreciation of law and order than all of the Little Rock preachers put together. When it is darkest, the stars shine the brightest.

Yes, the battle is very bitter, but there can be no doubt as to the outcome. Not only the Supreme Court of the United States, but the Christian ethic, the American Dream, and time itself are on the side of freedom and equality. And when this battle is over, the Negro shall have a second emancipation, the white man shall shake off the bondage of fear and guilt, the South shall at long last spiritually rejoin the Union, and "this nation, under God, shall have a new birth of freedom."

chapter IV

Science and Public Policy

Don K. Price
Harvard University

▬▬▬▬▬▬▬▬▬▬▬▬▬▬▬▬▬▬▬▬▬▬▬▬▬▬▬▬▬▬

FOR THE last decade, as a result of the spectacular developments of the second World War, we have become accustomed to seeing the physical scientist appear as an expert on international or public affairs, discussing issues of obvious national importance which the politician or political scientist can hardly claim to understand. This has led some people to fear that technocracy is just around the corner, and that our representative institutions are about to be abandoned for some shiny new set of scientific political gadgets. It has led others of a less traditional and more impatient temperament to think that our political system is poorly suited to the demands of the atomic age and that we will have to improvise a new constitution, as well as develop a new educational system, if we are going to keep ahead of the Russians. In the meantime, the Russians lose no opportunity to tell the world that their system of government is based on scientific principles, and gives scientists the fullest opportunity to use their talents in the service of a perfect society.

A discussion of "What America Stands For" is an appropriate occasion to take stock in this very timely and topical field. As we do so we have in the recent daily press plenty of current texts on which to base any number of sermons.

For example, Professor Teller, generally considered the father of the H-Bomb, has put forward very pointed criticism of our whole system of civil defense and of our national policies regarding scientific education. This may surprise those who think that people in state universities, being dependent on public funds, are not in a good position to criticize politicians.

53

Second, a staff at the Massachusetts Institute of Technology has recently presented a study to the United States Congress proposing a program of aid to less prosperous parts of the world. This is notable if only because the plan itself, which seems to be getting respectful if not effective attention from both congressmen and scholars, is of a grand enough scope to put to shame the plans proposed a few years ago by one of our eminent statesmen, who was immediately ridiculed as wanting to give a daily quart of milk to every Hottentot. It seems, perhaps to the surprise of some observers, that scholarship supported by great aggregations of private capital can come forward with bold and imaginative political ideas.

Congress is supposed to distrust the eggheads. Perhaps Congress does, because Congress is a multifarious representative body, some part of which at some time or another distrusts almost everybody. Yet now the Senate Foreign Relations Committee has been hiring eggheads by the dozen, and social scientists at that. It has paid for an elaborate series—a baker's dozen of them—of studies by a number of experts on the whole range of problems involved in foreign economic aid, and it seems to be paying earnest attention to their conclusions.

I do not really expect that we will ever completely understand "What America Stands For," but if we are going to try we shall have to puzzle over these oddities—why a state university like California should become a great arsenal of atomic weapons, and the source of vigorous and independent criticism of our military defense program; or why industrial profits go to support foreign agricultural missions; or why Congress should turn to social science researchers instead of party platforms in considering a new approach to international economic problems.

If we can understand the way such things work I do not think that it will lead us to believe that we are living, in the United States, in the best of all possible worlds, or that our governmental system has yet taken fully into account the problems caused by the rapid advances in technology. But I do think that it will suggest that our governmental system has some assets that have not been properly appreciated, and it will lead us to worry about the right things, rather than about theoretical issues that have no relation to reality.

To avoid the distorted perspective that comes with looking too closely at the current scene I will try to look back at least eighty or ninety years, to see where we started to rebuild our governmental institutions after the low point following the Civil War. No doubt it was a very low point indeed. By contrast with the great days of the intellectual leadership of Jefferson and Franklin and Hamilton and Adams—days when our political leaders were also in the forefront of international scientific and intellectual progress—world opinion put very little stock in the American political system in, say, 1867. The basic constitutional principles of the United States—republicanism, checks and balances, and federalism—had begun to seem naive and out of date. They involved a basic distrust of unlimited central power, and hence seemed old fashioned to those who joined the steady drift of liberal thought in continental Europe toward Marxism. But they involved, too, an assumption that the people generally were competent to have a hand in the establishment of their basic system of government. And this rationalistic assumption began to seem ridiculous to the conservative critics of democracy, who brought to their traditional prejudices the support of the new sciences which dealt with the irrational bases of human behavior.

Yet it seems to me that we may have passed the time when the general principles of American constitutional development appeared to be out of date. We can never recapture the simple confidence of a Jefferson or a Bancroft that American society has discovered a formula that insulates it from the political ills of the rest of the world. But if our constitutional system did not bring about the millennium, it still looks a lot better than some of the ideas which tried to supplant it. If it has had more stability and more adaptibility than one would have predicted a half century ago, I think that at least part of the reason may be that our political institutions from the very beginning have absorbed something in the way of openness to new ideas, freedom from vested interests, and disregard of mere traditional authority, from the independent educational and scientific institutions in our society.

Perhaps I should pause to note that I am not talking about science in its more precise sense, but science as a general approach to natural (including human) problems, as followed in the academic institutions and scholarly societies through which scientists bring their views to bear on human affairs. In this sense I think it is clear that the broad principles which have been the basis of our constitutional and political development have owed a great deal to the world of science.

One such principle was republicanism. We don't talk much about this principle today because we have become so accustomed to the idea that constitutional monarchies can help support democratic institutions, and that the main threat to freedom comes clearly from other forms of power than dynasties, that we do not remember what it once meant to be a republic. In 1776, to choose to become a republic meant more than to get rid of a king; it was to reject a system of government in which power was vested in an organized establishment rather than in the people. The kingship was supported by the organized nobility and the established church, and was to stand or fall with them. Much earlier James I had remarked, "No bishop, no king" as he undertook to defend the episcopate of England against the dissenters who were already speculating on the outlines of a written constitution with an elected executive.

When we in America abolished hereditary nobility and established churches, we also abolished the third pillar of royal power—the military and civil services which were set apart from the rest of society in their composition, and subject to little responsible political control.

In the United States we obviously overdid our jealousy of established power. Indeed we suffered from going to the other extreme, and giving too little account to the need for an effective governmental organization and a responsible public service. No American recalling the shame of our public affairs during the gilded age of the late nineteenth century can be proud that we came so near to destroying completely the idea of a corps of civil servants dedicated to the virtues of integrity and public service, nor can he fail to admit that we learned a great deal, as we sought to rescue our civil service from demoralization and party patronage, from the example of the more traditional establishments of Great Britain and continental Europe. But it is equally important to remember that when we did reform, we profited from their example but did not imitate their systems. We did not rebuild our system by creating a *corps d'élite* in the civil service corresponding to the regular officer corps of our military services, or to the British administrative class. While the main battle against partisan appointments below the top levels has been won, the American civil service in its fundamental structure follows principles that stem directly from our original republicanism and our distrust of an establishment. No federal department has an apex to its career pyramid; that is to say, you will find in no civilian department the career equivalent of the chief of staff of one of our military departments or of the permanent secretary of a civilian department of the United Kingdom, who is basically in control of all the department's career personnel and through whom they all report to their political superiors. Moreover, the non-political executives and administrators do not constitute a separate corps composed of people who must enter the service early and remain in it for most of their careers; a civil service executive position, unlike that in a military or foreign service position, may be filled by appointment from outside the government almost as readily as from within the career service.

Finally, and perhaps more important, the scientist and specialist may move freely up into general administrative, and even top executive positions. Indeed, the basic victory over the patronage system was won not by the reform movement so much as by the scientific and professional groups who were able to show that particular governmental programs had to be administered by people with particular scientific or professional skills. Almost everywhere it was the public health doctor, the geologist, the forester, the engineer, whose job was "taken out of politics" in the early days of reform as a result of the steady pressure of professional standards, measured against the plain requirements of the job. And still today the typical bureau chief in Washington is a scientist or specialist who is more concerned with the technical substance of his program than with government policy. Indeed the scientist may move not only to general managerial but also to top political positions if he has the ability and the taste for their responsibilities.

There are obvious disadvantages to this system, which puts incalculable strains on any formal coordinating machinery. But it has some of the merits of maintaining flexibility of political control, and maintaining an open system of administration in which new techniques and new ideas can be more influential than general bureaucratic considerations. In its basic structure our civil service has been kept open to the influence of new techniques and new ideas from both scientific and political sources, and free of domination by any bureaucratic hierarchy, much as the founders of the Republic wanted to keep it free from domination by the organized and established authority which they associated with royalty.

A second fundamental principle in our constitutional traditions is that of checks and balances. This is of course the despair of people who would like to see our government policies more effectively controlled in accordance with the consistent theories of responsible parties. But it is impossible for political parties to exercise a predominant influence on policies where the most effective lines of communication and power run from the individual committees of the Congress to the individual bureaus of the executive departments. And these bureaus are usually headed by men who have risen from the scientific and professional specialities to administrative positions and who remain more closely connected with their various specialties than with party interests or general concerns of government policy.

But this institutional description merely observes what has happened in many fields throughout our history. The whole story of the activities by which the Federal government furthered our early economic development—the geological surveys, the aids to navigation, and the policies on public lands, reclamation, forestry, and agriculture show how the scientific and technical services, working closely with their counterparts in private life, provided a large measure of the initiative in developing new governmental programs.

Much the same thing could be said in the various fields of governmental regulation of private business, beginning with the steamboat inspection service, which started with a federally financed research project at the Franklin Institute of Philadelphia. And the same type of initiative came from research workers and scientists (social scientists as well as their colleagues in the physical and biological fields) in the development of the newer types of federal services, whether in social security or the development of airports and highways.

Congress, unlike the House of Commons, has a system of specialized committees, simply because it is not willing to leave to the political executive the exclusive control over the shaping of new policy proposals. This means that its committees insist not only on dipping down within the executive departments to keep in touch with the subordinate administrators and scientists, but also on getting independent opinions of outside scientific authorities. This is a system in which private interests and independent scientists or engineers have the maximum opportunity to bring their ideas directly before the public political forum— much to the detriment of disciplined administration and neat political doctrine, but perhaps to the advantage of those who wish to take the initiative with new ideas. But for good or ill, it has been a system in which the institutions of organized knowledge have had an unusually powerful role, both with respect to the formation and development of the public service, and the initiating of new public policies.

The increase in the influence of scientists, particularly in crucial fields such as military research and development or atomic energy, leads many to wonder whether the great expansion of governmental functions, and the great importance of scientific and technical considerations, will make democratic politics impossible in the future. Are we becoming something like a technocracy in America?

This question brings us to the third great principle of American constitutional theory, that of federalism. The American federal system was set up in order to prevent the creation of a single center of power. The principle was later extended to insure a measure of independence to municipal as well as to state governments. And in the economic sphere the same desire for the distribution of power has strengthened the defenses of private business against encroachments by government. But in the opinion of many people, this healthy kind of pluralism is threatened by modern technology. This threat comes partly in the form of sheer destructive power, as in the case of the hydrogen bomb, and partly in new fields of knowledge which make the human being the object of technical manipulation, rather than a free and responsible citizen.

But before we assume that our Frankenstein's monster has taken command completely, let us take a look at one or two of the more hopeful signs in our history, especially at the types of institutions which government organizes for the production of new scientific knowledge, to see how they are related to representative institutions.

We might, for example, look at the history of the land grant colleges. They succeeded in creating something like a national system of higher education after the dream of Washington, Jefferson, and Adams about the establishment of a national university had failed. These colleges, now become full fledged universities, have been the source of most of the ideas and most of the personnel that have governed our farm and agricultural policies. They are entirely supported by governmental funds, and their research program and extension services have been made possible by federal money. As a result of the programs which their professors and their alumni helped work out, our national agricultural system is an intricate and marvelous combination of governmental planning, economic aid, and technical education. It is not socialist in a Marxist sense, but it certainly astounds every foreign observer who starts with the assumption that the American farmer is a rugged individualist who has nothing to do with government. At the same time it is a denial of a basic assumption of Marxism—that the fundamental changes necessary for the technical development and the control of the economy requires a strong central control, with no independence elsewhere. For if anything is obvious in American society, it is that the land grant colleges have not become mere appendages of the U.S. Department of Agriculture but, if anything, more vigorously independent and influential as time goes by.

I think we can see much the same thing happening in the more spectacular case of the industrial corporation in relation to the national military programs. Government pays for most of the research which is producing technical revolutions in fields like electronics, aeronautics, and nuclear physics. But the aircraft and electronic and power companies do not seem to be getting any poorer, less independent, or less strong. You do not need to study the situation in very much depth to be persuaded that more young men on the way up move from government agencies to private corporations than vice versa, and they do not feel that they are becoming any less influential in society as they do so.

Even more important, the federal support for the scientific research programs of American universities has been extended without putting those universities under federal control. The outlines of the system by which this became possible are obvious: the provision of support from a wide variety of federal agencies rather than a single center; the control of grants by advisory committees of scientists from private life; and within most of the scientific fields, a frequent exchange of personnel between government and private institutions to keep the government from developing a lack of sympathy with the private point of view.

All this has produced a general climate in which there is a genuine desire for the maintenance of many independent centers of study and criticism, and for entrusting to private corporations many functions that are public in their implications. As government expenditures have gone up in many of the newer fields, functions which in earlier days might readily have been undertaken by direct federal government management have been assigned by contract to private corporations or local governments. To advance the maritime business more than a century ago, the Federal Government began to clear the ports and install the lighthouses and inspect the ships and license the pilots; today in the aviation business, most of the comparable functions are left (or contracted) to municipal governments or private companies. For a combination of motives—managerial efficiency as well as anti-socialist principles—the Defense Department has been looking for opportunities to turn over to private firms many business operations which it formerly ran for itself. And in the uniquely modern field of atomic energy more than nine-tenths of the activity supported by government funds is carried on through contracts with private corporations.

In cases of routine management these actions are not very important or significant. But in some cases they touch on the basic determination of fundamental policy. For example, the military services have contracted with private universities, or have directly created independent private corporations, to carry on the scientific research that is needed for the planning of new weapons systems and their use in modern warfare. Thus the Rand Corporation was brought into existence to provide a quite independent source of criticism and planning recommendations for the Air Force. Supported by Air Force money, this organization can bring to bear on military policies the independent and informed criticism of scientists drawn from universities all over the country.

Thus even in industry and universities, and even in the most rapidly developing fields of new technology, power is not automatically being centralized, regardless of the need to deal with new problems on a nationwide basis. In effect we are developing a newer and more complex kind of federalism on the basis of our earlier experience with academic and scientific institutions. All this leads me to think that if we do not believe in having unlimited centralized power, no technological or financial trends need force it on us. And indeed the record of the past few years suggests that, as in the early days of our republic when Jefferson and Franklin combined governmental and scientific interests, scientists today are playing an important role in building a system dedicated to the decentralization of authority.

I would like then to turn to two questions about the future. How are we going to support science, and how control it? These questions lead to many issues that are as complex and significant as those that were involved in the old debates on the relation of civil to religious authority.

First of all as to the financial support for science. The figures on government appropriations are hard to get in precise terms but here precision does not matter very much. In 1900, Federal support of scientific research was running at about ten million dollars a year. We multipled this figure by ten over the next forty years, and then in the sixteen or seventeen years thereafter we multiplied the result by twenty or more, which brings us in 1957 to a Federal expenditure running about two and one-half billion dollars. It is a little less spectacular to show the same trend in terms of percentage of the Federal budget, but to do so shows that regardless of the broad movements in the level of government expenditures and the value of the dollar, we are putting more money into advanced scientific research: in 1940, research and development accounted for one per cent of the Federal budget; today it accounts for about four per cent.

Then who controls the distribution of these funds? As I have already remarked, they do not go through a single channel to the various universities and laboratories but through a wide variety of executive departments. I have already noted that quite frequently in the disbursal of these funds the advice of part-time consultants from the scientific or professional field in question is followed. The existence of such advisory machinery is a strong guarantee against domination of a scientific field by a governmental bureaucracy.

But equal care should be taken to state the opposite and balancing principle. The responsibility for the actual awards is usually firmly fixed in a full-time officer of the government. In the United States we have been much less ready than, for example, in Great Britain to delegate to a scientific or professional body control over its own status and privileges. Nowhere in America, for example, do the professions like law and medicine control themselves, and admit or deny admittance to applicants by action of their own professional societies, as is the case in Great Britain. A somewhat similar principle has been applied in the procedure of federal scientific grants, with a few exceptions, especially in the field of medical research. Part-time advisory committees may, in effect, make the decisions by their recommendations, but generally the ultimate legal responsibility is fixed firmly on the responsible full-time federal official.

This issue came up most clearly in the dispute over the organization of the National Science Foundation. The creation of the Foundation was delayed for several years by the dispute between those who wanted it controlled entirely by private scientists serving the government only part-time, and those who wanted it established firmly within the normal structure of government responsibility. The final outcome was a delicate balance, in which the part-time Board must vote the grant actions, but on the recommendation of the full-time executive who is Director of the Foundation, and who is appointed directly by the President.

It is customary to take note of the fact that the great motive for the support of science with federal funds is the motive of military defense. This is quite true, since by far the largest share of federal funds for research and development comes through military channels. But on the other hand the National Science Foundation, which was created entirely for non-military and basic research, has multiplied its annual budget more than tenfold in less than a decade of existence. And if anyone even at the end of World War II had ventured to predict that in a few years the government would be appropriating forty million dollars a year for grants to outside institutions for basic research he would have been considered a bold and reckless prophet. The continuation of such support now seems an assured feature of our national policy. And it rests on an assumption of a satisfactory balance between the need for responsible central administration of the grant making system, combined with a respect for the independence of the research institutions which receive the grant, and with guarantees of adequate freedom for the scientist.

With financial support of this kind the scientist must face the question what his responsibility should be for the effect of his research on public policy. A number of scientists like Bernal and Joliot-Curie have for years seen in Marxism the hope of a system which would govern society on scientific lines, as well as encourage the progress of science. Very few American scientists were ever of this opinion. Most of those who were, abroad as well as here, have now been persuaded by the logic of obvious events that a communist society is not necessarily a paradise for the scientist. They admire the tremendous resources which Russia has put at the disposal of scientists, and the high pay and status which Soviet scientists receive. But they know too the price the Soviet scientist pays in loss of freedom. Accordingly, when J. B. S. Haldane chose to leave Great Britain in disgust with British and American policy, it was India and not Russia which he chose for a residence.

But if hardly anyone believes any more that a dialectic can enable scientific methods to provide answers for all our social problems, it is equally clear that governments can no longer be managed according to the simple principle that experts must be "on tap not on top." Scientific issues are closely interwoven with the substance of high policy, and international news is made when the President of the United States sees visiting physicists. It is of course not always easy to tell whether the scientist is discussing a public policy issue in terms that come from his scientific knowledge, or that depend on his personal judgment in fields in which he is as much a layman as anyone else. On the whole it is generally true that the kinds of issues that have to be faced near the top of the governmental hierarchy are ones which involve a mixture of scientific considerations with economic issues, moral problems, and everyday garden-variety politics. Issues that can be settled by scientific tests or the quantitative method can generally be disposed of in the lower reaches of the hierarchical pyramid of a government department. The scientist can tell whether a certain type of aeronautical development can give a bombing plane a certain range, on the basis of scientific experimentation and engineering experience. But science cannot tell the Secretary of the Air Force how many planes the Air Force can afford to buy, much less tell the Secretary of State or the President whether those planes should be kept ready for attack in overseas bases, or given up in the course of disarmament negotiations or an economy campaign.

While science cannot answer these questions, this does not mean that scientists cannot. Indeed, by their greater understanding of one aspect of such problems, they may have an edge on their non-scientific colleagues. American business has certainly benefited by having engineers move into positions of managerial responsibility, as observers in many foreign countries would certainly concede. It may well be true, although on this point fewer foreign observers would agree, that American government has had a similar advantage from the movement of scientists into administrative positions.

But the application of scientific method to political problems involves more than simply getting scientists into administrative or political positions. Some phase or some aspect of a great many broad policy problems may be isolated and dealt with by the techniques of scientific research. But to make this possible, the problem must be defined by careful staff work so that the responsible executive can understand clearly on just what part of the problem scientific research can be done, and just what parts of the problem it leaves unanswered. This is not always possible. In some political or administrative situations basic conflicts exist which make it impossible to organize systematic research in an objective manner. These are situations in which competing factions really do not want to know the facts; they would rather submit to the ordeal of trial by political battle rather than submit their case to the dispassionate judgment of the scientific method. But if the situation is one in which there is enough orderly and competent administration first to define the issue, and second to see that the research is presented in a way in which its relevance is understood and not exaggerated, research techniques can make a great contribution to public policy.

Without trying to define this very complicated subject in precise detail, I may illustrate it by noting that it was possible several years ago to set up within each of the three military services a successful agency for the conduct of operations research, well before it was possible to do the same thing at the level of the Joint Chiefs of Staff and the Secretary of Defense. The existence of conflicts of jurisdiction among the military services made them each suspicious that operations research techniques would benefit the other services in their rivalries. But this problem was solved in large measure as the administrative structure within the Department of Defense gained in authority and expertise, and as it became clear that scientists could provide expert assistance without superseding the judgment of responsible executives.

A government which is organized on authoritarian lines, or even one which puts a high premium on permanent careers, might set up scientists in positions of special influence or control over public policy, just because of their status as scientists. But it is hard to see this happening in the United States. For this is quite a different matter from the freedom of scientists to move into positions of administrative responsibility, along with others. The whole system of government scientific careers, and the way in which all parts of the executive branch are subject to checks and control by Congressional committees as well as by the President and his Department heads, make most unlikely any form of technocracy in the United States. Science has simply become too strong and pervasive an influence in all parts of our national life to be organized as a guild apart from the responsible machinery of democracy.

The typical scientist in the public service is not a wizard controlling decisions of state, a Merlin behind the throne. He is more likely to be a man who complains at least twice a day that he wishes he were back in his laboratory. But having left it, he has taken on administrative responsibilities, as the price of acquiring administrative authority. This means that he has to compete with his non-scientific colleagues in handling issues every day in which he must reconcile scientific, budgetary, administrative, and political considerations, within the same context of constitutional responsibility that applies to the rest of the government.

There are plenty of defects and difficulties in this system which makes scientists into administrators, and puts them and their colleagues in a close working relationship both with private organizations and with the many centers of dispersed power within the Executive branch and among the congressional committees. One obvious one is that the system puts a heavy premium on the support of the applied sciences, so that by comparison our basic science suffers. Another is that it makes it hard to develop the coherent general administration which is so important to the country with respect to the democratic process.

Much needs to be done to overcome both these shortcomings in government, and to improve the educational system which is becoming every day more closely related to the world of public affairs. The close ties between the universities and government, and the fostering of many centers of independent ideas within them, will provide the best guarantee of a continuing fruitful relationship between science and politics.

In the days of the American Revolution the scientific spirit— as personified in such leaders as Jefferson and Franklin—went far toward helping to shape the nature of our new republican institutions. In a much less conspicuous but perhaps equally significant way the need to support science and technology and use them for the solution of our twentieth century problems is having a profound effect on the development of our governmental system.

For more than a century Marxism has offered itself to the

intellectual as a scientific approach to politics, and as a political approach that will give the scientist high status in governmental affairs. These pretensions are supported by the great successes that Soviet science has accomplished in limited and specific fields by concentrating its efforts on subjects of special interest to the Soviet regime. No one should underestimate the ability of Russian scientists, but no one should believe either that Marxism is the ideology under which science flourishes in freedom; that notion has been as effectively debunked by the commissar's control over the scientists in Russia as the general pretension of communist benevolence has been exploded by the Soviet intervention in Hungary. It is high time for us in America, and for the uncommitted world, to understand how deeply the future of science and of free government depend on each other.

If we can educate scientists with an appreciation of our political traditions and our social problems, and statesmen who understand the role of science in contemporary life, we may make this relationship as fruitful as the needs of the age require. We may then use the massive federal support for research to foster a flowering of basic science as well as applied technology, and we may strengthen our responsible administrative machinery to insure that our technology will serve as a shield of the Republic, and not a threat to its freedom.

part II

ECONOMICS AND LABOR

chapter v

Contemporary Problems of the American Economy

Karl de Schweinitz, Jr.
Northwestern University

▄▀

DESPITE THE massive capacity of the American economy to produce material wealth it holds an ambivalent position in the court of world opinion, being at once the object of great envy and great contempt. While acknowledging the productive achievements of the American economy by setting for itself the goal of surpassing them, the Communist Party in Soviet Russia has calumniated American society and pictured its citizens as helpless and poverty-stricken minions of rapacious capitalists. Even friendly nations, though eager to receive the benefits of its economic strength, are suspicious lest they become infected by an American ideological virus. The hostile critics abroad, of course, have not gone unanswered. Indeed, there has been a plethora of individuals and organizations who have sprung to the defense of the economy, laboring hard to superimpose on the invidious image of monopoly capitalism the pleasing image of a people's or democratic capitalism. Inevitably, the defense has been polemical and propagandistic, designed, one suspects, on the principle of modern advertising, to capture its audience with glitter and slogan.

The American economy, however, is much too complex a social organism to fit into the stereotypes which serve as weapons in the prosecution of the cold war. In view of the well-nigh universal tendency of academicians and publicists alike to couch contemporary problems in cold-war terms, one can grant a special need for a dispassionate interpretation and appraisal of the American economy. But because of the audience—the international community—to which the symposium wants to appeal, it is not easy to know how to make such an interpretation. The nations making up the international community include some with highly developed economies, such as those in Western Europe, and others with economies that are desperately struggling to break away from the tenacious grip of subsistence, such as those in the Middle East, Africa, and Asia. Since each nation is likely to view economic experience in light of the particular problems confronting it, American economic experience will not mean the same thing to each nation. Moreover, economies that are fundamentally different from the American economy in their resource endowment, ideological background, or population characteristics may neither be able, nor want, to aspire to the methods of American economic organization. An appraisal of the American economy, therefore, if it is to be anything more than a journalistic tour de force, must be made with a clear realization of the heterogeneous nature of the international economic community.

At the outset one must acknowledge the incredible wealth of the American economy. Since the turn of the present century it has produced the highest per capita income in the world and in the period of full employment since World War II has not only managed to maintain its lead but to increase it. With less than ten per cent of the labor force working on the farms of the economy, they nonetheless produce such a superabundance of agricultural output that we find ourselves embarrassed by crop surpluses. In the industrial sector of the economy we are not quite so prodigal with our resources, for the American consumers' demand for goods is not so easily satiated. Despite the limited capacity of highways and cities, the output of automobiles, for example, continues to grow as producers capitalize on the American penchant to live on wheels. And with the added leisure made possible by growing per capita income and the technological revolution in food-processing and home-services, the American family can roam far and wide. In consequence, the resort industry, drive-in theaters, residential construction, patio accessories, do-it-yourself kits and countless other goods and services have experienced unparalleled expansion.

But the wealth of the American economy is, or should be, evident to anyone who cares to notice it. American movies, trade fairs, and propaganda reiterate the story of abundance, and the ubiquitous American tourist in almost any season advertises, unhappily not always to our advantage, the benefits of material well-being. Notwithstanding the attempts of some countries to blur the picture of American wealth, it undeniably is the most universally accepted measure of what the American economy stands for.

Although high per capita income is something to be proud of and a goal for impoverished nations to emulate, it is an unsatisfactory measure by itself of what an economy represents. It is in a real sense meaningless, for it abstracts from the problems that an economy encounters and from the obstacles it surmounted in achieving its present state. I therefore propose to discuss some problems facing the American economy, concluding with a brief reminder of the historical conditions out of which it evolved.

CONTEMPORARY PROBLEMS OF THE AMERICAN ECONOMY

The Concentration of Economic Power. The American economy in the year of 1957 bears only a very faint resemblance to the model of the competitive order which has served as a norm for the present generation of economists. Neoclassical economists postulated a system in which no one individual would have influence over price; firms, as well as consumers and the owners of resources, were assumed to be too small a part of market supply or demand to be able to affect price by their individual transactions. Taking prices as given, therefore, and with full knowledge of the alternatives in the markets, they produced and exchanged goods and services until they had maximized their income, profits, or satisfaction. In so doing, the welfare of the community was also maximized for this consisted of the sum of individual satisfactions and if each individual in budgeting his income and allocating his productive effort had reached an optimum position, then the community could do no better. It seemed to follow from this hypothetical model that the size of economic units was a significant welfare norm. If, for example, the firm became so large relative to the market that it could influence price, it would restrict output and raise price and profits at the expense of the community. Monopoly, in short, was undesirable.

Whether or not there has been any conscious intent to monopolize, the typical American firm has long since transcended the limits of neoclassical competition. In the capital goods and durable consumers' goods industries, especially, a few large firms typically dominate the market. This is also true in the food-processing and meat-packing industries. And even retailing, with the rise of the supermarket and the gigantic chain stores, affronts orthodox economic standards. Only in the agricultural industry do we find large numbers of firms which have no control over the prices established in the markets. But agricultural prices are so distasteful to farmers that, with the aid of the agricultural senators and the Department of Agriculture, they have worked out parity pricing formulas to protect themselves from the rigors of competition. Moreover, as the economy grows, the agricultural sector becomes proportionately smaller so that even if competition prevailed in agricultural pricing, it would represent a waning part of the economy.

Undoubtedly, much of the growth of American business firms is attributable to technological developments which have made the optimum-sized firm so large that it reduces the number of firms that any given industry can contain. One cannot produce steel or automobiles at minimum cost in a cigar store. Firms that exploit these technological possibilities are but carrying out the mandate of the capitalistic market and can scarcely be accused of sinister design. Yet once having grown large, they become less subject to the pressure of competition, for the heavy capital costs of acquiring the assets essential for doing business make the entry of new firms more difficult. The predatory methods of the robber barons are no longer necessary corporate policies, for who can seriously contemplate entering the steel or automobile industries? Moreover, the modern large-scale corporation can marshal inordinate strength to protect the value of its assets from possible adverse decisions in the market. And rather than await the outcome of the market test with feverish anxiety, it much prefers actively to influence the judges—the consumers—through flamboyant, iterative, but seldom informative sales campaigns. Whether they are driving on the nation's highways, reading the press and magazines, listening to the radio, or watching television, American consumers are fair game for the blandishments of the corporation which tries to control their dollar expenditures.

Not only has the growth of the American corporation increased the discretionary power of business vis-a-vis the consumer, but it has attenuated the once strong relationship between ownership and control, a traditional characteristic of capitalism. The capital requirements of modern enterprise, which, as noted, restrict entry, also compel the corporation to seek the savings of increasing numbers of households. The ownership of American business is more widely dispersed in consequence; American Telephone and Telegraph is quite correct in its proud claim that America owns it. But ownership means little more than a claim to the net income of the corporation. The typical stockholder has no direct control over corporate policy. He is welcome to attend the annual stockholders' meeting and he probably receives in advance of the meeting a handsome brochure, designed by the best talent on Madison Avenue and containing a glib account of the successes (or failures) of the corporation during the previous year. But unless he has a significant bloc of voting stock behind him— unlikely in the extreme for stockholders other than the Youngs, Wolfsons, or Rockefellers of this world—he can only expect to be heard with polite interest and thanked with the usual assurance that his perceptive suggestions will be taken up by the appropriate committee.

Neither the consumer nor the stockholder, however, is quite so helpless as my remarks imply, for the existence of organized markets, whether or not competitive in the economists' sense, allows him a range of choice by which he can protect himself from products or corporate policies he does not like. That is to say, he can spend his income on competing products, or he can change the composition of his assets by selling some stocks and buying others.

The range of choice, the mobility in other words, of stockholders and consumers is not so characteristic of workers, upon whom the incidence of corporate power accordingly has fallen with greatest force. Immobilized by their unwillingness or inability to change employment rapidly, American workers have organized in the union movement and substituted their collective strength for their disabilities as individuals. And just as corporate power has grown in the past decades, so has the power of the unions. Although the entire labor force is by no means unionized, union strength tends to be at its peak at precisely those points where corporate power is greatest. And so each year we witness those great struggles—more often than not confined to the bargaining table—between labor and management which settle the pattern of wages for large numbers of workers in strategic industries.

Granted that the American economy no longer fits the neoclassical pattern of competition, that, to use the jargon of economics, it is characterized more by oligopoly, why should one be concerned? Is the concentration of economic power in the business enterprise, the trade union, and for that matter in agricultural associations a cause for alarm so long as the economy continues to expand? It is hardly surprising that the answers to these questions vary from one period to another and from person to person, depending on the particular vantage point from which he views the economy. Irrespective of time and circumstances, however, there are at least four issues which one might raise in connection with the concentration of economic power: its impact on 1) the discretionary power of persons in positions of responsibility and control, 2) the composition of output, 3) the distribution of output, and 4) the stability of output.

1) Strongly individualistic, indeed at times almost anarchistic, American ideology has fostered a profound distrust of authority. Nowhere did Lockean beliefs flourish with such vigor as in the United States. With a continent to conquer and with few restraints imposed on his conduct, the individual seemed to be, above all, the maker of his own destiny, and consequently he tended to be contemptuous and distrustful of anyone vested with the restraining authority of the state. Far from viewing the state as the custodian of the public consensus, he viewed it at worst as an impediment to, and at best something to be manipulated for, the achievement of his own goals. During war emergencies, when the government had to assume greater power over the economic system, the individual was either bravely forbearing or hurried to Washington to insure the business-like conduct of administration. But all the while he was confident that, after the emergency, normalcy would return and government would be reduced to its appropriate place in the national life.

For many people the New Deal was a bitter pill to swallow because it challenged the prevailing orthodox ideology. The welfare measures it sponsored were an open and unashamed disavowal of the notion that the individual was sufficient unto himself. In providing for income in old age and in times of unemployment, the government confronted the individualist with the possibility that it could provide some services that were beyond his capacity or the capacity of private organization.

The various legislative acts of the New Deal have to a considerable degree been accepted by all shades of political opinion. Very few people seriously urge the repeal of the Social Security Act, the Securities and Exchange Act, or minimum wage legislation. Yet the acceptance of these specific legislative acts does not necessarily mean that American citizens have embraced the state, thereby denying their ideological heritage. Much of the public discussion of the Federal budget revolves around the issue of its absolute and relative magnitude, the fear being expressed on many sides that the Federal Government intends to play too active a role in the economy. With the recent acceleration in the growth of population and the imperceptible growth of the capacity of schools, colleges, and universities, education faces an increasingly serious crisis with each passing year. But there is manifest reluctance to mobilize the resources of the Federal Government to help ease the crisis. One could go on citing innumerable examples, but the point is clear: although the scope of government is vast, the American people, or at least its most articulate representatives, seem to be apprehensive about its further growth.

But, curiously, the American people do not show quite the same distrust of concentrated economic power. On the face of it, it is not evident that a large governmental department is any more or less capable of arbitrary acts than a large business organization or a large trade union. Certainly General Motors or the United Automobile Workers has the power to proscribe certain kinds of behavior and demand conformance to standards which they themselves set. It may well be the case that these standards established by private economic organizations are in the main reasonable, but they have a wider discretion in setting them than ever would be tolerated in governmental organization.

Moreover, powerful economic groups not only control the behavior of their constituents, but they exert profound influence on individuals and organizations outside the limits of their jurisdiction. Referring to education again, it is undoubtedly the case that business firms are donating many millions of dollars to private universities and colleges. The motives for such donations are, I am sure, unexceptionable, but as schools become dependent on this source of funds, it may become increasingly difficult for them to retain that independence from vested interest which is the *sine qua non* of good education. To take another example, commercial advertising has become an extremely important source of revenue for the nation's newspapers and magazines, and it is unlikely, to say the least, that editors will apply the same standards to articles critical of wealthy clients that they apply to other articles. The United States Steel Corporation apparently has not yet forgiven *Fortune* Magazine for publishing a series in the middle-thirties by Dwight MacDonald which was less than flattering to big steel. A check of recent issues of *Fortune,* at any rate, does not reveal any advertising by the United States Steel Corporation. On a more serious plane, it was recently announced by Batten, Barton, Durstine & Osbourne, Inc., that it was not renewing its contract with *The Reader's Digest* because of a conflict of interest with the American Tobacco Co. *The Reader's Digest* had published an article critical of the effectiveness of filter-tips in removing tar and nicotine from cigarettes. On being notified that the American Tobacco Company was displeased with the article, the advertising agency decided to drop the magazine account. Surely this was something less than a subtle attempt to control the press.

It is useless to deny that the structure of the American economy endows some individuals with a great deal of arbitrary power. The president of General Motors or of the A.F. of L.-C.I.O. is not a man to be taken lightly. Far in advance of his times Karl Marx anticipated the growing concentration of power in capitalism and he hardly would have been surprised by the preeminent positions occupied by the leaders of large-scale industry. What he did not anticipate was the subsequent growth of the union movement and, perhaps more significantly, the independent influence the democratic political community could exert on the exercising of economic power. Within the capitalistic framework he could only believe that the state was a committee of the ruling class to oppress the proletariat. Legislative policies which seemed to be in the interests of the working classes were more apparent than real, so he argued, for they were nothing more than scraps thrown out by capitalists to divert workers from their true goal— socialism.

Marxism, more specifically historical materialism, has provided the rationale for the more doleful predictions about the consequences for American capitalism of the concentration of economic power. I am not sure that anything I can say here will convince the true believer in historical materialism that his analysis may be overdrawn. If he really believes that the present structure of the American economy represents an advanced but moribund stage in a teleological movement to a predestined end, then my remarks will seem trivial. Nonetheless, I should aver that the democratic political community imposes certain kinds of restraints on the growth of arbitrary economic power that in large measure account for the uniqueness of the American economy.

In the first place, the freedom of individuals in a democratic society to organize has, in the words of Professor Galbraith, created countervailing forces which limit the discretionary authority individuals can acquire from concentrations of economic power. If the growth of business enterprise gave corporate executives the opportunity to oppress and exploit workers, those opportunities could not be long exercised without being destroyed. Aside from its obvious economic purposes, the union arose to protect the worker from the arbitrary actions of management. Similarly, the Granger movement flourished in the 1870's in response to the oppression of farmers by banks and railroads.

In the second place, monopoly is, in a sense, always on trial in the democratic political process. For to the extent that democracy is viable, it continuously elicits the preferences of the community in its search for a policy consensus. Accordingly, when the community becomes concerned about monopoly problems, one may expect that the government will become similarly concerned. The trust-busting activities of Theodore Roosevelt were not fortuitous, but were a manifestation of the fear of arbitrary business power occasioned by the initial rise of giant industrial and manufacturing corporations early in the 20th century. The expansion of the anti-trust division of the Department of Justice under the guidance of Thurman Arnold during the New Deal reflected a persistent belief that the structure of American industry had something to do with the prolonged depression that was crippling the American economy. Neither of these eras of trust-busting had dramatic consequences as measured by quantitative criteria; relatively few corporations were prosecuted and even fewer were actually divested of assets in adverse court decisions. But quantitative criteria do not tell the whole story. The fact that the Federal Government will prosecute industry for violation of the anti-trust laws and that the courts may find for the government— witness the decision of the Supreme Court in its 1957 term on the DuPont case—surely acts as a limit to the discretionary authority of business organization. As someone once remarked, the ghost of Thurman Arnold sits on the board of directors of all the large corporations in the land. In short, corporations are not likely to court the inconvenience of a government suit.

Although monopoly may always be on trial in democratic society, it does not always excite the indignation of citizens. Significantly, the greatest periods of anti-trust activity in the country's history came as I have noted 1) following the merger movement and 2) during the great depression. Typically affected with a touch of megalomania, Americans apparently do not become alarmed by the concentration of private economic power so long as certain standards of economic performance are maintained. When the large corporations were new, they were apprehensive about them, as they were when the economy was in the throes of the great depression. But far from viewing their destruction as the best protection for society against the abuses of arbitrary economic power, they prefer to identify themselves with organizations that can meet the corporation on its own grounds. The structure of the American economy, therefore, becomes a matter of public censure when the economy does not measure up to more narrowly economic criteria. To these criteria I now turn.

2) It is a cardinal tenet of liberal economies that the individual is the best judge of his own conduct and that his preferences should guide the allocation of resources among alternative uses. The purely competitive market, as fashioned by neoclassical economists, allowed just such an allocation of resources, for it

contained none of the restrictions that would prevent resources from moving to points of maximum productivity as indicated by consumer choice. Monopoly, on the other hand, distorted the allocation of resources by imposing barriers to their movement. The notion of an optimal product mix being such an important dimension of economic analysis, it is hardly surprising that economists have been hypersensitive to the impact of the structure of economic organization on resource allocation. But because this notion is somewhat esoteric and hard to register as an empirical phenomenon, it also is hardly surprising that the public is profoundly unimpressed by the issue, if indeed it knows that the issue exists. Assuming, then, that the American economy is performing adequately in other respects, it is most unlikely that great public concern will be generated by the possibility that concentrations of corporate power or union power may prevent the achievement of an optimal composition of output.

3) If the composition of output is a problem that eludes Americen citizens, the distribution of output or income is not. Since the colonial period income distribution has been at the center of many of the great controversies which have shaped the American tradition. The debate over the Hamiltonian system at the formation of the republic, the struggle over the United States Banks, the clash between North and South leading to the Civil War, and populism all involved the divergent interests of creditors and debtors who either in defending the *status quo* or advocating departure from established practice espoused policies designed to influence the distribution of income. In our own day, the farmer protects himself against an adverse turn in the terms of trade through the inestimable help of parity-pricing formula. Not to be outdone, the worker through collective bargaining attempts to increase, and as a minimum to maintain, his share of the national income. Similarly, business firms through price policy, and where this fails, through governmental subsidy, seek to protect profit levels from the incursions of other income shares.

In truth, the structure of the American economy manifests the struggle of different individuals and groups over the distribution of income. While no one would assert that these individuals and groups necessarily get what they deserve, most people seem to feel that the institutions created in the competition for income are deserving, unless or until proved otherwise. The modern business firm, for example, undoubtedly has a significant influence on the real income of its managerial and professional staff through the largess of the expense account. Although it is difficult to quantify its effect on the distribution of income, it would appear to be great. The accommodations in hotels, restaurants, trains, planes, nightclubs, and sporting events preempted by business men working on the expense account at least give such an impression intuitively. Yet far from condemning the expense account, the American typically prefers to allow the individual to seek the privileges of an expense account in his own occupation or profession as best he can.

This example, inconsequential though it may be, reflects the expansiveness of the struggle for income shares in the American economy. Rather than different classes fighting over a fixed income pie and consequently being inalterably hostile to one another, different groups compete for the pieces of a growing pie, which, of course, permits a greater accommodation of conflicting income interests. And this surely is the key to an appreciation of the impact of the concentration of economic power on the distribution of income. The structure of the American economy has not been built according to blueprint. It has grown on an *ad hoc* basis as individuals and groups, each exercising the prerogatives of an individualistic enterprise order, have formed associations, corporations, and organizations incident to their attempts to maximize income. So long as the economy continues to grow, its structure is not likely to be condemned on the grounds that it creates an inequitable distribution of income. If in the short run, for example, corporate profits are relatively high, trade unions will attempt to increase wages in their negotiations with management. Or if trade unions have been able to increase money wages at the expense of profits, corporations will attempt to increase labor productivity through investment or they will raise prices. These are accepted practices in the American economy.

4) However free of censure the American economy may be on its distribution of income, it is far from being above criticism on the stability of income. The structure of the economy, which has been instrumental in stimulating a high rate of economic growth, may be a cause of aggregate instability because of its

reliance on administered prices. Where purely competitive pricing theoretically leads to price flexibility and stability of output, administered prices may lead to price inflexibility and instability of output. During the great depression of the thirties, at any rate, prices in the oligopolistic sector were observed to change less than prices in the competitive sector and output more. On the other hand, it has been argued that inflexible prices prevent precipitous inflationary or deflationary movements in aggregate income by placing a ceiling over and a floor under aggregate price changes.

One thing is unequivocally clear, however: the price level has risen persistently since World War II. This indisputable fact coupled with the observation that it has only been since World War II that trade union strength has been exerted on a wide scale in collective bargaining has led some analysts to conclude that the inflation has been cost-induced because the unions have been able to secure wage increases greater than increases in productivity. I do not care to dispute this view any more than I care to dispute the contrary view that holds the large corporations responsible for the inflation because of their discretionary control over price. The point is that it is not particularly fruitful to try fixing the blame for aggregate instability—in this case inflation—on particular individuals or groups. As I have tried to show previously, the economy has developed its unique structural characteristics because individuals and groups have obeyed the enterprise injunction to enrich themselves. The corporation is trying to maximize profits for the stockholders and the trade union is trying to maximize wages for its members. It is not the function of the corporation or the trade union to maintain the stability of aggregate income. Indeed, given the American economic system each would be derelict in its responsibility if it placed this social objective above the particular interests of its constituents.

Yet the price level continues to rise and it is at least plausible to believe that the structural characteristics of the American economy have accentuated the inflation and indeed have permitted it to continue unabated, even when there is significant unemployment. To the extent that this is true the society is confronted by a clear-cut conflict between the individual and social interest. It is one of the precious features of American society, unlike some societies in the world today, that we frankly admit the existence of such conflicts and view public policy in large measure as serving the function of working out a *modus vivendi* between the individual interest and the social interest. With respect to the particular problem I have raised here, the society is inclined to let the government assume responsibility for the maintenance of the stability of income through its power to create an economic milieu in which the behavior of individuals and groups as they maximize income will not cause undue instability. But the problem of stabilization is such an important aspect of the American economy that it must stand by itself in a separate discussion.

Stabilization of Income. It is a sad truth about the American economy that one of its greatest virtues leads to one of its most persistent problems: the instability of income. In a decentralized market-oriented economy the level of income depends upon the spending decisions of millions of individuals and it can only be fortuitous if the aggregate of these decisions yields the amount of income which will just fully employ the labor force without precipitating a rise in prices. We insist that individuals should be free to consume and invest according to their own preferences. But in economics as in many other things, you cannot have your cake and eat it too—the price of such freedom is instability. Since the early part of the nineteenth century the American economy has passed through a succession of crises culminating in the prolonged and deep depression of the 1930's. And since the '30's the economy has been plagued first by inflation and then, by the most unlikely of devils, recession-inflation. The historical evidence speaks with embarrassing clarity.

But the picture is by no means as black as these remarks suggest, for in the past twenty-five years a great deal has been learned about fluctuations in income and the stabilizing role public policy can perform. Public policy, of course, cannot perform miracles. Some instability is, as I have already pointed out, the price of individual freedom. It is also the price of material progress. The adoption of new techniques and products into the economy cannot always be expected to proceed evenly over extended periods of time, and to the extent that there are cycles of investment with the growth of the arts and sciences one should anticipate uneven growth in income. But having made this caveat I can assert with confidence that it is technically possible through public policy to modify, if not to eliminate, the instability of income in an enterprise system. In short, there is no need for the American economy during the second half of the twentieth century to repeat its performance of the first half.

This sanguine assertion is prompted by the potential stabilizing influence of the fiscal-monetary powers of the Federal Government. So long as it possesses ultimate control over the money supply it is in a position to compensate for undesired changes in the level of spending in the private sector of the economy. If expenditures on private investment and consumption are too great, the government can raise interest rates, cut back its purchases of goods and services, decrease transfer payments, or raise tax rates. On the other hand, if private expenditures are not large enough to generate full employment, the government can lower interest rates, increase its purchases of goods and services, raise transfer payments, or lower tax rates. I am fully aware that these policy variables are not as flexible as a governmental stabilization program would ideally require—tax rates can hardly be changed at will and a high proportion of the expenditures of the government on goods and services represent long-term commitments—but the point to be made here is that such a program is a feasible goal. We now know that the federal budget, aside from influencing the distribution of income and the allocation of resources between the private and governmental sectors, affects aggregate income, and that in evaluating a particular budget, whether it runs a deficit or a surplus or happens to be balanced, the position of aggregate income in relation to a full employment level of income is a relevant consideration. Thus fiscal policy has joined monetary policy as the great enemies of the fluctuations in income which tend to inhere in private enterprise.

But notwithstanding the noble presence of these policies, inflation, as I have already indicated, is very much with us. If the government can be responsible for the stability of income, one might reasonably ask why it does not exercise such responsibility properly. The answer to this question reveals a lot, I think, about the nature of economic policy in a democratic society and therefore is particularly relevant to the question of what the American economy stands for. Although extremely important, stabilization of income is but one of many goals which legislators and administrators are trying to achieve. Since these diverse goals will inevitably conflict, compromises will almost certainly characterize the formulation and execution of policy. For example, the desire of governmental officials to maximize the external security of the United States has led them to demand staggeringly large appropriations from Congress for the maintenance of the military establishment. Whether or not this is the most appropriate way of obtaining this goal is perhaps debatable. What is not debatable is the fact that such expenditures have an inflationary impact when business firms are hard pressed to satisfy the demands of the private sector of the economy. Yet to reduce military expenditures in the interests of stabilizing income could conceivably jeopardize the external security of the country. As long as the American economy is embedded in a democratic political matrix, one must expect that different goals, representing the values of many different people, will compete for consideration and that no one goal can dominate all others. In such a society it is not possible to solve an inflation problem as, for example, Russia did after World War II, by suddenly reducing the quantity of money in a currency revaluation which discriminated against the hoarders of cash.

Summary. Let me pause here and summarize the relevance of the problems I have discussed to the issue with which this symposium is concerned. All of us carry in our lexicons flamboyant words such as capitalism, free enterprise, socialism, or communism for describing economic organization. It is doubtful, however, whether these words are really capable of conveying substantive meaning because so often they are subordinated to the ideological intent of the person using them.

The American economy is a mixed economy, its most important ingredient being the market mechanism through which economic choice is decentralized among firms and households. It is capitalistic to the extent that there is private ownership of capital and production for profit; it is socialistic to the extent that collective decisions of government supplement, or are substituted for, individual market decisions. It is an economy which is highly responsive to the preferences of the individuals and groups in the community, for the private sector produces to meet market demands, while the public sector meets the unfulfilled demands of the former. The problems I have discussed are among the issues which set the boundaries of the private and public sectors. The concentration of economic power and the instability of income are manifestations of the conflict between different individual interests and between individual and social interests. Far from denying these conflicts, we articulate them and proceed in pragmatic fashion as best we can to resolve them. The process, no doubt, may often appear to be sloppy, since publicly-aired dispute inevitably is noisy and discordant, but thus far it has worked. Various individuals and groups have an opportunity to express their views on these issues through the political mechanism and in consequence policies are formulated that establish the working relationship between the market and the government. The impact of this relationship on the national income is never satisfactory to everyone. Some people want more government goods and fewer market goods produced, for example, more earth satellites and fewer Edsels. Others want fewer military goods and more schools and hospitals produced. Still others want more subsistence goods and fewer luxury goods produced. If the resolution of these preference conflicts is not always neat and tidy, it is because we want to accommodate many different interests and are unwilling to specify one as paramount. In short, the American economy responds to the interests of workers, farmers, and business men as well as consumers, all of whom exert their influence through both the market and the government.

CONCLUSION

It should be apparent that the virtues of the American economy are attributable in no small degree to its unrivaled wealth. We can allow different interest groups to compete for their shares of the national product because the latter is large enough to tolerate inefficiencies in the economic system. We are so far removed from subsistence, in other words, that we can afford the conspicuous waste of advertising and public relations or the lost output of a prolonged strike.

But in all candor, one must acknowledge that this has not

always been the case, even though there has never been an economy in the history of the world blessed with such propitious conditions for economic growth. Located in the favorable middle latitudes of the North American continent and possessing a rich and variegated storehouse of natural resources, the American economy only needed the energies of an enterprising people to develop its economic potential. This was provided initially by the settlers and immigrants from Europe, many of whom came to these shores to escape the political, religious, or social restrictions of the old world. Enterprise was what they had to have to leave the old world. And because they found no established feudal system with its rigid class structure in the new world, the successful exploitation of the vast public domain promised them not only wealth but social status. America was truly the land of opportunity.

When one looks back over the past two hundred years of American economic development, however, one cannot help but be aware of many conditions which today we tend to associate with underdeveloped economies. The labor force, for example, did not come into being full grown, with all its rights fully established. One cannot overlook slavery and during the colonial period the system of indentured labor. Nor can one blink the fact that labor organizations were oppressed and harried in an unconscionable manner until comparatively recent times. It is therefore risky and, I think, inappropriate to make comparisons between the American economy and other economies, without at the same time specifying the stage of development each economy happens to be in. One must be exceedingly cautious about generalizing the significance of American economic experience for other countries today. It does not apply everywhere.

chapter VI

Managing the Managers—The Distribution of Power in American Industrial Society

Clark Kerr
University of California

▄▀

AMERICA HAS been an industrial society for only about half a century—a relatively short period of our history. In 1900 the United States was still a predominantly rural nation. In the short span of time since then we have become predominantly urban and fully committed to an industrial way of life for most of our people.

As we have gained experience, we have been shaping and re-shaping our views about the nature of the good industrial society. In changing our views, we have re-structured our society very substantially. In particular, we have greatly increased the power of the state to control the economic system and the flow of income within that system. This control has been exercised in several major areas. The Federal Government has been given the responsibility for the general level of employment and for certain techniques to be used in fulfilling this responsibility. The government has undertaken a massive redistribution of income, especially through income and inheritance taxes and levies on corporation profits. It has regulated industry, trade, and finance to prevent the economic exploitation of consumers. In the labor market, it has introduced minimum wages and supported the rights of employees to bargain with their employers about wages and working conditions. It has provided a system of social security for workers and for farmers.

Viewed broadly, the management of an industrial society has been considered essentially an economic problem. The task has been to stabilize the over-all level and even out the internal distribution of income. Economic stability and the reduction of economic inequality have been the goals.

The economic problem has existed and will continue to exist, but with a shift of emphasis. Our primary economic concern in the future will not be so much the achievement of greater internal stability and equality, but rather the means of assuring an adequate rate of economic growth within the developing world-wide context. This growth will depend on the rate of investment and the adequacy of our educational system and its related research activities, more than on any other factors. In fact, these two factors will be virtually the sole determinants of our national economic progress.

But there has been a political problem, as well as an economic one, as industrialization has swept over the United States in the past half century. The political problem has been, by comparison, largely neglected, and it is growing in significance. I refer to the distribution of power in our society. As we have been dispersing income more widely among our people, we have been allowing power to become more concentrated. In our absorption with economic equality, we have neglected true political equality.

The question of political equality is more complex than we have thought it to be. Traditionally, we have been concerned with the relation of the individual to the state. We have established our federal system of government, our checks and balances within each level of that system, popular control of government, and the rights of individual citizens. By and large, we have done very well in safeguarding the freedom of the individual and the group from the overwhelming dictation of the state. But we have paid less attention to the growth of private governments such as the corporation and the trade union which now range alongside public government in the influence they have over the lives of individuals. Individual freedom is not affected solely by the relationship between the individual and the state, but also by the relationship between the member and his trade union, and between the employee, the consumer and the corporation.

Thus, managing the managers in industrial society is not alone the age-old question of making the political leaders responsive to the wishes of the people. It is also the question of making the private association—the trade union, the corporation, or whatever group—responsive to the people it is intended to serve. This is a newer problem in the life of man, and he is only now grappling with it in the United States and around the world. For the big state increasingly has as companions the big corporation and the big trade union, and all of them confront the smaller individual. The distribution of power in society has taken on new dimensions and new complexities.

Industrial society is new to man. The final form it will take, even in the United States, cannot yet be fully seen. In our own country, industrial society has changed greatly in the past quarter of a century, and we can hardly expect that change is a monopoly of the past. How will it change in the future? There is at least some basis for prediction, for it is certain that industrial society has some logic to itself different from the logic of a hunting and fishing society, or a herding society, or an agricultural society.

Inherent in its logic are at least two imperatives: there will be large-scale organizations, and there will be a web of rules.

There will be large-scale organizations because many efficiencies flow from such organizations in numerous areas of production and of control. The large steel company and the large automobile company are the more effective producers, and it takes large unions and a strong state to match their influence.

There will be a great web of rules because they are necessary to govern and channel the actions of men in an interdependent society where the acts of one person affect so many other persons. A tremendous amount of discipline in society is essential to assure that we all produce and act as we should among the millions and millions of people mutually dependent upon each other.

Thus the logic of industrial society requires that there be fewer managers and more managed, and that the managed be subject to a growing burden of rules. The eternal conflict is not between the farm and the city, or the rich and the poor, or the hereditary class and the hereditary mass, for all these historical distinctions which have set men against each other in the past are being obliterated. The inevitable and undying conflict is between the manager and the managed. And it is a real conflict, because there are real issues to fight about.

While industrialization has a logic, it has no single form for carrying out this logic. Recent history reveals a number of forms, sometimes widely varying.

Industrialization can be operated by a dynastic elite, as in pre-war Germany and Japan, among other countries. Here the emphasis is upon the paternal community where the employer is essentially the father of the employees in the family enterprise, upon the perpetuation of a class structure, upon a tie of loyalty between employer and employee, and generally upon social stability.

An industrial society can be developed and managed, at least for a time, as in Indonesia or India, by a colonial power. Such a society will be designed primarily to serve the needs of the "home" country, however far away "home" may be.

Industrialization can also come under the control of the revolutionary intellectual, as in Russia and China. The communists base their control not on heredity or the free choice of the people, but on the conviction that their ideology has the greatest survival value in an industrializing world. Their ideology requires forced-draft industrialization under the firm control of the state.

Contrasted with the state-controlled industrial society is the state-guided society as we see it in Israel or Turkey or Egypt or Ghana. A strong nationalist urge is often the basis for guidance by the state.

Finally among alternative forms, industrialization can be organized by a new middle class of entrepreneurs, as in Great Britain, the United States, and elsewhere. Here the emphasis is placed upon the open market—the open labor market and the open consumer market—with the maximum choice for individuals within the market. The goal is economic freedom rather than social stability.

There are, of course, many variations on these themes; and among them, some have more survival value than others. In particular, the dynastic elite and the colonial power appear to be transitory forms of leadership in industrial society. Of the three more or less permanent forms, the "middle class" approach obviously allows more freedom to the individual and to groups of individuals than does the state-controlled or state-guided economy.

The world is currently witnessing the greatest ideological struggle of all history—the ideological struggle over how best to organize industrial society. Essentially, this struggle concerns the distribution of power. The communist view is that all decision-making power and all rationality reside with the state. The "Western" view is that decision-making authority and rationality should be widely diffused among the people. The "state-guided" approach lies somewhere in between. Only the Western approach is committed to the supreme value of individual liberty.

There can be no question about which of these forms of industrialization best serves the freedom of the individual. But there is a question about whether it yields in practice the maximum individual liberty consistent with its effective operation. This is an issue which we should examine frankly and carefully. We should be concerned not only with the preservation of our system for its great values, but also with its perfection for the sake of these same values.

How, then, can our American industrial system best preserve the freedom of its individual members in the face of large-scale organizations and the necessity of complex and confining rules? How can we best keep power dispersed as broadly as it is today, or disperse it even further?

To begin with, we must develop as much concern for the appropriate distribution of power as we have had for the equitable distribution of income. Our nation began with the concern for the distribution of power, and our founding fathers handled the problem extraordinarily well within the context of their time —the relationship of the citizen to the state. We should return to their central concern and treat it within the context of our time—the relationship of the individual to both public and private power organizations. In the past century, which might be called the Socialist Century because so much of the world was debating and responding to the Socialist demands for more power to the state and more equality of income distribution, this earlier concern was partly obscured. It is high time we bring it again to the forefront, for it is the more enduring and more basic concern.

Our nation is what the political scientists call a pluralistic society—that is, a society in which there are several or perhaps many centers of authority rather than just one. A pluralistic society, in and of itself, contributes to freedom by fractionalizing authority. But the problem does not end there. For each center of authority, such as the corporation or the trade union, can make and enforce its own rules and, in doing so, can limit the freedom of the individual. Consequently, it makes a great deal of difference how these rules are made and what they are.

I should like to state briefly seven principles which I think are essential to achieve a reasonable distribution of power within a pluralistic society:

1. There should be as many power centers as possible, consistent with the effective functioning of the society. We must preserve local governments as well as state and federal. We must preserve the maximum number of firms in an industry consistent with efficient operation. And we must preserve the identity of individual unions and of the locals within them.

2. These power centers should be roughly balanced in strength, where they face each other in conflict, so that no single one can dominate the others. This principle applies particularly to the equality of bargaining power in labor-management relations. Neither the company-dominated union nor the union-dominated industry is desirable if the contending positions are to be freely expressed.

3. Power centers should be separate one from another. Along with the doctrine of separation of church and state should go the doctrine of separation of state and industry, of state and labor, of industry and labor. There are some current tendencies toward the breakdown of this principle of separation and toward the creation of collusive alliances among power centers.

4. Individuals should be given as much choice as possible among these power centers. In particular, this means the open labor market and the open product market.

5. Each power center should provide for at least an essential minimum of control by its members over its leaders. Stockholders should have a measure of control over their Boards of Directors; union members over their officials.

6. Each power center should have an adequate judicial system to protect the rights of the participants—a grievance machinery in the corporation and the trade union alike.

7. Finally, each power center should exercise only the min-

imum control over the lives of its participants consistent with its survival and effective operation. Today there is a contrary tendency for power centers to grow not only in size but in the depth of their penetration into the activities of their participants.

If these seven principles are observed, our pluralistic system will remain reasonably responsive to the wishes of its members and will yield them a reasonable degree of freedom. To the extent they are violated, responsiveness and individual freedom will suffer.

You will note that these principles for the operation of our industrial society have their counterparts in the governmental arrangements established by the Constitution and the Bill of Rights. What I am suggesting is that those rules, so well designed to handle the distribution of power in our political system, be extended to apply to problems of concentrated power in other areas than that of public government alone.

None of my comments is meant to suggest that our American pluralistic system has not worked adequately, for it has obviously served us extraordinarily well. A pluralistic system can break down if its power centers fight excessively among themselves and grant no accommodation to one another, as we have seen happen from time to time in France or during the days of the Weimar Republic in Germany. In the United States, despite past periods of excessive industrial conflict, we have achieved a high degree of national consensus and social peace. A pluralistic system can also be subject to economic sabotage if individual power centers act like the Robber Barons on the Rhine in the late Middle Ages and exact a maximum toll from all who pass their way. They can restrict output and prevent the introduction of technological improvements. The United States has witnessed some of these activities, it is true, but never on a large scale. Our rising level of productivity attests to this fact.

Our pluralistic society is evidencing some deterioration not in these areas but rather in the slow erosion of the conditions essential to individual liberty, broadly defined, and perhaps also to continuing economic progress in the long run.

There are several current developments which may result in weakening the protective structure of our pluralistic system. One of these is the tendency for more and more of our national production to be concentrated in the hands of a smaller and smaller number of corporations. These corporations become increasingly autonomous. The market sets less precise limits for their actions. They are more in control of their own corporate lives and less responsive to the pressures of other elements in society. What good substitutes exist for the checks and balances normally provided by the competitive market? It is one of the wonders of the economic world that the corporations behave as well as they do, given such considerable latitude. Markets do not set the narrow limits nor do profits constitute the single goal assumed by orthodox economic theory to be essential to the effective operation of a corporation. Perhaps it is all explained, as some have suggested, by the corporations' having acquired a "soul." Whether they have or not, competition is still "the life of the trade," as Adam Smith pointed out so long ago, and it is safer for the consumer in the long run to be protected by competition rather than by the self-chosen "souls" of corporations. Thus the anti-trust laws are still essential to the preservation of a truly free enterprise system.

Another cause for concern is the increasing number of government officials and even agencies who are being captured in whole or in part by private industry or trade unions or other economic-interest groups. Agencies which were established to regulate an industry gradually come to protect that industry instead. Some agencies "belong" to labor, some to industry, some to farmers—rather than to the people of the United States. We must remember that it is just as important to protect the independence of government as of private groups and individuals.

The balance of power centers in our industrial system is being endangered by the growing areas of collusion in labor-management relations. Prices, entrance to the trade, business practices are jointly controlled in a surprising number of industries already. The old conflict of industry against labor is giving way to a new conflict of industry plus labor against the consuming public.

Another possible danger lies in the growth of paternalistic control by the employer as the welfare corporation competes with the welfare state. This trend has not gone to such lengths as it has in a country like Germany, where paternalism is traditional, but it has gone far enough to have disturbing effects.

During the past decade many industries have introduced private pension and welfare plans which serve to tie a man to a particular plant. In this period of time the voluntary quit rate of American workers has dropped in half, according to a recent study of the Bureau of Labor Statistics.[1] This fact is very significant, for it shows that individuals are losing their freedom to move and that our labor market is losing some if its dynamic aspects which have been so great a national asset.

One more development which deserves close scrutiny is the current role of our trade unions. In the United States, trade unions were intended in part to secure a better balance of power within our pluralistic system. They have made a most significant over-all contribution. They help balance alike the power of the corporation and of the state. They have introduced into many employment relationships the "consent of the governed" in the formulation of rules and judicial machinery to handle grievances. But they have also, on occasion, curtailed the freedom of the individual worker, sometimes necessarily and sometimes unnecessarily. Without endangering their security or their effective operation, it should be possible and even essential for all unions to do, as many already do, these things: open their memberships to all qualified workers without reference to race, religion, or creed; provide for secret elections at reasonable intervals; allow the maximum measure of autonomy to their locals consistent with effective bargaining; institute independent judicial protection for members who dissent against the leadership; and avoid extending their influence or control beyond those areas essential to the effective representation of their members, especially through compulsory political contributions which infringe on the political liberties of members.

None of this is intended to conjure up visions of *1984* or *Brave New World*. But man has some choices he can make about the distribution of power in industrial society, and these choices are important to the freedom of the individual. There is no cause for alarm but there is cause for serious thought. Industrial society

---

1 Ewan Clague, "Long Term Trends in Quit Rates," *Employment & Earnings* (Bureau of Labor Statistics), December, 1956. More factors were at work on the reduction of the quit rate than the growth of pension and welfare plans alone.

can be molded either with more or with less restriction on personal freedom. If it is important to preserve our pluralistic system against the monolithic alternative, it is also important to develop it to its utmost capacity as a liberating force in the life of the individual. The citizens in the industrial society of the future must learn how to manage, not only their political leaders, but also the managers of all important aspects of national life, so that society may remain responsive to their desires for "life, liberty and the pursuit of happiness"; so that they may continue to have in the future as in the past the greatest of wealth and the greatest of freedom.

chapter VII

American Agriculture

Charles M. Hardin
University of Chicago

■▪

IN THE diverse humanity that makes up the United States of America many groups such as the farmers appear to be both separate and integrated, at once distinct and blended in the common image. Others have been more despised and mocked than farmers, and occasionally some have been equally praised. But none other has been the subject of as much idolatry and contempt as the hayseedy son of honest toil and sweat, the noble yokel, the independent and thoughtful clodhopper, the bucolic philosopher, the industrious sucker, the indispensable hick, and the God-fearing, hell-fire-and-brimstone breathing last stronghold of woolhatted democracy—the farmer. Let us look at his political, economic, and cultural significance.

FARMERS IN U.S. POLITICS

Paradoxically, the shrinking numbers of farmers still weigh heavily in politics. Evidence is in the national budget with current annual agricultural outlays of recent years averaging about four and three-quarter billions of dollars. For 1957–58 agricultural expenditures are projected at 4.9 billions as against the combined total of 5.3 billions for highways, natural resources, housing and community development, education, and health.

Part of this fiscal concern for agriculture reflects the fortunate political access of farmers and their flair for organization. Congressional redistricting, performed by state legislatures typically apportioned in favor of rural areas and small towns and against the cities, lags behind urban growth. Moreover, the loyal rural voters commonly re-elect their Congressmen and Senators who thus climb the seniority ladder into places of preferment; consequently, rural law-makers fill a disproportionate number of committee chairmanships and of other powerful positions in the Congressional hierarchy. Again, the farmers' exceptionally successful access to the Federal Government has been improved by three general farm organizations, the Grange, the Farmers' Union, and the Farm Bureau, as well as by a host of commodity organizations many of which are members of the National Council of Farm Cooperatives. In this paper references to farm organizations will be to the powerful Farm Bureau which is organized in all states and has 1,600,000 family memberships, perhaps three-fourths of them held by families whose chief occupation is farming. In its internal politics the Farm Bureau exhibits many of the strains and stresses that afflict the nation.

Farm politics affects not only the budget but, more significantly, the constitutional system itself. Consider the political parties. Despite a number of important partisan Congressional votes on agricultural price supports, the economic program symbolized by parity for agriculture stems from a bipartisan coalition generated by the Farm Bureau and the farm bloc in the 1920's. The firm but divided partisanship of farm voters produces a nice distribution of Democratic and Republican Congressmen whose constrained bipartisanship weakens party lines in Congress generally and thus works against the development of a responsible two-party system as recommended in 1950 by a committee of political scientists—who, it must be added, have been vigorously controverted by a number of their colleagues.

Another effect of rural politics is in a kind of crude balance which emerges between the farm-small-town constituencies of many Congressmen and the heavily urban constituency of the President. Farmers have lost their one-time position of arbitrating between the parties. No longer does the farm vote decide which party controls the White House or Capitol Hill. The effect that I am seeking to express has to be stated precisely. Presidential elections, in the absence of landslides, are determined in the heavily metropolitan, two-party states. Which party shall control the House of Representatives is also decided in essentially the same states—and, on the whole, within these states in the same areas. But the *general* constituency of Congress, if we may so describe it, has a different center, especially in non-presidential years, a center in which rural areas and small towns figure disproportionately. Out of these two over-representations then we may say that a crude balance in our national politics emerges. This balance (sometimes, perhaps, a stalemate) is manifest in the customary preference of farm leaders for Congress as against the President—and if this be thought inconsistent with recent rural enthusiasm for Eisenhower, if not for Secretary Benson, I need merely mention that FDR's first term was a continuous honeymoon with cotton and corn growers. In the secular trend of rising executive power, this entrenchment of farm interests in the legislative branches acts as a counterweight. Let me stress again that I am referring to contributions by the farm sector to *national* politics; and in view of the international situation I do not want to foster complacency about our national institutions. Even more pointedly I am not referring to politics in the states which V. O. Key has shown (in *American State Politics*) to be declining in their responsiveness to shifts in political sentiment. His criticisms should interest farm politicians whose liability for this unhappy development is considerable.

Another great historical effect of farm politics has been to thrust aside the restrictions which a conservative jurisprudence once imposed upon the powers of government. Twenty years ago this would have headed our list; today the effects which current Farm Bureau leadership would like to soften, and even to reverse, are still significant. But let us glance at the influence of farm politics in the salient policy fields—strengthening reciprocal trade, on the whole, and lowering tariffs; sharpening the government's fiscal and monetary policy tools; historically supporting the drive to regulate business monopoly; and, more recently, applauding and even spearheading governmental attacks upon organized labor—indeed, farm pressure may have been determinative in passing the so-called "right-to-work" laws in eighteen states. When they are not pressing for price supports or for subsidies for the soil bank or for surplus removal, Farm Bureau spokesmen usually oppose federal expenditures, such as for education, public works, or the relief of depressed areas. In general, farm politics is presently conservative—in spending, except when agricultural programs are involved, and in restricting governmental powers, except when calling down the law on rival groups.

Another political consequence of farm politics is even more ambivalent: the effect on the federal system. Farm Bureau leaders have advocated decentralization even to the extent of supporting the Bricker Amendment which in its extreme form would virtually restore the Articles of Confederation. On numerous issues farm spokesmen urge vesting power in the states. On the other hand the major farm problem of economic adjustment is obviously national and even international. The prime policy instruments are the Agricultural Adjustment Administration and its successors and the Commodity Credit Corporation; both have to be national agencies and the centralizing tendencies are profoundly disturbing to many farm leaders. Similarly, farmers form part of the bloc which in nearly every state profits from the entrenched inequities of legislative apportionment to limit and confine the cities. But the result is to drive the cities toward Washington: the National Conference of Mayors is an advocate of national power, not of federal decentralization.

A final effect of farm politics (and I omit one or two) has been the early and persistent application of publicly-supported science to farming. Socially and culturally the land-grant college system has helped weave the rural strands into the American pattern. Economically, science has facilitated an ever-increasing flow of farm produce at relatively favorable prices—all this to the advantage of the innovators among farmers and of consumers generally. Simultaneously, however, science has helped increase the imbalance between the productive capabilities of agriculture and the demand for farm products. In turn, this imbalance has created a surplus of farm produce which under Public Law 480 we are currently distributing abroad at the annual cost of one billion dollars. This controversial program hurts some friendly nations of which the economic and political well-being is highly important to us; at the same time the program does channel American farm produce to needy peoples.*

* In a previous version I recommended that Public Law 480 might be continued if its adverse effects could be minimized. On reflection, I think that this approach should give way to a thorough reappraisal of our foreign policy in light of our radically worsened power situation. Public Law 480 would then be examined in terms of its consistency with the national interest rather than essentially as an instrument for ameliorating the domestic farm surplus problem.

In the same vein science-in-agriculture has provided trained personnel for staffing technical assistance programs. "Point Fourism" like "Do-Gooder" has become a term of contempt, perhaps especially for those who are unconsciously impelled to compensate for their own extreme overbenevolence. Meanwhile, agriculturalists and other scientists carry on, making some mistakes, it is true, but doing generally far more good than evil. Like surplus disposal, technical assistance concretely attacks the staggering differences in *per capita* productivity between the United States and most of Africa and Asia as well as much of Latin America. Countries in these areas need our help and in the light both of our political interest and of our religious obligations we need to give it. Many of them profoundly need technical agricultural assistance which we can offer, thanks to an unforeseen dividend of historical farm politics.

In the economy

Economically, the technological revolution in United States agriculture has many meanings. In 1956 each American farm worker supplied the food, fiber, and tobacco demands of himself and twenty other persons—twice as many as his predecessor even twenty years ago could provide. And in the same period the Bureau of Home Economics reports that the number of "poorly fed" households has declined from one in three to one in ten. While food costs have risen, consumer incomes have risen even faster—in 1956 an hour of factory labor would buy three times as many eggs and almost three times as much bacon as in 1929.

Other economic consequences flow from the fact that, come fair or foul weather and even during depressions, farmers keep on producing. In 1956, despite the long-standing drought that in the previous year had brought 1,055 counties in nineteen states into the "disaster area" category, and despite also the twelve million acres removed from commercial production in the acreage reserve program, we had the highest total farm output in all our history.

More important, by maintaining production even in deep depressions farmers have softened the hardship of those terrible years since much of what is produced somehow gets distributed and consumed. Likewise, farmers have responded (in part to zooming prices) to the extraordinary demands of war production. Meanwhile the farms have been a constant source of urban labor, already reared to a productive age and given "basic" training.

At the same time, historical farm production has been neither rapidly increasable nor decreasable. On the side of increases this is now much less true. With the ongoing technological revolution our national farm plant could very well add another fifty to sixty per cent to its production in the next decade. This is the present shape of the farm problem: an overexpanded plant in view of the prospective demand for the next twenty years. At the same time, historical stickiness of farm production in face of wide shifts in demand has acquainted farmers with unstable prices, both in their exhilarating rise and in their heartbreaking fall. The avidity of farmers for some kind of price support is as understandable as their willingness to accept the consequential production control.

And so we have our major governmental farm programs of which the heart has been price supports and production control. What have they cost? From 1932 through the current fiscal year the cost to government of all agricultural programs will be (very roughly) twenty-eight billion dollars. This figure seems staggering, and theoretically it could have been considerably lower; nevertheless, it is only six per cent of the current gross national product. Without condoning unnecessary extravagances in the farm program or advocating that we should long continue the present rate of expenditure, I think that we can afford the cost up to now in view of the contributions of our agriculture.

AND IN THE CULTURE

In 1910 nearly thirty-five per cent of American population was on farms; currently this figure is less than twelve per cent. The farm population hovered around thirty million from 1910 to 1940; today it is about twenty million. The exodus continues, the Census Bureau having just reported the 1956 off-farm migration as "one of the largest . . . ever recorded." What are the remaining farmers like? Large groups of them, as cotton, corn-hog, wheat, and dairy farmers, have much in common including their family quarrels; but the aggregate has great variety. Let us look at the differences first.

Farmers differ in their preference for political parties. Rural Southerners have been tenaciously Democratic, the more so in old plantation areas with the highest percentages of Negroes; nevertheless, a strain of Republicanism rides the Appalachian ridge even into the deep South. The rural Northeast and much of the rural Midwest are strongly Republican, although Democratic preference rises in the southern counties of states east of the Mississippi. In Iowa farmers have been more equally divided with a bit more Democratic tendency in the northern half and with flourishing Republicanism in the small towns. Farther West high-risk, one-crop farming has helped produce violent partisan swings—an extreme Republicanism in recent years, despite some disillusionment in 1956, follows a radically Democratic swing in 1932. Earlier the middle border displayed a yen for Fighting Bob, for the Rough Rider, for the Prairie Avengers, the Silver Dicks, the Progressives, the Greenbackers, the Populists and, in general, for anyone who promised to skin the fat cats of Wall Street.

Farmers are often separated by clashing economic interest. Western cattle breeders and Midwestern feeders; Midwestern cash grain growers and Eastern dairymen: for such pairs the price of the final product of one is a cost-of-production of the other. Eastern dairymen shore up their markets with barriers which Western dairy producers try to destroy. For many years conflict grew between cotton seed and soybean producers and dairy farmers who were barricaded behind discriminatory federal taxes on colored margarine. Today the federal law has fallen and so have similar state laws until butter legally monopolizes the golden appearance only in Wisconsin and Minnesota. The fact that so many of the major agricultural products have, in effect, their own special laws—cotton, corn, wheat, rice, tobacco, wool, and sugar—indicates the special interest as well as the political power of the groups which cluster around each of them. Major battles have occurred within Farm Bureau ranks over the conflicting views of cotton and corn farmers respecting price support levels. A statesmanlike stand in favor of flexible price supports has been maintained by the Farm Bureau leaders especially in the Midwest against strong internal opposition, the attacks of most Democratic party spokesmen, and a constant barrage from the kings of the wild frontier in the western wheat belt.

Fortunes of different economic types of farms vary considerably. During the golden years of 1910–14 corn producers enjoyed better terms of trade than cotton; hence the parity formula, based on these years, has tended to over-price corn—this fact explains in part, but does not wholly account for the Midwestern Farm Bureau leaders' stand on price supports. During the 1920's tobacco farmers prospered as women reached for Luckies and dairy farmers profited from rising milk consumption, while many other agricultural groups were frustrated by failing to share in the blessings of "normalcy." Immediately after World War II livestock producers were coining money. But between 1947–49 and 1955 the net farm income of corn-belt corn-hog and beef fatteners fell sixty-four per cent while that of tobacco-cotton farms in the Southern Piedmont was gaining forty-three per cent and that of central Northeast dairy farmers was rising fourteen per cent.

To these many differences among farmers may be added a variety of religious beliefs—Baptists and Methodists nearly everywhere and especially in the South; Lutheran and Catholic communities in the Great Lakes region and scattered through the Corn Belt; the white box churches with the slim spires dominate the Northeast and mark the westward trek of Congregationalists and Presbyterians.

Finally there are differences of attitude. A government psychologist once told me that in the deep South tenants or sharecroppers, asked about government programs, would refer to the "Big House"; the Middlewestern owner or tenant, taciturn at first, could be drawn out. The western rancher would say, "You want to know what I think about the government; Boy! Let me tell you . . ." And he would. In the same way, tastes differ. Edward A. O'Neal of Alabama, long president of the American Farm Bureau, loved to tease Iowans about growing so much corn but not knowing what to do with it— "They don't liquefy enough of it," he complained. But when he made these remarks in Iowa proper—or in proper Iowa—the reception was a bit cool. And yet there is striking variety in these matters even in the Southland. A North Carolina Agricultural Extension man may be invited to cocktails by coastal plains vegetable growers; offered nothing stronger than coffee by the piedmont yeoman for whom alcohol is the devil's brew; and, in the western Smokies, given a swig of mountain dew and a chance to help sing "The Criterville Jail."

And so there are many differences, but they should not obscure important similarities within the two great groups that make up American farmers—on the one hand, the middle-class to well-to-do; and, on the other, the hard-pressed to impoverished. Exact division of the 4,800,000 census farms (in 1954) into these two groups is impossible. But the first would include the half-million who produce half the commercial farm product and enjoy the lion's share of benefits from governmental programs. It would embrace the top two million farmers whose net money incomes in 1953 averaged $5,600 as compared to slightly under $5,000 for all non-farm families. The second group, on the other hand, would take in the half-million farms with less than $1,200 farm sales in 1954 where the operator worked less than one hundred days a year off the farm; and it would include many more part-time and other low-income farms. The middle-and-upward income group would include up to two and one half million farms; the poor-to-impoverished group would aggregate perhaps a million and a half.

Consider first the better-off farmers. The chief commercial producers, the staunch farm organization members, the architects-critics-administrators-benefactors of governmental farm programs —these are (in the recent phrase of Secretary Benson) the "new agricultural community that might be described as city life widely spread." They are catching up rapidly on home-freezers and TV sets, and they are rapidly learning to purchase their food at the supermarket.

Wherever such farmers are (and they occur in all settings, although there are proportionately fewer in the South, in the Appalachians, in the Ozarks, and in some cut-over northern timberlands), they have much in common. They must buy both their producers' and many of their consumers' items in the market, and the spirited fluctuations of farm prices in contrast to the stickiness of the prices of things bought are well-known to them. They embrace the best customers of agricultural science and include some with an intense interest in economic analyses of the farm problem.

And yet they are still farmers. Some of them may make an agricultural conference "sound like a seminar in physics" in the amazed description by a research director in Washington state. Others may be much less conversant with scientific developments. But nearly all of them are rooted in the soil and still think in terms of biological processes, of the life cycles of plants and animals. When Henry A. Wallace declared that above all a plant breeder needs "sympathy for the plant," he spoke for millions of farmers.

These similarities have historically drawn commercial farmers together in common distrust of the middleman. Investigation of the price-spreads between farmers and consumers has been a perennial favorite of farm politicians at least since the Grangers formed a posse to chase the elevator men and the railroaders in the 1870's. More recently the common situation of farmers has aggravated their suspicion of organized labor. Farmers tend to attribute the high prices of things they buy both to monopoly profits and also to what they think are inflated wages. Wedded as they are to biological processes which cannot be stopped, farmers view the strike as a mischievous economic weapon—although they have no scruples about using their own political weapons which laborers may consider equally mischievous. Acknowledging that widespread prosperity is essential for agriculture to thrive, they are learning that prosperity in itself is not enough. As urban incomes grow, proportionately less of the increase is spent for food—and much of the extra expenditure goes for additional services rather than to the farmer. What sharpens rural receptiveness to attacks upon business and now especially upon labor "monopoly" is the farmer's consciousness of his declining share of the consumer's food dollar: from over fifty per cent in 1945 to forty per cent today—and with no end in sight.

Farm price support programs benefit agriculture's have-nots little, for they have little to sell. The Farmers' Home Administration and its predecessors have helped them; but FHA is wisely centering its efforts on families who can reasonably expect to develop economic farm units. To extend FHA assistance to extremely hard-up farmers would be to permit the exchange of a mean and uncertain existence for a kind of protected poverty.[1] Much has been made of the Rural Development Program currently under way in sixty counties and nine trade areas in thirty states and Puerto Rico. While this program attempts to improve low-income farmers as farmers it commendably and courageously stresses the development of non-farming alternatives. I say courageously because there are many who, from their luxury apartments or split-level dream houses, lament the passing of the "small family farm." And yet a serious problem of rural poverty still remains. And a perspective of the attack upon it may be seen by referring to the agricultural budget for fiscal year 1957. In it the Rural Development Program has approximately $2,000,-000 plus $15,000,000 earmarked FHA loans—as against a total outlay of over five billions! I realize that juxtaposing these figures is a bit unwarranted. But suppose that we double the first figure and halve the second—the result would still dramatically show the disparity with which this nation helps the better-off farmers while ignoring their poor relations.

Many of the have-nots in agriculture are Negroes. Over half the 1940 farm population were Southerners and twenty-eight per cent of these were Negroes. Nearly forty per cent of southern rural farm Negroes migrated to cities in the 1940's, and the outflow continues heavy. But proportionately more Negroes than whites still live on farms; and Negroes compose a large fraction of farm labor which, whether casual or permanent, is perhaps the lowest American population group in income, prestige, and opportunity.

Negro-white relations are currently of the highest significance, both in domestic politics and in international relations. Agriculture by no means monopolizes the responsibility for reducing the tensions involved, but it cannot escape a sizeable share. Can farmers and their representatives facilitate the gradual integration of public agricultural services, including agricultural research and extension? What is more important—*will* they? These ques-

---

1 Following an analysis of W. E. Hendrix this should be qualified. Some farm families, not now dependent, are unable because of age or health either to move or to expand very much; they may be thrust into dependency by the loss even of one cow. For such farmers the FHA has a special function.

tions are directed toward organizations with both Northern and Southern members, like the Association of Land-Grant Colleges and Universities (which in 1954 took the long-deferred step of inviting Negro institutions in sixteen states to be members); like the United States Department of Agriculture, the federal partner of grant-in-aid agricultural research and extension programs which are still segregated; and like the Farm Bureau.

Such organizations may mitigate intersectional and intergroup conflicts so that their entire resolution need not be thrust upon our primary political institutions. At present hardening antagonism leaves little room for statesmanship, but some remains. Thus certain Midwestern state Farm Bureaus might issue invitations for annual conference speakers to moderate Southerners rather than to extremists who happen to favor flexible price supports and the American Farm Bureau might show more discrimination in its Distinguished Service Awards. In the same way the American Farm Bureau Federation should revise its current resolution which advocates the radical decentralization of governmental power to the states, for the present wording [2] embarrasses the moderates and strengthens the reactionaries. Beyond such organizational actions and unspeakably more important are the countless chances for farm leaders and for farmers generally to bind up the old wounds rather than to open new ones. In this way they may achieve the moral identity of which Robert Penn Warren wrote in the noble conclusion to *Segregation.*

CONCLUSION

In conclusion let me comment briefly on certain publicized beliefs about farmers and their roles. Some think that because farmers are near to nature they must be exceptionally close to God, but since Christianity holds God to be omnipresent this belief can have little theological standing. Again farmers are sometimes held to be more innocent of evil than urbanites, but habitués of both town and country know that sinfulness is distributed between them with generous impartiality.

2 "We recommend federal legislation to establish the principle that state law continues to be valid and enforceable in state courts unless there is a direct and positive conflict . . . with federal law." AFBF policy, 1957.

Another absurd argument is that agricultural prosperity is fundamental to national prosperity "because national income is seven times agriculture's income"—as is obviously untrue. Still another misinterpretation is that the democratic demands of farmers are misrepresented by the organized groups which have sprung up to speak for farmers in Washington; in the first place, group action in politics is probably essential and is certainly inescapable in a constitutional democracy; and, in the second place, the presumption that leaders should properly confine themselves to reporting to government "what their constituents want" misconstrues the function of political leadership—a function commendably performed, for example, by the Farm Bureau respecting price support policy and, on the whole, respecting international trade. In contrast the Farm Bureau has sometimes used its power to maintain the disadvantages of disorganized, low-income farmers.

In another vein the populists and progressives, heavily recruited from disgruntled ruralites, have been described as prime sources of the anti-intellectual, the nativistic, and the authoritarian contortions that occasionally disfigure the face of America. This description may please those urban liberals whose stereotypes about farmers are unconsciously derived from Marxian designations of the peasants as barbarous, primitive, stupid, and subhuman. While some evidence does identify some rural spokesmen with some of the seamier social movements and ideas in the United States the general indictment is unsupportable: both common sense and numerous analyses tell us that socially and politically vicious tendencies have been nourished by many kinds and conditions of men in diverse social settings. Similarly I have passed over the mass-psychoanalyses of society which tag farmers as exceptionally tradition-bound, rigid, and authoritarian. Generally I should reject these interpretations as resting upon the questionable scientific pretensions of "national character" analyses and of "modal personality type" theories. Specifically I should reject their application to farmers as depending upon flimsy evidence and leading to fuzzy inferences.

Traits imputed to farmers as farmers are often more properly attributable to other characteristics which may be but are not inevitably associated with farming—such characteristics as isolation and the intensification and persistence in particular communities of common ethnic derivation, of similar religious commitments, and of received standards respecting the proper organization of the family or the role of education. The distinguishing influence of the United States pattern of farming as such, I think, is rather different and stems from the farmers' common economic advantages and disadvantages, their strategic location in federal and state-local politics, and their unalterable conjunction in earning a living with the wheel of the seasons and the biological process. Such mutual experiences influence—I say *influence* rather than *determine*—the beliefs, attitudes, and actions of commercial farmers as, individually and collectively, they participate in the socio-politico-economic life of the United States.

In a word, the farm sector has contributed greatly to the productivity and stability of the country's economy and considerably both to the dynamism and to the equilibrating influences of its politics. The price of these gifts is unnecessarily high, but it is still supportable. On the other hand, farmers share the responsibility for the decline of state political institutions. Also on the debit side is the persistence of disadvantaged rural groups whose members considerably overlap: low-income farmers, hired workers, and Negroes. These failures are by no means attributable solely to farmers. But the degree of the failure and an appraisal of the farmers' share in them temper the note of acclaim on which one would otherwise conclude.

part III

CULTURE AND RELIGION

chapter VIII

The Meaning of Literature in America Today

John T. Frederick
University of Notre Dame

▄▀▄

IN APPROACHING the subject, "The Meaning of Literature in America Today," perhaps a first responsibility is one of definition. Shall we understand by "literature" the body of writing which is generally accepted by critical readers as marked by qualities of literary distinction? Or shall we consider the vast area of "popular" literature: the fiction in periodicals of largest circulation, the "bad majority" of paperbacks on drugstore stands, the confessions magazines and the comic books? Certainly these have meaning as expressions of American culture—meanings possibly depressing and even frightening, though somewhat less so if they are viewed in the perspective of popular literature of the past, and of the rest of the world. Those meanings are, however, perhaps more properly objects for consideration by the sociologist and the social psychologist than by the student of letters. In any case, I shall limit this inquiry to writings which appear to deserve application of the term "literature" in the usual sense. I shall proceed from the premise that a national literature is organic: that the work of writers of a given generation rests upon and is shaped by the work of their predecessors to a degree rarely recognized by the writers themselves. This means that in attempting to discover the meaning of literature in America today we cannot separate arbitrarily one part or branch of that literature from the main body and hope to view it with understanding. While I shall consider chiefly the writers of the present century and the literature of our own time, I shall endeavor to place those writers and that literature in their historical context. Indeed, I shall develop the thesis that more than a century ago American writers

115

formulated in criticism and realized in creation two cardinal principles which have marked and distinguished our national literature as a whole to the present time, and afford the basis of its meaning today.

The assertion of American political independence took but a day, and its attainment less than a decade. The achievement of our cultural independence took much longer and was in some ways more difficult. Indeed, so far as literature was concerned, the first half-century of our national existence was largely devoted to the mere declaration—in varied tones and terms to varying degrees of dissent—that American writers "are and of right ought to be free and independent," and that an American literature should be brought into being marked by qualities and characteristics which would distinguish it from British literature. It remained for a second generation of writers, born and educated as citizens of the young republic, to establish positive definition of those distinguishing characteristics, and to realize them in practice.

By 1850 this process of definition was substantially complete. American literature was to be particular, in the sense of immediate and intimate contact with and response to the actual texture of American life in the varied regions of the country; and it was to be marked by moral earnestness, by concern for ethical and spiritual values, by social purpose either immediate or ultimate, as distinguished from purposes of mere entertainment or self-expression. The first of these principles was no more than a logical recognition of the effects of geography and climate in a continental nation, with the resulting diversification of occupations and ways of life, and of the diversity of cultural background and inheritance which has marked Americans from the beginning. How much the second of these principles owed to the religious preoccupations of the Puritan founders of the culture which shaped most of our early writers, and particularly to the Puritan doctrine of stewardship, is a question which must await more searching consideration than it has yet received.

These two concepts were defined rather precisely and clearly through the critical contributions of Bryant, the elder Channing, Longfellow, Emerson, Lowell, and the theory and practice of such editors as John L. O'Sullivan of *The Democratic Review*. They

were given integrity and substance by Cooper's careful documentation of his earlier regional novels and by his often polemic
treatment of moral and ethical issues in his later work; by the
fiction of Hawthorne—"as parochial as the town pump," in the
phrase of James Gibbons Huneker—and by his intense preoccupation with ethical and religious values; by Thoreau's triumphant
discovery of universals in the minute particulars of New England's land and life; and by the obvious prevailing characteristics
of the most representative writings of Bryant, Whittier, Emerson, Longfellow and Lowell. Only the work of Poe, in the period
before 1850, offers a substantial exception. In the succeeding decade, Melville followed Hawthorne and the established directions of
American literature both in specification of fresh areas of American experience and in a penetration into its ethical and religious
problems which only now we are beginning to measure. Whitman's passion for particulars is all too evident to any reader of his
catalogs of American experience. His conscious dedication to social purposes is equally obvious.

As we pass the historical benchmark of the Civil War and find
the creation of our national literature passing into new hands,
evidence of the continued potency of both of these basic principles is ample. Most striking is the richness of consciously
regional writing in this period, with Harriet Beecher Stowe, Sarah
Orne Jewett, Mary Wilkins Freeman and Philander Deming in
New England; Joel Chandler Harris, Thomas Nelson Page, Mary
Noailles Murfree, Sidney Lanier, and George Washington Cable
in the South; Edward Eggleston, Bret Harte and Mark Twain
in the West. In the regional fiction of Hamlin Garland and Edgar
Howe in the middle west, and in that of Stephen Crane, Frank
Norris, and others, critical realism became naturalized in the
United States, in terms of definite social purposiveness integrated
with regional particularism.

But what of the three major writers of this period—that unique
triumvirate united by the common friendship of such different
men as Mark Twain and Henry James for their editor and friend,
William Dean Howells? In all three the thoughtful reader finds
displayed, as clearly as anywhere in our literary history, the
distinguishing marks of Americanism. Though Twain ranged far
for some of his subjects—to King Arthur's England, to mediaeval

Europe—he viewed these remote times and places with incurably American eyes. It will surely be generally agreed that his finest achievements—in *Huckleberry Finn, Roughing It, Life on the Mississippi*—are as intensely particular in texture as is Whittier's *Snow-Bound.* Nor, as the study of Twain has advanced, will many now be found to view him as a mere entertainer, a "funny man." Rather we see him as one of the most notable examples of the endemic moral earnestness of American writing: in his best work profound and sensitive in his perception of illness and error in American life and of the frailty of human nature. Extravagantly wrong as he could sometimes be, he was always terribly in earnest and terribly effective: the adverb is used here advisedly. With the best of intentions he dealt an all but mortal blow to the literary reputation of Cooper; achieving in his case something of what much lesser men with far lower motives did a generation later to the reputation of William Dean Howells.

Howells made the mistake of living too long. A prophet and a leader in his own generation—in the forefront of the fight for a sound realism in fiction as opposed to the cheaply and falsely romantic, the mentor and patron of such younger writers as Garland, Crane, and Theodore Dreiser—he lived on beyond the end of his period while the procession passed him by. To the petulant critics of the "roaring Twenties" he was "old hat"— his moderate realism weak and insipid to admirers of Hemingway and Sherwood Anderson. Though a clearer vision of Howells now begins to emerge, our criticism in general still signally fails to realize the range and depth of his understanding of the America of his times, his energy of understatement, and his frequently exquisite craftsmanship. Nearly all of Howells' work is American in setting, and these various settings are observed and recorded with precision, insight, quiet humor, and sensible sympathy unmatched in the whole range of American fiction. Usually his ethical convictions and social purposes are veiled or muted by his extraordinary understanding of and sympathy for the contrasting and conflicting characters who dramatize the issues of his novels—Old Dryfoos and his son in *A Hazard of New Fortunes,* for example, or Bromfield Corey and Silas Lapham in *The Rise of Silas Lapham.* But his conviction that literature has an ethical responsibility and a social function is expressed overtly and vigorously in his criticism and is almost everywhere implicit in his novels and short stories.

Henry James, whose work is now somewhat belatedly recognized as one of the chief ornaments of American literature, illustrates the major directions of American writing with certain modulations and special applications which have proved misleading to some critics. Because James so often dealt with Americans in the context of European culture, and because many of his major characters display a measure of family resemblance, it has been assumed that his vision of American life was obscured and truncated. However, the attentive reader will find that in his direct presentation of America, as in *The Bostonians*, the delightful *The Europeans*, portions of *Roderick Hudson* and *The Portrait of a Lady*, and some of the short stories—as also in the nonfictional *The American Scene*—he was a most sagacious and penetrating observer. Moreover, his Americans in Europe, from Daisy Miller and Roderick Hudson to Millie Theale of *The Wings of the Dove* and the Ververs of *The Golden Bowl*, are essentially and irretrievably American in most significant ways. In the whole body of James' work, no sensitive reader can miss the moral and ethical overtones—the never obtruded but always informing concern for ethical values. To some readers it seems that these are ultimately religious values.

The period between the Civil War and the end of the nineteenth century again affords but a single example of a major American writer whose work shows little trace of regional particularism and no evidence of social purpose: Emily Dickinson.

With the turn of the century there appeared in the United States younger writers of important promise, most of whom were to bridge the end of the period and to do at least some of their most distinguished work after the First World War. Among these we may note two poets, one of whom was destined to only a brief career and slender production, the other to a long creative life and many volumes: William Vaughn Moody and Edwin Arlington Robinson. Moody's religious impulses and classical studies gave some of his work qualities wholly divergent from what we have noted as prevailing American characteristics. But in "Gloucester Moors" he achieved a fusion of particular local detail with a broad sense of social responsibility rarely matched in poetry; and his "Ode in a Time of Hesitation"—written when the issue of imperial expansion following the Spanish-American War was paramount—is the noblest poem of its kind in American literature. Though no one can doubt that the central themes of Robinson's earlier lyric and dramatic poems are those of poets everywhere, their specific terms of character and detail are emphatically those of his New England "Tilbury Town." The best of these—such poems as "Isaac and Archibald" and "Mr. Flood's Party"—achieve richly satisfying integration of local incident and detail with universal experience. Just at the end of the period the mildly salacious fables of James Branch Cabell attained a temporary celebrity—partly by the help of the New York Society for the Suppression of Vice, in preventing the open sale of *Jurgen*. That Cabell's fame seems wraithlike now is in part, I think, the result of failure to recognize the quality of his particularized portrayal of actual American life, as in portions of *The Cream of the Jest* and in *The Rivet in Grandfather's Neck*.

Censorship of alleged obscenity in *The Genius* had something to do, too, with the high estimation placed on the work of Theodore Dreiser by spokesmen of the 1920's. Dreiser, the most important of the young writers encouraged by Howells, had forged for himself a new approach in fiction to American life, deriving something from Howells, something from Zola, more from his own materialistic determinism—"chemism," he called it—which was vaguely drawn from Darwinism *via* Herbert Spencer. In each of his major novels—*Sister Carrie, Jennie Gerhardt, The Financier, The Titan, The Genius*, and after World War I in *An American Tragedy* and *The Bulwark*—he undertook, with increasing clarity of purpose from book to book, a microscopic analysis of restricted areas of American life in terms of representative characters. In each case he gave the chosen area exhaustive and documented treatment by means of particularizing details; and in each case—at least after *Sister Carrie*—an obvious purpose of social criticism gave the book its reason for being, and a dogged moral earnestness, which could not spare a single scrap of evidence, its reason for being so long.

Robert Frost had to go to England for his first accurate appraisal and generous recognition; but to insist on the essential American character of his work would be carrying coals to Newcastle with a vengeance. There can be little dispute, I think, about the relative perfection of such purely lyrical poems as "Stopping by Woods on a Snowy Evening," "Come In," and "Mowing." Even these are marked by a pure and positive particularism of detail, even of phrase. These poems rest, however, upon the solid structure of the main body of his characteristic work—the narratives like "Home Burial" and "Brown's Descent," the incidental and reflective pieces like "A Drumlin Woodchuck," "Mending Wall," and "Birches"; and it is of course obvious that these are as native in thought and motive as in external detail. In the whole body of his work Frost has compiled an encyclopedia of New England comparable to that in Thoreau's notebooks—with far more emphasis on the human elements but without neglect of their physical environment. Never by any means the evangelist or exhorter—though sometimes in his later poems notably and even garrulously argumentative—Frost is as clearly an American writer in his inveterate concern for ethical issues and moral problems as in his lyric and dramatic materials.

Of all the American writers who began their work in the decades just before the first World War, Frost in poetry and Willa Cather in fiction seem to me most likely to be read in the future. After a partial false start, too obviously influenced by the powerful example of Henry James, Miss Cather found the material that was peculiarly her own in the untouched life of the Nebraska prairies, later in the American Southwest. She had aesthetic sensitiveness comparable to that of James, reticence and control and economy like Hawthorne's at his best, and a richer sense of the beauty and meaning of the American earth and a deeper appreciation of ordinary American men and women than any other novelist of her time.

One of the distinctions of H. L. Mencken was his early and generous recognition of the quality of Miss Cather's fiction. He performed a like service for Sherwood Anderson, for Sinclair Lewis, for Dreiser, for Ruth Suckow, to name but a few. It is at least arguable that Mencken was the most directly influential writer who has ever practised the art of literary criticism in the United States. One must have lived through the Twenties as a member of the literary community to testify adequately to his influence. The point I wish to make about Mencken, however, is that a dynamic, indeed, a militant earnestness was the man's most distinctive mark. Even when he wrote with tongue in cheek, as he frequently did, it was with a very real purpose, and definitely, as he saw it, a moral purpose. H. L. Mencken was in fact a writer as wholly dedicated to a characteristic American ideal as any I have ever known.

The First World War, like the Civil War, ended an era in the United States. The damage wrought by the war to our material economy was less immediately apparent than that of the Civil War—except in the field of agriculture. But the cultural dislocation, the spiritual trauma, were immediately evident. The swift disillusionment of those who actually believed in a war to make the world safe for democracy, and the quite different disillusionment of those compelled to fight in a war they did not believe in, are but crude and general verbal approximations of what had happened to the millions of young men who were freighted back from Europe in the transports and released from the mushroom training camps in 1918 and 1919—and, almost equally, to the millions of young and older men and women who had stayed at home. The climate was right for the full release of the energies of critical realism which had found their limited expression in the work of Garland, Crane, and others thirty years before.

In the perspective of another thirty years, it appears that among those who with implements of varying precision and with varying degrees of technical skill undertook in this decade of the Twenties to remove the hide of the corpus of American society and probe what lay beneath, the most overrated was Sinclair Lewis. The obvious hollowness of his too-voluminous later work underlines the superficiality of his earlier and better novels— *Main Street, Arrowsmith,* and *Babbitt.* He gave the times a word and emphasized an attitude; but his work already holds scarcely more than historical interest. More durably interesting are the novels of John Dos Passos—*Three Soldiers, Manhattan Transfer,* and the massive three-decker *U.S.A.* It is noteworthy that both of these men adopted in some measure the method of Dreiser: the roping off of defined areas of American society, and the close critical examination of those areas in the dramatic terms of people and their experience. In use of this method Dos Passos was measurably more sensitive in observation and more dependable in documentation than Lewis.

Also like Dreiser's fiction in its painstaking accumulation of particularizing detail and in its profound sympathy for "little people," as in its acute concern for social and economic tensions, is the slightly later work of James T. Farrell. More searching than the fiction of Dos Passos in its treatment of specific areas of American experience, and less objective, the best novels and stories of Farrell illustrate pointedly both the particularism and the moral earnestness which are the persistent hallmarks of American literature.

F. Scott Fitzgerald was a better craftsman than any of these— at his best, an artist of no mean stature. The essential difference between his work and that of Lewis and Dos Passos, especially, springs from a difference in its source, its reason for being. Fitzgerald's studies of contemporary America are not artificial in conception, but essentially lyrical in their origin from the inner experience of the writer, like the so different work of Willa Cather and Ruth Suckow. This makes for limitation, but also for concentration and for intensity. The best of Fitzgerald is slender in volume, but it provides the most adequate self-revelation of the Twenties in their "roaring" aspects. Less overt but no less genuine than that of Lewis, Dos Passos, and Farrell, is Fitzgerald's concern for ethical and moral values in a world which took them very lightly. All four were censors of the American scene.

Like Fitzgerald's fiction in its lyrical impulse, its personal reference and revelation, and in far more extreme degree, is the work of Thomas Wolfe; in all other aspects, unlike indeed. Wolfe was a writer unquestionably gifted, capable of rising to real poignancy and power. But among the gifts withheld were the sense of order and proportion, and the realization that two words are not always better than one. Great editors—Maxwell Perkins, and later Edward Aswell—labored mightily to give shape to his mountainous manuscripts. Probably the time for accurate appraisal of Wolfe has not yet come. In the present perspective, it seems that the work in which the editorial participation was most potent—his first novel, *Look Homeward, Angel,* and the posthumous *You Can't Go Home Again*—is his best. It is marked by intense particularism in setting and social nexus, and by vague but strong resentment of injustice, sympathy for suffering, and indictment of false values.

Sherwood Anderson had no more sense of form than did Wolfe, so far as the novel was concerned, though his terminal facilities were better. His novels are flabby patchworks, from *Windy Mc-Phearson's Son* to *Dark Laughter*. Also he was as much a lyricist as Wolfe, dipping every spoonful of his material straight from the kettle of his own experience and ego. But these very qualities combined to make him one of the best short story writers in American literature. His is not the traditional short story of Poe and Hawthorne, of course. Learning much from Joyce and at least a little from Gertrude Stein, he largely initiated and established in *Winesburg, Ohio, The Triumph of the Egg,* and *Horses and Men,* the volumes he produced during and just after the First World War, the direction the serious short story has taken in this country in the last thirty years. It is needless to emphasize the particularism of these stories—the rather painfully accurate, for one who has known them, recreation of the streets of a little midwestern town, the races at the county fair, the cornfields at night. Anderson's title to the other pervasive quality of our national literature lies in the fullness of his sympathy for his people—the warmth of his vision of their lives and of what limits or mars and mutilates, from within and without. He is not, except when he is at his worst, as he frequently is—witness *Marching Men* and *Many Marriages*—a preacher or a prophet. But very rarely in Anderson's pages can the reader imagine that the writer's purpose was mere entertainment, or doubt that he is profoundly in earnest in his desire to share his vision of the pathos and the occasional ecstasy or tragedy of American life.

Ably but most ungallantly Ernest Hemingway (in *The Torrents of Spring*) parodied Sherwood Anderson, after learning from his obvious master all that he could. Hemingway is one of the most inconsistent of the American writers of fiction who emerged in the 1920's, and partly for that reason one of the most difficult to assess. At his worst he can be flagrantly sensational and abysmally sentimental. At his best his work has a classic spareness and sureness of form and effect. A reason for this inconsistency may be found in his abundantly demonstrated inability to achieve sound characterization of women—except in such rare cases as that of the admirable Pilar in *For Whom the Bell Tolls*, in whom sex is largely irrelevant. For whatever reason, the moment Hemingway approaches feminine character in the aspect of sexual love he becomes either sensational, in the sense of exploitation of the sexual for the presumed excitement and gratification of the reader, or sentimental, in asserting attitudes and values obviously incompatible with the characters as given. To measure the gravity of this defect and the resulting inconsistencies in Hemingway one need only look from the extreme example in *Across the River and Into the Trees*—a novel redeemed from utter worthlessness only by two chapters on duck-hunting—along a vista of diminishing impairment at the characterization of Catherine Barkley in *A Farewell to Arms*, Maria in *For Whom the Bell Tolls*, and Brett Ashley in *The Sun Also Rises*. Perhaps it was not without double meaning that Hemingway titled one of his books *Men Without Women*. Certainly his best work, his only consistently sound work, is to be found in those short stories, like the early "Big Two-Hearted River" and "The Undefeated," in which women appear only incidentally or not at all; in similar parts of novels like the retreat from Caporetto in *A Farewell to Arms*, the fishing chapters in *The Sun Also Rises*, and El Sordo's defence of the hilltop in *For Whom the Bell Tolls*; and in his finest book, *The Old Man and the Sea*. Stylistically, for his chosen purposes and when he is at his best, Hemingway is the peer of anyone who has ever written fiction in America. Curiously, unlike Henry James in every other aspect and dimension of his art, he parallels James in writing largely of other lands than the United States, and in viewing them through American eyes and illuminating them by what he conceives to be American attitudes. He is far too much the artist—usually though not quite always—to let his moral purposes and convictions obtrude. But clearly in his most distinguished work he celebrates human values of moral and ethical significance.

Perhaps one other American writer of fiction whose best work was done in the interval between the two World Wars demands attention here: John Steinbeck. To the critic and historian of American literature, Steinbeck appears to afford a striking example of a melancholy fate too often exhibited in modern American literature: to put it bluntly, the stultifying and destructive effect of too much money. The American reading public gives generous material reward to its favorites—too generous for the well-being of the less truly dedicated among them. The later novels of Steinbeck are for the most part feeble and fatuous imitations of his own earlier work. But in the 1930's Steinbeck deserved the eminence he achieved. Perhaps his most distinguished work was in the short stories of *The Long Valley,* marked especially in such stories as "The Leader of the People" and "The Red Pony" by a rich and intense particularism in its presentation of the fresh setting of a California Valley, and in its deep and compassionate understanding of character. These qualities are strongly evident in the three short novels written in the same brief period, which are the most consistently satisfying of Steinbeck's books in their integrity of theme and expression: *Tortilla Flat, In Dubious Battle,* and *Of Mice and Men.* These novels are marked by a particularism as notable as that of the short stories in their realization of limited areas of the American scene, by firmness of structure rarely matched in American fiction, and by the typical American moral earnestness in approach to and exploration of social problems. This last-named quality was fully and eloquently expressed in the more famous and influential novel, *The Grapes of Wrath.* Though this novel is less satisfying as an artistic whole than its immediate predecessors, it is even more vivid in its detailed and accurate portrayal of American localities, and distinctly more positive in its definite espousal of a moral purpose.

The complex field of American poetry in the forty years since the beginning of World War I clearly defies analysis in a study of the present scope. We may note, as a single example of the difficulties it presents, the case of Robinson Jeffers. Whatever the future may think of his work, we can safely observe that in its most characteristic aspects it is vigorously regional, and is marked by an acute preoccupation with moral problems—with sin and its consequences—that approaches the frenetic. The most important poet of American origin in the period, to contemporary eyes, is one to whom our national title is not clear. T. S. Eliot is regarded by many readers as the most acute and articulate critic of modern life in all modern literature; not only of American life, of course, but of the whole culture of the western world. To what degree, if any, his qualities and attitudes are traceable to his American inheritance is a problem which must await a far more searching inquiry than is possible here. I shall merely suggest that if we do tentatively view Eliot's work as American, we may find in it the clearly demonstrable religious base which marked the work of Hawthorne and Melville, submerged in various degrees and disguised in various forms for two generations, now emerging again to visible primacy.

Critical writing has been abundant and fruitful in the period since the First World War, to a degree unparalleled in our literary history. In part it has been motivated by the desire to rescue our literary practice from the vigorous impressionism of Mencken and to achieve a criticism of greater precision and authority, as in the work of John Crowe Ransom, Lionel Trilling, Cleanth Brooks, R. P. Blackmur and others. It has also rendered distinguished service in reappraisal and illumination of American writers of the past, as in the work of Henry Seidel Canby, Perry Miller, F. O. Matthiessen, Yvor Winters, and many others.

To some readers, myself among them, it seems that much of the most distinguished writing done in the United States in recent years has been in the fields of biography and history, as in James Southall Freeman's *R. E. Lee,* James G. Randall's *Lincoln the President,* Esther Forbes' *Paul Revere and the World He Lived In,* Samuel Eliot Morison's *Admiral of the Ocean Sea,* and many other comparable volumes; the field of science approached as experience, as in Esther Carson's *The Sea Around Us;* and even in journalism, as in John Hersey's *Hiroshima.*

Viewing the whole period since America entered the First World War, however, the most prominent aspect of American literary production has been in the field of fiction, and most notably in that of fiction emphatically marked by the traditional American quality of particularism. The decades between world wars witnessed a harvest of regional fiction exceeding not only in volume but also in variety and general quality the similar outpouring after the Civil War. Historical fiction holds an important place in this body of writing. Region by region, the American past has been revitalized and brought into significantly illuminating relation to the present: and region by region that present has been closely analyzed and critically viewed. The reader can find the indivisible present and past of New England in the fiction of Kenneth Roberts, Mary Ellen Chase, Granville Hicks, and John P. Marquand; of Pennsylvania and the middle east in the novels of Joseph Hergesheimer and, more recently, in the finer achievement of James Gould Cozzens; the middle west in the work of Conrad Richter, Ruth Suckow, Josephine Johnson, and Richard Sullivan; of the far west in that of H. L. Davis, Wallace Stegner, A. B. Guthrie, Jr., Paul Horgan, and Walter Van Tilburg Clark.

Preeminent among these bodies of regional fiction is that which has come from the South. Perhaps this is because the South is more consciously a region of the United States than any other. Being a Southerner—I speak seriously—is a serious business. Certainly the unduly neglected work of William March, and the varied contributions of James Boyd, Caroline Gordon, Eudora Welty, E. P. O'Donnell, Carson McCullers, and others would be enough in themselves to create a new and vigorous regional literary tradition. They are surpassed, however, by the massive achievements of Robert Penn Warren and of William Faulkner. I submit that in the work of these writers the desiderata established more than a century ago as the marks of a distinctive American literature have come to their most mature realization.

Particularism—the most acute and accurate observation of specific men and events, the utmost richness of concrete local detail—provides the stone and mortar of Warren's fiction. Deliberate examination of the case of modern man and of its historical roots and determinations dictates its architectural design and gives its reason for being. What may be called historical density —the active recognition of the interaction of generations, is perhaps the most valuable element in Warren's fiction in constituting its eminent service to a national consciousness in search of itself.

There is of course no need to labor the presence of historical density in the work of William Faulkner. It is pervasive and in one sense paramount. Nor need we remind ourselves of his all but parochial particularism in the limitation of his major fiction to "Yoknapatawpha County" and largely to the members of a half-dozen families. It is equally clear upon any adequate reading that the whole body of his work is primarily moral and ethical, if not religious, in its orientation. Certainly there is no lack in the work of Faulkner of that quality the absence of which, in the judgment of William Butler Yeats, vitiated the American achievement of Emerson and Whitman: the vision of evil. Not even Hawthorne and Melville were more obsessed by the theme of sin: viewed by Faulkner not only in terms of the sins of persons but in those of region against region, race against race, and of man himself against the earth. So constant is this vision and so consuming this preoccupation that it is sometimes hard to see through their dramatic projection into ultimate and positive meaning.

Throughout our history, the makers of American literature have portrayed and expressed an America not smug and complacent but profoundly self-critical. But if the attention of many of our ablest writers has seemed to dwell, like Faulkner's, upon the faults and failures of America, that emphasis has but measured and underlined for most of them their dedication to truth and their vision of potential good. They have chastised America because they loved her. They have denied the finality of fault and failure because they have believed in the future of America and of mankind. In their picture of America today, neither the dollar nor the machine nor the state represents the supreme value, but the human spirit. This central fact has been best expressed by a chief among them, in the words of William Faulkner's speech in acceptance of the Nobel Prize in Literature: a formulation which would have been not unacceptable to the Puritan founders of the culture which first shaped our national literature, and one which expresses with exceptional precision the essential character of the totality of American literature in its prevailing purpose and practice and its consequent meaning for the world today:

> I decline to accept the end of man. . . . I believe that man will not merely endure: he will prevail. He is immortal, not because he alone among creatures has an inexhaustible voice but because he has a soul, a spirit capable of compassion and sacrifice and endurance. The poet's, the writer's duty is to write about these things . . . The poet's voice need not be merely the record of man, it can be one of the props, the pillars to help him endure and prevail.

chapter IX

Higher Education in the United States

George N. Shuster

Hunter College

BY WAY of prologue let me recall that Montaigne said for the emulation of all of us that his book had been written "in good faith." In spelling out what follows, I have abandoned well-nigh every hope or aim save this. It is difficult to attempt to describe the spirit of American higher education, see it clearly in terms of virtue or fault alike, and venture then to compare it with schools elsewhere. Far easier to do would have been a kind of catalogue, with statistics appended. The very thought of such a thing has been put from me, quite as if it were deadly temptation. I speak rather of ideas and ideals, of men and their patterns of thought, of culture as the necessary background of educational effort. The reader may perhaps wonder why I have been so candid. The excuse offered is that so many of us who represent American schools have thumped each other on the back so hard and loud abroad that we have sounded like Hollywood real-estate salesmen rather than earnest masters of the educational process, knowing weakness and strength alike. On the other hand there is nothing here of the critic for whom all we do is wrong and who strikes off in something akin to Rimbaud's *bateau ivre* to explore educational dream worlds which never have been and never will be.

The truly educated person will, I believe, seldom be very doctrinaire about education. Naturally he will take it for granted that schools of all sorts exist in order to prepare the young for a reasonably adequate use of their future years. He will also contend that those who supervise education must shirk no scholarly duty required to keep themselves in training for the task. But whether one way of doing all this is necessarily the only right way remains another matter. Young people are by no means alike, so that a mental headdress which fits one will look bizarre on his fellows. It is also apparent that "life" changes, and that therefore scholarship which loses awareness of change may come to lack proteins and vitamins. In support of these views so much writing and experience can be adduced that one may safely conclude that even "democratic" education will not inevitably make the world safe for democracy.

Perhaps, however, we should evaluate at the beginning of what must of necessity be a comparative discussion—for the meaning of higher education in the United States cannot be made clear unless it is placed in context [1]—three views of education currently expounded with vigor. First, it is contended that brains are our principal treasure and that the future will depend on how well we use them. This assertion no doubt contains a good measure of truth, but it is fortunately a fact that brains can be expended on tasks not devised by formal education. The pilot of a long-range bomber, for example, can survive only by being very intelligent, but it would probably do him little good, in a technical sense, to take time out in order to acquire a Ph.D. degree. The theory that a pool of brains exists from which every possible ounce of mental energy must be extracted dominates, so far as one can see, Soviet education. Yet this seems not to have proved that human intelligences are apples the juice in which can be squeezed out in a scholastic cider mill. Indeed, the intellectual energies which are noblest and most creative cannot be brought under any formula of coercive use. Educators must rather always humbly admit that some of the most promising of young minds will be in constant rebellion against what the schools have to offer.

---

1 No comparative typology of higher education will be attempted in this paper, though some attention will necessarily be paid to certain basic differences of purpose and structure. The various nations have appended to their school systems a vast number of specialized programs in order to meet as best they can the requirements of a growingly complex society. Thus professional training in France reveals a bewildering maze of curricula and degrees through which a foreign student of such matters will find it as difficult to move as Hercules did in his labyrinth. On the other hand, Austria, which has a comparatively simple plan at the professional level, has tried any number of experiments designed to adjust the lower schools to the varying needs of pupils emerging from the elementary schools. There is no handbook which adequately sets forth all these differences. Perhaps one is needed.

Second, there is a widespread view that since individuality is a basic characteristic of man, education must while imparting knowledge concern itself plastically with intuition in every sense in which this difficult word can be understood. This view has been expounded with brilliant insight by Jacques Maritain,[2] and one may note with satisfaction that it seems to underlie much impressive writing about education which has come out of England. To "glow, glory in wonder," as Father Hopkins' phrase has it, is surely to be a human being in the highest sense. And Vachel Lindsay was right when he said of so many people, sadly, that their trouble is

> Not that they sleep, but that they sleep so dreamlessly,
> Not that they die, but that they die like sheep.

Since one cannot understand either art or science unless one grasps the luminous significance of intuition in the making of both (who will cease marveling at say, the sudden glimpse of the formula of Relativity which was vouchsafed to Einstein as a young man, or the intuition of the meaning of Justification which was Newman's at an early age?), it is self-evident that awareness of intuitiveness in one's own life ought to be developed in as many human beings as possible. Nevertheless such a concept of education, when isolated from all other views, as Maritain of course does not isolate it, may lead to forms of teaching which fiddle around with "pupil creativity" and forget that the individual must be made, if need be, to hammer his little nail into the wall of society. This obliviousness seems a peculiarly modern temptation in the West. For example, in order to shut out from their imagination the shoddy symbols employed by the world about them, many painters end by excluding themselves from the world of accepted symbols altogether, and therewith from any form of adequate communication with their fellows.

Third, we ought to take a fresh look at what in our own country is termed "education for citizenship" and in other lands may take on different names without in essence being very disparate in character. At the level of the lower schools, this concept results in things as diverse as sharing in student government and pledging allegiance to the flag. Behind it lies, for many of us, the

2 Jacques Maritain, *Education at the Crossroads* (New Haven, 1943).

philosophy of Dewey and Kilpatrick. This philosophy has, however, two sides and it may be helpful to differentiate between them. The one side is that which developed from a quite simple social ethic, which in large measure was that of the United States during the period between the Civil War and 1914. Emphasis was placed here on the community working together for worthy common causes, and in particular on the cooperation between elders and youngsters in the business of education. It will do no harm to recall that Dewey was until the turn of the century professedly religious, and that Kilpatrick often cited the Biblical injunction, "Suffer the little children to come unto Me." Their commitments were, however, without adequate theological underpinning, so that the crisis of belief which was experienced in the United States after 1900—a crisis extending all the way from Winston Churchill's *Inside of the Cup* to the development of the Naturalistic Philosophy and of American Marxism—profoundly affected both men. But the other side, the later non-theistic doctrine of Dewey, which in the end led to cloudy books that are really nebulous variants of the great philosophy of Spinoza, should not now lead us to forget that the vision of a "community working together," whether in education or otherwise, was perhaps as notable a contribution as pioneer America has made to human experiential thought. It happened to be optimistic, but this is not an overpowering argument against it. Only when devotees of the Dewey-Kilpatrick doctrine, admittedly not without encouragement from the author of *Democracy and Education,* began to declare that the community should work together minus any kind of direction which did not take for granted an absolute relativism of values, that great harm began to be done. The dimensions of the injury cannot yet be fully estimated but are no doubt vast. Gordon Keith Chalmers dealt with this problem so well that a reference to his book will suffice by way of commentary.[3]

The three philosophies of education thus outlined have concerned all the countries of the Western world in varying ways. But upon different interpretations of them the cleavage between what we in the United States mean by education and higher education and what is believed and practiced elsewhere in large

3 *The Republic and the Person* (Chicago, 1952).

measure reposes. And so it is no doubt natural that the outside world should judge us by the weaknesses in our theory and practice rather than by our virtues. We have encouraged that judgment, perhaps, by endeavoring to impose our system of education on old countries like Germany and Japan. At any rate, the discussion begins by assuming that there is a marked difference between what is with us understood by culture and what is meant by this word in Europe and the Orient. Eastern views we shall not discuss by reason of the present writer's limitations. Insofar as Europe is concerned let us observe first of all that the strictures are not new.

Here are a few words about the city of Berlin as it was in the nineteenth century, written by the Swiss novelist Gottfried Keller in 1882. It may be added that Berlin is younger as cities go than New York but for a time bade fair to becoming the most popular urban center in Europe.

> Strictures on the condition of contemporary culture in Berlin (wrote Keller) have made a painful impression on me, primarily because I realize that for all who live in that city things are beginning to be decidedly uncomfortable. Disregarding for the nonce the miserable blocks of houses, together with what is in or around them, I have for my part been tempted to believe that the good old Humanism of Berlin, once so genuinely universal in outlook, was drowning in murky grandiosity, fed by numberless rivulets streaming in from all sides. A million small town folk, who every night have rushed together in a heap, cannot produce a great spirit all at once, through some sort of collective effort. Rather they will at first only make a good deal of noise or even a raucous alarum. And if the available talent runs after the crowd and tries to please it, the results can only be what they now are.

This is a fairly accurate description of what is currently being said about the culture of the United States in a good many places. As a result we, too, are "decidedly uncomfortable." Nothing about us do other peoples seem to like less than they do our culture. To a great many Oriental intellectuals we seem crassly materialistic in action and utterance. Many well bred Europeans, on the other hand, believe that we are ruled by mass psychoses, engineered by personalities as diverse as the late Senator McCarthy and the directors of television programs. Underlying this more or less impulsive response, which of course is in part the result of Communist propaganda, is the feeling that the "good old Humanism" of the United States has in turn been drowned in "murky grandiosity." In earlier times the writers and scholars of Europe experienced a sense of intimate comradeship with their fellows in America, very likely for the reason that men on both sides of the Atlantic approached the life of the mind in the self-same way. The great universities of Germany were revered by New Englanders and Middle Westerners now in their seventies with filial homage; and in turn the men who were the stellar lights of those institutions were grateful indeed for the comradeship of admired colleagues from across the sea. This sense of association in the business of the mind, which could easily be exemplified in instances as diversified as those of Lowell and Henry James, William Hocking and Sidney Fay, now exists only in feeble measure.

But it is also true that not every foreigner who sees us embroiled in a cultural mob scene is rebuffed by the spectacle. An educated American is often startled by Europe's cultural importations. The most flamboyant of all writers about the Wild West was the German Karl May. So popular do his books remain that the East German Communist regime was compelled to permit the publication of an edition of his works, which is now in great demand. The same author is also a major financial resource of a Bavarian publisher. Again, when a representative of a large Foundation made a tour of Polish universities in 1957, he found that "rock and roll" was a favorite pastime. When he confessed that he had never previously witnessed a demonstration of this bacchanalian rhythm, he startled his youthful acquaintances almost as much as if he had undertaken to recite a passage from Lenin.

One may venture the generalization that the strong appeal of certain aspects of the culture of the United States to wide segments of the population of Europe is based on a love of the exotic. That is certainly true of the continuing interest in the Wild West. It is undoubtedly in part also an explanation of the vogue of jazz, though this is a music having its own status as an art form. But what the educated seek is solidarity in the common quest for freedom, beauty, and truth. The fact that Americans do actually in the main share the same intellectual treasures and seek the same goals has unfortunately been obscured by a spirit of contentiousness difficult to account for. To some extent it is probably unavoidable. Since we have had to exercise military, political, and economic leadership, the cultural quality of those to whom it has been delegated, particularly in the lower echelons, has unfortunately often revealed our less desirable rather than our best qualities. On the other hand Europeans often manage to be stiff and unapproachable as well as prone to exaggerate what they term the "mass suggestibility" of our culture. The significance attributed to Senator McCarthy, has, for instance, been caricatured out of all semblance to reality.

It is for this reason above all that a candid confrontation of the two educational systems, Europe's and our own, may help to remove misunderstandings. What you will read has been set down without a semblance of a claim to finality. The literature which might be considered pertinent is very extensive, ranging all the way from statistical compilations to the proceedings of such bodies as the West German *Rektorenkonferenz,* but its existence will be taken for granted rather than adduced. For it is so easy to get so bogged down in an examination of the various pieces in the mosaic that the pattern cannot be seen with any clarity.

The first thing to note about the European system is that its most distinguished representative, the professor, is a Civil Servant in a society which turns far more than does ours round the Civil Service. It is in nearly all countries save ours the Ministry of Culture which determines not merely the fortunes of higher education, but those of the arts, the theater and the opera as well. The controls it exercises, however, will normally be circumscribed by the stature and independence of the professorial group. In Russia of course, although the basic organization remains the same in several fundamental academic respects, such as the function of secondary education in the thorough preparation of candidates for higher study, the powers of the Cultural Ministry are virtually absolute except that it must perforce adapt the curriculum to whatever ideological or political commitments are currently in vogue. But in the West European countries the prestige of the professor is very great—greater, perhaps, in countries like Poland, where no comparably prominent social figure seems to have emerged—and certainly generally much more impressive than is the case with us. If we take Germany

as a convenient example, we shall see that the professor, protected by the well established principle of *Lehrfreiheit,* is not
only likely to view his students with an indulgence ranging all
the way from zero to infinity but is ready to apply whatever
methods he can to the curbing of the Ministry. Among the means
adopted to serve the second purpose is one which entrusts the
administrative leadership of the university to professors chosen
in turn, usually for a year, from the several faculties. Thus a
theologian may be triumphantly succeeded by a veterinarian.
This procedure results in a lack of continuity which would be
fatal to American institutions of higher learning, and saddles
the victim with duties he is often poorly prepared to assume. His
tenure in office is therefore likely to be exceedingly burdensome,
even if it brings prestige and at least temporarily a not un-
appreciable grant of power. So strong is the resistance to possible
domination by a non-academic administration that the faculties
have blocked, and no doubt will continue to do so, all suggestions
for a change in this respect.

The status thus conferred on its corps of professors gives the
European university a position as arbiter of the arts and other
cultural activities which it does not possess in our society. Although fortunately a tradition of scholarly leadership is still
widely respected amongst us, many of the administrative heads
of our institutions are chosen from the company of businessmen,
experts in public relations and retired officers of the armed forces.
This may be the case primarily because even colleges and universities which rely for the financing of their ordinary budgets
on states or municipalities need private benefactions. This need
is a symbol of the glory and the weakness of American higher
education. It is "private enterprise" and so must seek out friends
even while organizing protection against them. Great educational
centers like Harvard University are corporations often possessing
resources which rival those of industry in magnitude and are
managed with exemplary skill. Additions to their capital or
endowment funds represent investments from which adequate
returns in terms of research and personnel are confidently expected. Not a few smaller colleges are similar in structure and
character.

We may cheerfully concede that in such a system the professor usually has the status of a trusted employee. The word "usually" is adduced advisedly because some states and cities confer civil service status on their educational appointees, though this normally implies nothing save tenure rights. When conditions are favorable, the professor's salary will be compared with what is paid to assistants to major business executives, with an implied suggestion that improvement is indicated; and upon occasion a notion will even be advanced that he be placed on a time schedule similar to that prevailing in industry and be paid accordingly. If the demand for instructors is greater than the available supply in a given field, a well qualified individual will profit as a result of competitive market conditions. This is now quite generally the case; and it seems probable that since ever-increasing numbers of students will seek admission to colleges and universities, the relatively small—indeed in all probability calamitously small—number of instructors who possess the traditional degrees and other attainments can choose between handsome offers for their services. The plight of financially less stable institutions will therewith become extremely serious as a matter of course.

But for the time being, the academic report must be optimistic. At all levels and in virtually every area, the American professor has the conviction that whatever effort he expends will earn a handsome dividend, to be paid not merely in dollars and cents of enhanced well-being for himself and his family but also in terms of notable contributions to learning. The resources available for research, supplied by federal, state, and local governments, by foundations and corporations, and by private individuals eager to assist scholarly endeavor, are lavish beyond all dreams of the past. Indeed, it is quite likely that more money is wasted in this country on futile and poorly conceived projects than is available to any country in Europe for scholarship. Grants-in-aid for travel and study are likewise stupendous in comparison with what was the custom, say, during the years prior to the Second World War. Granted a modest amount of initiative and diligence, the American scholar is now assured of the tools and the time he requires for research. In short, the American Maecenas has no peer in history; and it may be said by way of encomium that he has not expended his substance in vain.

Nevertheless it must be hastily interposed that at no stage have recruits for the academic fraternity been mustered in in any large number because of the material inducements held out. To be sure, a number of men and women not well suited for any other activity have been attracted by the security, the amenities, and the vacations provided by the University. But by and large the ablest of our faculty members have been motivated by sincere dedication to their tasks. Many have been or are sons of rabbis and ministers of the Gospel who have preferred secular learning to the lore of Scripture. These have given to the universities and colleges they have served a very special impulse to achieve innovation and even reform. Perhaps they are primarily responsible for a quality no one can dissociate from the American campus and which is virtually unknown in Europe—a characteristic to be defined on the one hand as an almost bellicose addiction to freedom and on the other as a commitment to a "liberal position," not quite a dogma this but almost one, which assays the Devil according to the degrees of his "conservatism."

The free enterprise system produces in addition many more kinds of educational institutions than are known abroad. This spectrum is not easy to delimit or describe. First come the colleges and universities under religious auspices, Catholic, Protestant and Jewish. They manifest startling differences of quality, outlook, and envisioned purpose. Some are little more than appendages to the major endeavors of religious Orders or of Protestant mission bands. Others proudly claim equality with all but the very best of secular institutions. In some the clergy exercise complete control; in others the religious profession is perfunctory. Next one must note the complexity of the course of study at the college and university level. For example, though the great institutions in the East, and some in the Far West, do set apart the Institutes of Technology or the Schools of Science, many universities blend the two, not always happily, so that they come to resemble cafeterias of higher education in which virtually the whole of a student's time is devoted to vocational studies, often taught without intellectual distinction. Certainly this situation clamors for change. But that Technical Institutes, even when not infused with love of higher learning for its own sake, are necessary in an era which depends on applied science for its very existence scarcely needs proof. If it were needed, the multiplication of such institutes abroad would provide it.

Finally there is a great diversity in method and orientation—a multiform flowering of educational philosophy—which in my judgment is the most impressive characteristic of higher schools in this country. What is it that a given institution is trying to do, and what means does it employ to reach this goal? Here leadership blending wisdom and tenacity can create patterns and tendencies which in the long run will bear fruit elsewhere as well. It is true that sometimes a gifted president will mount his barricade so imperiously that in the end little that is tangible will remain to prove that his revolution took on concrete form. This has been the case, no doubt, at the University of Chicago, under Robert M. Hutchins. Nevertheless it would be quite impossible to ignore the fact that the thinking which was done at Chicago has greatly stimulated educational reflection on many other campuses. And quite generally one may say that the American "system," about which there is nothing systematic, with its polarities of public and private, religious and secular, experimental and traditional, institutions, not only affords scope for creative minds but gives youth a far wider range of choice than is made available in the Old World.

Here one may as well discuss the major formal difference between the organization of higher education in this country and in Europe. The College as we know it has no counterpart elsewhere, while the graduate divisions of the University, insofar as they adhere to the four-faculty structure traditional in Germany, is distinguished only by pedagogical practice from those of Goettingen or Freiburg. The College has slowly evolved, with often curious or it may be inexplicable mutations, from the pattern furnished New England by the University of Cambridge in the seventeenth century. As is well known, it carries the student farther than does the Continental *lycée* or *Gymnasium*—a year farther if one is stringent, two years if one is not. Until quite recently, it was assumed that only a relatively few students would enter the University proper, an exception having duly been made for the science of medicine. Therefore it was normal to include in the program courses—amounting usually to these of the final two years—designed to prepare young men and women for the bar, teaching, and engineering. Therewith the College course of study became an amalgam of Liberal Arts and professional studies.

This practice reflects the character of a society which was still close to its pioneer origins. It believed in improving the mind, in opening vistas for the imagination, in acquiring the historical perspective needed for the proper adjudication of civic issues. But it was also normally acutely conscious that a living must be made, a wage earned. Since it was not a society respectful of social caste, in the sense sons would follow in the footsteps of their fathers, but was committed rather to constant freedom of opportunity, it desired to see its young men rise in the world. The farmer dreamed that some of his boys would become teachers, doctors, lawyers. Storekeepers in small towns thought of their children being at home in the glamor of cities. Thus the college became a sort of stock exchange in which investments could be made in two kinds of security—the one that of intellectual acumen and moral outlook, the other that of success in practical life.

It is true that, as critics were not averse to observing, the vocational purpose frequently left small room for the Liberal Arts. The most glaring instance, perhaps, was the stress placed on methodology in the training of teachers. Certainly it has not been as infrequent as is desirable that the fledgling pedagogue knew much more about how to instruct in a subject than he did about this itself. More generally the student was prone to ask what this or that course would "do for him," with the result, for example, that the study of Latin and Greek all but disappeared from the curriculum and even the Modern Languages were considered perfunctory and meaningless forms of academic torture. It was also no doubt inevitable that in a national community which expected of its citizens, at every level of government, active participation and a measure of unemotional judgment, the Social Sciences, as they came to be called, should figure prominently in the bill of fare. In short, the College seemed destined to become the exponent of Pragmatism *à l'outrance,* and the trend was aided by widespread acceptance of the doctrine, sponsored by President Eliot of Harvard, that the student should be permitted freely to elect whatever studies pleased him.

Note further that the College clung tenaciously to the quasi-monastic form which was one of the legacies of Cambridge. It was rural whenever it could so be; and when of necessity it functioned within the framework of city life it attempted to be as much of a rustic enclave as possible. The visitor to New York can still find one admirable survival of this mood—the College of Mount St. Vincent, into the beautiful campus of which one enters with the sensation of suddenly having stepped from the teeming metropolis into a tranquil countryside. Here young scholars and teachers lived in a community. There was fostered an admirable if upon occasion fretful solidarity, with its rule of life and its matching of wits, its long hours of companionship and its perennial exercises in adjustment. This college was a coming together in friendship of young and old for the purpose of hammering out together an approach to life. An institution was thus fashioned of which one can only think with nostalgia. No doubt it was rarely without its crudities and its provincialism; and sometimes its young fledglings rubbed themselves raw against the bounds that hemmed them in. But at its best it knew great teachers and noble spirits whose memories would be cherished always, as well as young companionship beyond price. When the College flourished as part of the University, as was the case at Princeton, Yale, and Harvard, it developed its own solidarity and loyalties, often surpassing by far those fostered in the more individualistic realms of post-graduate study.

Such colleges rarely exist any longer in the simpler form of yore. Urbanism has modified virtually all of them. Week-ends and short holidays siphon the students off to their families or the cities, and in turn bring to the campuses throngs of parents and friends. Sex segregation has become almost mythical, as a result of the commingling fostered by games and proms. In turn the number of strictly urban institutions, catering to young people who live at home or off campus, has become a dominant development. But America struggles hard not to permit its dream of a constant, very personal association between college teachers and students to die. It is true that "counsel" has now become "guidance," wearing professional, psychological guises not known before. And in its turn there has come into being almost everywhere an earnest effort to restore the Liberal Arts to a commanding position, to improve the quality of what is offered and done, and to awaken in students and faculty alike a sense of the true character of the intellectual life. Thus what we have lost in terms of simple commingling we seem to have gained in coinage of scholarship and earnestness.

One reason why such progress has been made, while not destroying the basic social character of the College, is of course that more students are now preparing to enter graduate schools. To be "accredited" as an institution the graduates of which will freely be admitted to the University has therefore become not so much a coveted mark of distinction as an assurance of survival. Good colleges now select their freshmen far more rigorously than used to be the case; and they must also elect to their faculties instructors who are thoroughly familiar with what the University does. One significant fruit of this concern is the scholarly achievement of the college professor. In some fields the College actually produces more writing of merit than does the University. A survey of publications in the realm of English Literature, for example, indicates that the faculty of a single college is outranked in productivity by three universities only. Among the reasons why this is so is probably that the universities still very rarely appoint women scholars to posts of academic importance. However that may be, the best colleges in the United States sponsor far more scholarly activity than does the European *lycée* or *Gymnasium*, though many of the teachers in these have been superbly trained.

It can be argued, and has been, that the "college habit" is wasteful of the student's time, and that the net result, in terms of preparation for the university, is not superior to that achieved in Europe. Dr. Hutchins and others have as a matter of fact attempted to shorten the span of pre-university study. But I believe we shall have to take the American youngster as he is, and not expect him to submit to the hard formal discipline of the Old World. He is more interested in becoming mentally supple, social-conscious, and ready for a wide range of life experiences than is his European counterpart. That he is able to work hard is true, but he indulges in shrewd, skeptical appraisal of what the aims of education are. For better or for worse, he has grown up in an environment which correlates the learning process with "interest," and if he is not somehow really gripped by the nature of the task assigned he will shirk it. In short, there is more of the soldier in the European student, and more of the civilian in ours.

No doubt it is the highly problematical high school which must be considered at this point. I am aware of the unending discussion which has grown up round an institution which is now in the grip of a profound dichotomy between the purpose which was in the past assigned to it and the uses which it serves at present. This school was seldom asked to consider training for admission to college its major function. On the one hand, it was an enlightened humanitarian device for keeping young people out of the labor market until they had reached a certain measure of maturity. On the other hand, it was expected to produce the "good citizen" conceived of in either secular or religious terms as somebody who desired to make his own contribution to the common good. The notion that democracy is the basic virtue and that it is undemocratic to separate brilliant young people from the mass just because they look forward to college, for a long time made it virtually impossible for the public schools in particular to provide the training on the basis of which the College could build. The clamor for a change is now so loud that it cannot any longer be ignored.

Yet I am bold enough to think that there is a more fundamental difference of outlook between ourselves and Europeans. We have developed a concept of puberty and the meaning of the years that ensue which, though new and unexplored, is widely accepted amongst us as the summit of all wisdom. The Old World practice of segregating boys and girls during their adolescent years of study is manifestly imperfect. It undoubtedly fosters its own forms of prurience and even unhealthy eroticism. And so a widespread American recourse to coeducation, which at the outset was resorted to because local communities could not afford to maintain independent schools for both sexes, affects even monosexual preparatory schools by making collective inter-school dating routine. Nobody knows the merits or demerits of this practice, because no one has seriously studied the situation. We cannot, for instance, tell whether there is now more immorality or less than there used to be. But unless all signs fail this much can be said;—the American system of dealing with the puberty period means that more time must be expended on education in order to obtain the same results. No one has as yet attempted to prove that "going steady" is a process to which a young person need devote only a few moments a day. Unquestionably somebody ought to take a good look at a social change which is at present compelling even Catholic and Protestant high schools to become coeducational. It will not be a popular inquiry, nor can one predict that the results—whatever they may be—will induce people to change their minds. But certainly only good could come of an objective inquiry into the discernible facts.

We shall now come finally to the University proper, conceived of as an institution of higher learning devoted to the training of candidates for the doctorate. There are notable differences in the American approach to this obligation, which from the intellectual point of view is the most important educational enterprise to be faced in any modern society. I should say that the principal cleavages are twofold. First, the average candidate for the degree receives more personal attention in this country and incidentally has a more difficult time meeting the course requirements. Yet in both situations it is the quality of the dissertation which ultimately decides. The American candidate is held more strictly to routine class attendance, but in both cases what the candidate can be considered able to do on his own responsibility determines his fate. I am inclined to believe that from this point of view it is easier to obtain a doctorate in Europe than in the United States, exception having duly been made for certain faculties.

Yet we have nothing to impose by way of discipline that is comparable to the severity of the examinations given in the École Normale Supérieure or the quite drastic selection processes in vogue in the *Instituten* of a good German University. The first probably constitute the most exacting of all academic winnowing devices, and rightly so since the few survivors constitute the élite of French intellectual life. The German *Institut,* which from a pedagogical point of view subjects the *Assistent* to a discipline of the utmost rigor and severity, depends for its vitality on the wisdom and objectivity of the professor in charge.

There is no denying that it is not as impersonal as is the scythe with which a French academic jury mows the incompetent down, less in the sense that it acts unfavorably to most of the candidates who present themselves than in that it frightens off all but the most resolute. The German system is more paternalistic. Yet it too makes virtual slaves of those of the men and women who seek through the guidance accorded them to ascend the narrow ladder which leads to the Ordinariate. Few will, however, deny that these exacting methods of selection have through generations insured the value and integrity of European scholarship.

By comparison the American method seems decidedly more leisurely and considerate. The best students are noted by their professors for appointment if not to the faculty of the institution granting the degree, then to those of colleges and universities in which it is deemed they will have an opportunity for development and advancement. To use a current phrase, the individual is aided to be "on his own." He is expected to make his way both as a scholar and as a teacher. Not a few fall by the wayside, including some for whom great hopes were initially entertained. Those of us who have grown grey in the service of American higher education will often have observed this phenomenon, which may well be a by-product of the formula of academic "free enterprise." Young men run afoul of their teaching assignments, or lack the patience to deal with students often distracted by the recreational lures of contemporary life. Others of whom much was expected later on never manage to complete a research project. They flit from topic to topic, staking claims on several moons but never getting their spades deep in any soil. To tell this mournful part of the story briefly, the roster of American higher education contains the names of many whose mature mediocrity contrasts strangely with their early promise. Perhaps the failures are in part attributable to the environment —a social situation in which the great rewards seem to pass the campus by, in which inflationary trends do not permit family budgets to balance unless the breadwinner takes on additional chores, and in which relatively so little glamor surrounds the person of the scholar. Yet it is also to a certain extent the result

of an optimism which often leads us to assume that what glitters
may be gold.

Nevertheless the gold we do produce—the roster of our illustrious professors and scientists, as well as the story of their
achievements—does not, it seems to me, lose any lustre when it
is placed beside the best which the Old World affords. Perhaps
we infrequently excel in fields which no doubt must be tilled
by men and women trained in early life in the basic techniques
required. Thus there are too few American theoretical physicists,
and perhaps even fewer native-born philologists of stature. On
the other hand, there are areas in which our leadership now excels
—for example, medicine, administration, military and diplomatic
history, political science, agronomy. In many branches of the
natural sciences we have demonstrably held our own, so that
our Nobel Prize winners are veritably not few in number. More
likely to be overlooked is the first-rate work being done in the
humanities. Newer forms of literary criticism and history have
been fostered. Above all, the number of poets who are also
scholars and teachers of distinction is large. We have only
recently begun to rear theologians and to develop a corps of
philosophers who will call to mind the great days of Santayana
and Royce, but we have clearly undertaken to do so.

Let us refer also to the hospitality of the American University.
It has accepted into its company of scholars very many of Europe's best, has given them homes in which they feel at home,
and has sat many grateful students at their feet. On the one
hand this places the American University greatly in Europe's
debt. If one thinks only of books which resulted from Nazism,
such as for instance the development of musicology and art
history, it is apparent that the total obligation is very great. Yet
on the other hand a University which can be cordially receptive
to men as diverse as Albert Einstein, Werner Jaeger, and Robert
Ulich, to mention only a few names, must assuredly be an institution in which such leaders could find a full scope for their powers.
Some of our European guests have as a matter of fact admittedly
made greater contributions to scholarship because they have felt
the challenge of the United States.

I conclude, therefore, that the American University properly

defined—that is, a University not in name only but committed
to the long-range and illustrious purpose of higher education—
is not immodest when it proclaims its readiness for the company
of its peers abroad. As has been said, it owes very much to the
German University in particular for example and inspiration.
But it has not wasted that patrimony. And so, whatever may
somewhat petulantly have been said during times of war and
political crisis, our higher schools are fully aware of the fact
that learning is truly international. This is to be kept in mind
when we say finally that our *national* achievement is the success
we have had in passing on to very many ordinary citizens, who
would never dream of considering themselves allied with scholars,
some of the fine wine of academic endeavor. The University has
played its goodly part in inculcating standards of objectivity and
combatting the disease of commitment to half-truths. In this
sense it is constantly at work, knowing that so very much remains
to be done until the scholar need no longer view the ignorance
about him contemptuously and in turn the public does not lock
the scholar in his ivory tower. This dream of the interpenetration
of learning and living is as old as Emerson and as young as the
youngest doctor of philosophy, standing in a classroom for the
first time and wondering whether the youth about him will dub
him monarch or fool.

chapter x
The Meaning of Architecture
John Ely Burchard
Massachusetts Institute of Technology

THE MOST important thing to say about Americans and architecture is that if we value the art of building at all it is usually when it is ancient or exotic or preferably both. This is simply one facet of the general American attitude toward the arts which, if it is changing at all, is changing slowly. Menotti observed some time ago that the typical American father was not very happy if his son asserted that he intended to be a composer. The same uneasiness develops if the son is interested in becoming a ballet dancer, a painter, a poet, an actor, a sculptor, or a physicist, although the sputnik-induced respectability of science and the consequent improvement of the scientist's economic status has, at least for the moment, quieted the parental fears about science as a profession if not as an art. We have to face the fact that at least until very recently the arts and the intellectual pursuits have been peripheral to American life. Calvin Coolidge was true to the current American attitudes when in 1925 he informed the *Exposition des Arts Decoratifs* that America had no representative contemporary paintings to send. Although there has been some change in the American view of the arts and of artists since then, some increased curiosity about the products, even some improvement in the popular critical taste; although there has been a comparable improvement in the respectability of the artists, the gain has not been great. There may be no country in the civilized world in which the artist is, in the last analysis, held in lower esteem. All this affects what American architecture is, what it has been, and what it is likely to be. For architecture is an art and that must never be forgotten.

149

It is an unusual art because it has to be made out of buildings that are erected for practical social purposes. The pragmatism may be that of supplying emotion in a memorial or at a shrine, of helping to induce the appropriate reverence and mystery in a church or temple, of providing healthful conditions of light, air, and sound in a schoolhouse or factory, but the pragmatism is always there. There never has been a time when people have been willing to lavish the amount of effort demanded by a building simply to produce an abstract piece of art. This not only limits the architect's freedom of fantasy and of self-expression, which may not always be a handicap, but it tends to make us confuse architecture with building. America is full of buildings that are sturdily built, easily maintained, comfortable to live or work in, efficient, if you like, but unfortunately lacking art. They are not architecture.

It will not help us much, in trying to evaluate what American architecture stands for in the present world, to look back at what American architecture may have been in the past. This is easy to understand if we think of other countries. No Western countries have greater architectural pasts than France and Italy and it would be hard to say which was the greater. In the present moment, though, save for a few churches such as the Dominican Convent by Matisse at Vence, the church at Assy by Novarino and Malot or the chapel of Notre Dame du Haut at Ronchamp by Le Corbusier, France is not offering much in the way of exciting new ideas whereas Italy is full of them. It will not do us much good in assessing what France stands for today to lay too much stress on her great thirteenth century when in a short span of time and in the short radius of a hundred miles or so from Paris she built the greatest cathedrals man has ever made. Twenty-five years ago much of the most interesting and human architecture of the day was being built in Finland, Sweden, and Denmark but even in so short a space of time something of the spark has died away, much of the new work is uninspired and dull, and these countries today mean less architecturally than Mexico, Venezuela, and Brazil.

The heritage of history is not entirely expunged, of course, from the current image of a nation—the Gothic churches of France and their Romanesque forebears are still a part of the picture of France; Italy may gain from the palaces of Florence and suffer from the architectural reminders of Mussolini; the great days of Gropius and Mies van der Rohe or Oud and Berlage are a part of the impression of Germany or Holland, and the brilliance of the elder Saarinen, of Asplund, of the young Markelius, and the young Aalto are still treasured in Scandinavia. But these bear little of the weight of the current image. For the world image of today's America this may be particularly fortunate. With whatever sentiments of love and pride we may regard our architectural past, the plain fact is that it has few moments of distinction after 1820. A sophisticated European will not even value highly some of the more ancient monuments we properly prize most, such as the quiet dignity of the early New England village, the manors of Virginia, or the white mansions of the Greek Revival as they spread along the Ohio River or nestled in the groves of Natchez and the bayous of Louisiana, or even in the more exotic adobes of the Southwest and of California, for the simple reason that to him they are only pale evolutions, in typical colonial fashion, from the more robust prototypes of England, France, Italy, and Spain. That this is an oversimplified misunderstanding of the full architectural meaning of a New England village green will not help us in these matters. Art fails if it requires essays to support it.

Many of us must have had the experience of guiding foreign visitors to some of our finest architectural shrines, the genuine ones like the Capen House in Topsfield, Massachusetts, or Westover in Virginia, and the spurious ones like Williamsburg in Virginia, Sturbridge in Massachusetts, only to find that they are fairly indifferent to both. On the other hand they are often excited about what we are doing now. They are also excited about one part of our recent architectural history, the buildings of one American, Frank Lloyd Wright, stretching over the last fifty years. They recognize him as one of the few authentic architectural artists of the century and America gains in their esteem because he is an American. For those who know the history of his life in America this situation contains more than a little irony. Europeans have generally acclaimed this man and many American critics admit him to be the greatest creator in the visual arts America has ever produced. Yet he has never been commissioned to build in his homeland a really important official building, school, church, hospital, university, even a factory at the scale, say, of Ford or General Motors. He has, to be sure, designed houses, churches, schools, colleges, factories that are important because of the creative gifts he brought to them but this is a very different matter.

We do not need to concern ourselves very much with the harm this has done to Mr. Wright but we might concern ourselves for a moment or two with the harm it may have done to America. Of course he is a thorny, sometimes vain, sometimes arrogant person who on occasion (as in the case of the Air Force Academy chapel dispute) has made unfortunate public statements about his architectural contemporaries, but so were Leonardo da Vinci and Benvenuto Cellini and Michelangelo. The difficulties and the possible extra costs involved in supporting genius, however disagreeable, are difficulties and costs that perceptive patrons have gladly accepted in all the historic times that we admire. Individual American patrons like the Larkins and the Johnsons and the Prices and the Kaufmanns and the Guggenheims have found it worth while to pay the extra costs, financial and nervous, but the great institutions of church and state, of education and industry, in America, have either been unable to sense Wright's genius or unwilling to tolerate the minor troubles involved in employing him in important work. He has not built one of our new and refreshing embassies abroad although some fine ones have been created by lesser men. The advisers to the State Department were too timid to invite him to compete for the design of our new chancellery in London although it is impossible to believe his solution would not have had more art in it than all the actual submissions put together. There is no escaping the historical record in this matter and there is no amending it now.

So far as America and Frank Lloyd Wright are concerned, it is too late. No amount of present recognition can change what the moving finger has written. All we can hope is that we may learn a lesson for the future. As for what the world may think about our failures with our world-renowned genius, we shall simply have to accept and seek to correct it not by pretense but by our subsequent actions when another genius comes along, if he does.

I am not trying at all here to suggest that Wright's architecture has been *the* "American architecture" in any classical sense. It has been the architecture of a poetic individualist who happened to be born in America. Despite some of his own confused writing about American democracy the great characteristic of all of his work has been its relation to the site and to nature. Sites and nature are present all over the world and Wright is one of the few living architects, far more than Le Corbusier for example, who could build successfully in high Nepal or on the shores of the Dead Sea. But it is not a national architecture. It contains an essence of America but not *the* essence. As Wright himself has often said, it is not capable of imitation; he has not founded a "school" or a "style"; his apprentices have seldom been distinguished and none really has come close to casting the shadow of the master. His influence on other architecture and on other architects has been extensive but it has been subtle, not obvious, and there is no prospect that it will be developed by others into a classic American style.

Wright himself would be opposed to such an effort for he has proclaimed the somewhat dubious doctrine that the West is now so shaped that we cannot expect to produce another classic form. What Wright's architecture asserts is a different principle to which Americans give much lip service—the principle that this is a country which tolerates and even encourages diversity and that in diversity from time to time men will emerge who have a special flavor of genius which is typically American only in that it does show this diversity. Our record with the one architect of our own who has given us the greatest chance to show that we believe this in a big way is not convincing. But I am not so pessimistic as to believe we have learned nothing; and it seems to me that greater tolerance and interest are now present in our society so that we are giving greater chances than we once might have to men whose designs have personality and are not cast in the accepted American mode, men like Yamasaki, Weese, Stone, and Pei, and others like Saarinen, Stubbins, and Rudolph.

Even for these men the way is not easy. They may have a satisfactory number of commissions and enough work to do but the great social institutional buildings which at least state the official position of the society too often elude them. Still, we may permit ourselves a mild optimism about our attitude toward some future genius.

How we use our architectural poets is only one of the ways in which America's architectural posture will be judged by the world. It will also wonder about the quality of our general architecture and the imagination that goes into it; and it will ask what building types we seem to value most as a guide to what our deepest values are.

There is little doubt that American architects are now producing some of the finest buildings that are being built in the world—and some of the worst. If as the wealthiest country in the world we were not producing some of the finest we ought really to despair. Whether we are producing our share of the finest is open to question; and whether we are producing our share of the new suggestions is hardly debatable—we are not.

No one should be sidetracked in examining the problem by chauvinistic considerations. Many of the most distinguished architects living and working in America are foreign-born—Neutra, Gropius, Mies van der Rohe, Belluschi, Saarinen, Stonorov, Sert, Breuer, Raymond, and so on to a much longer list—but these are all American architects now and we should never have any hesitation in claiming them as part of our artistic force. No matter where they were born, no matter what their prior successes elsewhere, they have had their greatest opportunities on the American scene and they have been affected and changed by their life as Americans. They account for a substantial amount of the American work that is most praised; and they have influenced much of the other praiseworthy work but they have not provided all the work and all the influence and they have to be joined to the ranks of native Americans, with varied ancestry, like Wurster, Stubbins, Weese, Stone, Bunshaft, Netsch, Rudolph, Armstrong, John Lyon Reid, Yamasaki, and many younger men to provide a roster of architectural talent far more distinguished than America has ever presented to the world before.

From their hands in the past decade has come a remarkable range of impressive buildings of many kinds. There have been the great new office buildings of metal and glass such as 860 Lake Shore Drive or the Inland Steel Company in Chicago, Lever

House and Seagram's in New York, or the Mile High Center in Denver. These evolving from early suggestions by Mies van der Rohe and Le Corbusier are not unique to America, of course. They are part of an international movement. Very often and particularly in South America they are treated with more variety and gaiety and many innovations in the way of brise-soleil devices have been proposed. But largely under the influence of Mies van der Rohe and from the boards as well of Skidmore, Owings & Merrill, the best American work has achieved a dignity of proportion, a refinement of detail, an aesthetic austerity and integrity that is unmatched in the more exuberant productions of other lands. Unfortunately, the principles of such designs, clear enough to Mies, to Bunshaft, and to Netsch, have been mistaken by countless other often reputable architects who have not been artists and who have endeavored to build buildings that would not seem Miesian (copies would have been better). Thus, they have tried to combine the flat-plane principle with setbacks, to replace the glass with pressed-metal shapes which are extraordinarily ugly, and have experimented insensitively with fenestrations less bold than the great sheets of glass, even using windows smaller than those of a modern railway car. I will not risk libel by naming any of these unhappy men or their productions but you can see examples almost anywhere, perhaps most clearly in Chicago, Pittsburgh, and New York. Still we have a right to be judged by our best work and not our worst, and our best office buildings can stand comparison with any.

The same general treatment of frame and panels applied to horizontally disposed buildings usually in a decentralized park has produced some remarkably fine institutions not really to be duplicated anywhere else in the world. The General Motors Research Center by Saarinen near Detroit and the Connecticut General Life Insurance Company by Bunshaft near Hartford are excellent examples. The pressures for decentralization are not yet felt as strongly in other parts of the architecturally active world as they are felt here but we are setting fine examples of what can and must be done in this direction. If only the leaders of rapidly growing cities like Karachi could imitate the nobility of our finest work of this kind, instead of our more easily imitated urban sprawl, they might spare themselves the later expensive and convulsive efforts we are now making to reclaim our older cities.

Consistent with looking at our best we can also take pride in our very best shopping centers such as the whilom decentralized Northland by Victor Gruen near Detroit. Here the architect has combined convenient parking with pleasurable walking to a variety of attractive stores, places for children to play, trees, fountains, sculpture, so that the fine arts seek to play a role in ordinary life as they have in every other time when they have flourished. There are not many Northlands in America but North-land is a success and there can be more if we demand them; the recreational spaces of Northland are limited and you cannot lunch to the music of a military band as you can in Göteborg but that is not beyond the possibilities of tomorrow. The art of Northland is not the finest that America can produce and there is no good reason why the finest art of a nation should not appear in a nation's market places; there is every good reason why it should be there and not in the nation's museums. But this too is a question of degree and not of principle and America's face to the world is enhanced by its best shopping centers and stores.

The same thing can be said for our private residences but the idea of really fine private houses, extending well down into the middle class, is not an idea that is well imagined by much of the world, which is more likely to judge us by our group housing, public or private. Aside from the physical conveniences provided by American skill in the manufacture of domestic appliances which are not a question of architecture, we cannot insist, I think, that our results in this area are calculated to enhance our prestige. I am not attempting here to catalogue all of our fine architecture and can pass by some excellent achievements by men like de Mars at Easter Hill Village, Neutra at Channel Heights, and Goodman at Hollin Hills to say that we have not achieved any such pleasant groupings as those at Vallingby near Stockholm where, at the end of the rapid transit, shopping, amusement, recreation, schools, churches and housing of a wide variety of types and cost live successfully together. The fact that other nations are performing more brilliantly in this important area than we is less a criticism of the competence of our architects, I think, than a comment on what we ask them to do but the result is nonetheless part of the architectural face we present to the world and not one of the more impressive parts. The underlying cause is no doubt that Americans do reject and always have rejected urban life as understood in Continental Europe and this is an ineradicable part of the American image.

On the other hand our schools are distinctly impressive. The record here is quite consistent and of late years quite brilliant. Under the early lead of Californians like Ernest Kump and John Lyon Reid who took advantage of the Californian climate to break the problem open, under the stimulus of skillful designs like that for the Crow Island School in Winnetka by Perkins and Will, and under the constant prodding of architects like Caudill who studied the needs of schools in Oklahoma and Texas, we are achieving a nationally high standard. There are of course good new schools in some other parts of the world, notably in the Scandinavian countries and in England, but it is not chauvinistic to assert that the architecture of American schools leads the world. It is the greater pity therefore that influential, reactionary, and architecturally ignorant writers like Miss Dorothy Thompson employ the columns of influential magazines like the *Ladies Home Journal* to declaim against the "extravagance" of our school buildings. I think it is not extravagance, but if it is it is one of which a wealthy nation should be proud. It is perfectly true that what happens in the school is more important than the architecture of the building and I have no doubt that the architecture is superior to what is happening inside, but our task is to upgrade the education, not to downgrade the architecture.

Of our other educational buildings we may be less proud. Our earliest universities like Harvard and William and Mary have a few fine and admirable Georgian buildings. Yale has one or two, Princeton has Nassau Hall. The loved old "mains" of most of our middle-aged colleges are bad Victorian. Princeton, Yale, and Chicago Gothic is no more honest and little better-looking than the "schoolboard" Gothic of brick and stone so popular in Indiana and Minnesota. California's classic, Rice's Venetian Gothic drawn into what Cram imagined a Spaniard might have built had he come to Houston, and the pseudo-mission of Caltech are scarcely better. They will not impress a European who knows Oxford or Cambridge or even the Sorbonne whose antiquity is genuine, whose buildings were built in the spirit of their times. University trustees are a timid lot when it comes to architecture and although it is possible to get up quite a list of isolated examples of contemporary architecture at universities, they are isolated and seldom first-class. For all its faults, the University of Mexico is architecturally more exciting than all the universities of the United States put together. The descent of a boy or girl from a contemporary secondary school building into the archaic buildings of the college or university is a descent into the slums— the university gymnasia, stadia and hockey rinks are naturally good but these would be more impressive to an ancient Roman than to a contemporary European or Hindu or Arab.

We are building some interesting churches in various parts of our country. The small ones are finer than the big ones. The most daring is displayed by the Roman Catholics and the Lutherans; the least by the Mormons and Christian Scientists and Episcopalians. But despite the work of men like Belluschi, Lloyd Wright, Murphy, Byrne, Saarinen, and many less well known architects, no one who knows the new churches of Finland, France, Switzerland, or South America is likely to be impressed with ours as anything but derivative and weak. They are pretty good but they are not the best.

They do offer one curious insight into our life. Many people think that the large increase in national church-going and church membership is due less to an increased need for faith than to an increased need for belonging to something. One demonstration of this is the growing amount of the area of the new church complexes which is devoted to the social services of the church. Often these peripheral activities have become so great that their architecture dominates, even overwhelms the architecture of the shrine. Our foreign visitors from everywhere but Scandinavia are bound to find this interesting whether or not they judge it admirable.

We are ambivalent about our governmental buildings. As in the case of the church the new office buildings housing administrative services have begun to dwarf the ancient symbols of the legislative and judicial branches. This is particularly noticeable in a state capital like Topeka where the quite contemporary office building overshadows the traditional domed expression of the bicameral legislature. This is an honest expression of our times, of course, when bureaucracy outweighs statesmanship in all spheres, and it would be obvious in Washington as well if the administrative buildings like the Pentagon were not so spread around that the White House, the Capitol, and the Supreme Court continue to express an architectural importance equal to that they once really had.

Perhaps our attitude toward governmental architecture has even more sides. There are not many capitols or executive mansions yet to build even at the state level but there are still courts and city halls and these we generally continue to set forth in bad classic. The office buildings we are likely to put up in cautious modern which means they are inferior both to the classic and to the modern. Very few recent public buildings in America offer us any occasion to be proud except the budding Air Force Academy which in my judgment will be finer than West Point or Annapolis, especially if Congressmen are wise enough not to step in to stop the building of the chapel.

When we build official buildings abroad we do better some of the time. We were not considerate of the feelings of the people of Stockholm when we built our chancellery there and we perhaps paid too much attention to the personal tastes of our ambassadors in one or two other places but Stone's filagreed Embassy for New Delhi, Weese's native Embassy for Ghana, Yamasaki's Consulate for Kobe, and, perhaps especially, Gropius' brilliant modern-classic for Athens all show us what our governmental buildings might be at home if only the Congress could refrain from the aesthetic judgments in which it is so incompetent.

We can be proud of many of our Federal buildings abroad and these buildings far outshine the larger, clumsier, stuffier, and tasteless work of our Russian competition but at home our governmental work is often not distinguishable from that of the Soviet and we would do better not to show it. Here we are beset by the inability of American politicians to divorce their private taste from the public taste. Indeed, one of the humorous aspects of the official architectural situation, if it is possible to find humor in it, would be that some of the most zealous Congressional protectors of America have attacked modern architecture as un-American while asserting a personal taste in the arts which has seemed quite in accord with the aesthetic line adopted by the Kremlin until its very recent switch to modern. Thus bad and untutored taste has made strange bedfellows.

Our factories are second to none in the world, our hospitals technically elegant and innovative enough but not as full of suggestion, as for example Paul Nelson's hospital at St. Lo in France.

In fact, the architectural face we present to the world is spotty. We score a big plus and can create some excitement with our factories, shopping centers, office buildings, schools and some of our governmental buildings abroad; we are displaying a reasonable if unexciting average with our churches, hospitals, and museums; we are disappointing or worse in our group housing, universities, and governmental buildings at home. We do not on the whole seem to the rest of the world to have supplied many of the inventions in the new buildings; we do not seem bold about our structures; we seem to them absurdly parsimonious about our architecture in view of our manifest riches; and on balance our total showing seems only fair to them—better than it was twenty years ago, less good than it might have been. We build more solidly and design with fewer awful mistakes than the Mexicans, Venezuelans, Brazilians, and Italians but it is not certain that a trip to the contemporary architecture of Italy, Brazil, Venezuela, and Mexico is not more stimulating.

Yet we must not overdraw the indictment against what we are in terms of what we might have been. The solid fact is that until 1940 American architectural students went abroad to finish their studies whenever they could, usually to Paris or Rome but in later years to Scandinavia too. Today the tide sets the other way and our good graduate schools of architecture have more foreign applications than they can serve. These men from over the world do not come merely to study our building techniques; they expect to study our art as well. This is more convincing than any criticism and leads to the conclusion that much of the world anyway thinks we may be moving toward the eminence which Bertrand Russell predicted for us in architecture if not in any other of the arts.

So far in this look at our architecture through foreign eyes I have been speaking only of individual buildings. The integration of the individual buildings into cities is far less convincing or happy. It would be a brave man or a blind one who would contend that the visual effect of our cities is not declining rapidly despite the individually distinguished additions we are making to the urban scene. South Bend is ugly and so is Shreveport. But so is Chicago whose single avenue will not save it. The tip of Manhattan and downtown Fifth Avenue and a few fine buildings here and there on the heights will not weigh down the long desolate rows of houses on Long Island or the Jersey flats which are also a part of New York. Despite the efforts to rebuild the Golden Triangle of Pittsburgh, the waterfront of New York, the University area or the near North Side of Chicago, we are losing ground everywhere. This is of course the subject of quite another paper but if you will only keep your eyes open as you enter and pass through even the loveliest American city you are not going to be happy. Here is where we have made our greatest failure. Architecture can no longer be considered in terms of single buildings. Perhaps it never could. But it cannot so be considered in the modern world. To work with large groups of buildings especially in existing cities which have much to be demolished requires wealth, and resourcefulness, and strong will, and a spirit of cooperation. These are assumed to be the American virtues par excellence and if the American architectural posture is to be favorably viewed it must express these virtues—it cannot express them unless they are truly our virtues—our cities as they stand today deny that truth—and the new ones of Texas and California deny it even more noisily than the old ones of Massachusetts and New York.

*   *   *

Within our culture we have a number of pressing questions to resolve. I have spoken of them at length elsewhere and will merely summarize them here. On the aesthetic side I think we can say that the rearguard actions of those who would lure us back to another eclectic revival cannot succeed whether they are commanded by Dorothy Thompson or Henry Hope Reed or some new and more formidable leader. We have not worked out the controversy between those who would like to refine the Miesian cages into a classic form, useful and admirable for all building types, and those who are straining to break the bars of the cage. The latter seek many outs, overstraining at novel structure as Saarinen and Stubbins seem to do, overrefining screens as seems to be the present manner of Stone, working with structures and patterns resourcefully as Yamasaki does. All these men are brilliant and sensitive. Perhaps the classicists like Johnson are too dogmatic; perhaps the others overvalue innovation at all costs. In any event this is the great debate of current architecture all over the Western world and it will offer interesting listening and looking for some years to come.

I think we can expect some revulsion from the austerity of Gropius and Mies even in further Miesian buildings. Many experiments with color and materials are yet unmade. Most of all perhaps we need to find out how to bring artists back into architecture in a really serious way, as the collaborators they have been in every previous great period of architecture. The artists do not make it very easy for they have carried the cult of individuality and of the private message to an absurdity. The society does not make it easy if, as seems likely, it is so content with verbal messages that it discounts visual communication and has no further need for iconography. The architects do not make it easy if they arrogantly assume that they are fully competent to be architects, painters, and sculptors all at once or if they retreat into overmodesty or overpraise by asserting with Mies van der Rohe that the problem of architecture is so difficult in itself that the consideration of art should come afterwards. These considerations can no longer be postponed.

There are also social difficulties. Why do Americans still regard economy, even parsimony, in building as virtuous? Most great architecture has cost more than the minimum. Why are Americans so timid about color and gaiety and brio in their buildings and even in their lives? We are a sober lot at bottom— even sombre. Who are to be the arbiters of our architectural taste? We have lost aristocrats like Jefferson who might have been listened to. We mistrust, perhaps rightly, professional experts who obviously can be as far apart as Christopher Tunnard and Sigfried Giedion, or Henry Hope Reed and I. Certainly we do not need to rely on the aesthetic judgment of Speaker Rayburn in determining what to do about the National Capitol, especially when this is in conflict with all informed architectural opinion.

How are we to achieve a sensitive and reliable democratic taste? Especially how are we to do this for a nation of people who are largely ignorant of and apathetic to the arts?

For answers to all these questions I confess a mild optimism. I think we will work out a modified set of forms which will be representative of our times and which will rank with the great architectures of history; I think we will find a way to bring painters and sculptors back to architecture. I think we may dare, at least sometimes, to "waste" money on fine buildings; I think we may learn the value of color and water and trees and open space around buildings; I think we may find a way to a good democratic taste and do a good deal to dismiss public ignorance and apathy. On all these counts even now and in the area of architecture at least our competitors in Moscow are not to be mentioned in the same breath.

But when we have done all that, when the blinders fall from the public's eyes, will it like what it sees? Of this I am much less confident. Suburbia and exurbia and sprawl seem to me to be gaining every day; the fish-and-chips restaurant, the doughnut stand, and the used-car lot are a commoner part of our visual experience than that beautiful new icicle of Chicago, the Inland Steel building. America is witnessing a deadly struggle between a new highway culture, the culture of the strip, and a new and potentially brilliant urbanity. The leaders of the bold new highway program seem as little disturbed by the prospect of defacing them with super billboards as by the majestic indifference with which they are content to divorce the planning and redevelopment of cities from the planning and building of the strips which exist not in their own right but only to take people from city to city. The strip seems to me to be winning all the skirmishes; and I do not see how anyone can be very confident of the outcome of this aesthetic Armageddon as it is being approached in our country unless the rebound from satisfaction with highway life to a demand for urbanity and repose and even elegance is more violent than it shows any sign of becoming. Great cultures of the past have had great roads; no great culture before ours has tried to live and die on the road. We are gradually reducing the chance of death on the highway; but it is not so obvious that we are enhancing the art of living upon it. This is our greatest architectural problem.

chapter XI

Film and Television in the United States

Thomas J. Stritch

University of Notre Dame

▀▗

BOTH AMERICAN films and television are paradigms of American culture. The words ordinarily used to characterize them, production, mass entertainment, money, success, have a familiar American flavor. Both are primarily giant mass-production businesses; films have made thunderous use of advertising and public relations and television lives on revenue derived from them; behind both are huge capital investments, directly in plant and personnel, indirectly in electronics and optics. Both are objects of deep suspicion to American intellectuals. Both are uniquely ingrained in the national experience; indeed they are among the few experiences in our pluralistic society universally shared. The things that ordinarily bind people together, common traditions, race, education, religion, climate, are all so diverse in the United States that films and automobiles serve cultural functions. Films and television especially propose powerful images to Americans striving for the good life, and as powerfully reflect what are, perhaps, the only common goals of the strife.

Although the peak movie attendance of seventy-five million a year has shrunk to about half that, television watching, which serves the same cultural function, has more than made up the difference. Only one family in five lacks a television set. But though a single television program may in one evening have a greater audience than a film in its whole history—the successful "A" feature was seen typically by twenty million, while as many as seventy million, nearly half the population, may have watched Mary Martin in *Peter Pan* in 1955—television's influence is not as strong. The relatively small screen and home reception dilute

164

its impact. Television has sparked scarcely a fad or fashion; the films started hundreds. Television exudes casualness, and is so taken; the movie theater had about it a little of the atmosphere of a temple.

But it was a temple at whose door, enthroned, sat a money-changer, and behind whose garish facade was the atmosphere of business. The American film industry is a peculiar marriage of art and business, a union more deeply imbedded in American culture than is commonly supposed. Art, or style, or design, or "beauty" have roles in American business scarcely second to finance, to a degree which astonishes Europeans. It is surprising to note that Metro-Goldwyn-Mayer historically is very like General Motors; it is more surprising to note that General Motors is very like Metro-Goldwyn-Mayer. Both use, or, more accurately for M-G-M, used mass production methods to create stylish, or artistic, products. They have similar histories, largely of mergers towards giantism. It is fanciful, but revealing, to compare the roles and careers of M-G-M's Samuel Goldwyn and GM's William Durant; Louis Mayer and Alfred P. Sloan, Jr; William S. Knudsen and Irving Thalberg. When Loew's Theaters owned M-G-M, the relation was similar to GM and its dealers, and posed similar problems. Both constantly face the necessity for new models, the films more frequently and more desperately. Both are occupied with the same problems of advertising, finance, search for new markets, research, and, above all, the kind of creativity business can put to work. And both are harassed by constant criticism which ignores this basic mass-industrial pattern, which assumes that the products are custom made. To compare a Buick to a Ferrari is like comparing a Warner Brothers' "B" movie to *Potemkin* or *Nanook of the North*. And to expect of any of these the qualities of a Cezanne is absurd. To make a Ferrari or a *Potemkin* requires large resources; Cezanne used only his imagination and a basket of the simplest materials. Yet film criticism especially often assumes all of them are doing essentially the same thing.

American films and American automobiles are basic industries. They are made largely in the two most typically American cities, Detroit and Los Angeles, as alike as cities can be, and the models toward which all other American cities, whether they like it or not, tend. They attract the typical American talent, the creative mechanic. They promote, one by example and the other by manufacturing the means, the American standard of living, the family from its own home riding long distances to school and work in its own car—or two.

No understanding of American films is possible without this starting point. The chief achievement of the American film is mass production and distribution which after long struggles arrived in the early 1920's at vertical integration: that is, the functions of production, distribution and exhibition were handled by a single integrated structure, thereby eliminating to some degree financial risk and making possible a steady flow of product. Nowhere else in the film-making world was this done. People who enjoy the best English, French, and Italian films and disparage ours are really comparing two very dissimilar products. They see only a few carefully chosen foreign films, not the awkward average. Occasionally they see a superb example of film art, and they assume it was made as films are made in Hollywood; actually, in most instances it was made by an organization especially put together for the one film and disbanded afterwards. A majority of celebrated foreign films were made in creative spurts of brief duration with the help of government subsidies; the attempts to stabilize such spurts resulted in bankruptcy or a level of production quite as standardized as the American one, but much worse: as witness the current English and Italian films after the brilliant achievements of 1945–1952. The American film has been the only constant of the film world, and its constancy has been the result of smooth mass production and efficient distribution—granting, of course, as with Chevrolet, the quality of the product: the film's universally appealing story material and the swift pace of its action.

Mass production means team work. A film is made by a team, and even the most personal and independent film makers, like Cecil B. DeMille and John Ford, play the roles of coach and captain in the creative process. These men—and Chaplin, Rossellini, Eisenstein, McCarey, Vidor, and many others—made films by a slow process of gestation, with the cooperation of writer, cinematographer, art director, and the other team members at all stages. But the team assembled for many films in the hey-day of Hollywood production was made up mostly of old hands at the general type of film desired, permanent studio employees. Individuality was thus often lost to imitation, and stock situations, characters, and even dialogue seem sometimes clipped from other films of the same type. One of the most telling comments on mass film production comes from a short made about 1950 by the Motion Picture Academy of Arts & Sciences on film making. Documenting the work of the director, the film shows him explaining to the actors that the scene he is shooting comes after the hero knows that the girl has double-crossed him, not before, as he had thought. The scene is then re-shot. Such must be the methods of mass production: actors, assistants, electricians, art directors shuffle from one film to the next, without any real participation in the life of the film. Only the director and, perhaps, the writer and producer know its nature.

From this kind of mass production there follows nearly every "Hollywoodism" film critics complain of. The monotony of the Hollywood film, its over-use of patterns and stereotypes, its slickness, its phony glamor, its insipidity, tastelessness, and sentimentality, are all traceable to the methods of big business—and are nearly all applicable to General Motors' cars. In particular, the flavor of personality, the touch of eccentricity even, that delights in a writer or a painter is filtered out of many films by the smooth assembly line. Too often one feels that the film is assembled rather than imagined, turned out rather than created, precisely as automobiles are. Yet, because the investment required by a new car or film is so huge as to check experiment, such faults are in the nature of the case; and the real wonder is that they are not more widespread and more crippling.

What has kept the films alive, and infused so much vitality into them, is their sensitivity to public taste. It is astonishing how successful so many of the best films have been. The delightful American screen musical has had a long and honorable history; it came in with sound and Ernst Lubitsch turned it into an authentic film genre. Then came the Astaire-Rogers series, and the charming early Crosby films, which combined song and story with a highly sensitive use of the camera. With color came *On the Town* and the Kelly films, more ambitious and more lavish, yet still superlative. They are flourishing still in *Funnyface* and

Seven Brides for Seven Brothers. The enduring popularity of westerns is surely owing in part to the long list of really good ones, from James Cruze's *The Covered Wagon* and John Ford's *Stagecoach,* down to *High Noon* and *Bad Day at Black Rock.* Films about war have the highest general level of all: no matter how trite the story the action scenes make superb filmic material. Films of satire and fantasy, too, have reached great heights in art and, much more rarely, in popularity, from Chaplin to Disney. In dramatic films, especially those of everyday life, the American product has been consistently weak: but so, too, has the American stage.

Recollections of this sort suggest that in the long run the public has had unconsciously a better sense of film esthetic than the intellectuals, and in certain stages a better one than the film executives. The weakness of the dramatic film, in particular, suggests that perhaps the films are not a very good vehicle for the drama of character. The close relations of stage and screen pose a very difficult problem for the critic. Films began on stages, and most serious film critics—a surprisingly small crew in the U.S.— think they have stayed too close to them. In the U.S. films were made outdoors very early, and they tended to stay there, flourishing in the California sunshine, until sound drove them indoors again for a brief period. By comparison European films stay indoors, especially in the harsher climate and soft light of northern Europe.

It is probably true that good films can be made indoors or out. But to the American taste the European film is too tainted with conventions borrowed from other arts: theater, circus, dancing, painting, pantomime. It is certainly true that the highly stylized mannerism of many famous films made in Europe has prevented their being popular in this country, and prevented many American films from being made in their image. As one re-views Murnau's *The Last Laugh* or Dreyer's *The Passion of Joan of Arc* one cannot help feeling that even these landmarks of film art are not quite within the range of the medium, are trying to do what the camera can't do. Dreyer's sound films, though highly praised and lovingly made, notably *Days of Wrath,* confirm the feeling that he works in the direction of symbolic photography rather than *Motion* pictures, in statics rather than dynamics.

The sub-conscious esthetic of most American films is that motion pictures ought to *move;* that of many foreign films that they ought to be *designed.* The American view holds that the camera is an extrovert, ranging far and wide, a visitor, a traveler, not a settled resident; the garrulous salesman or filling station attendant of the town, not its sage. European films often make the camera an introvert, searching out motive and delicate feeling, a heavy burden for so direct a medium.

William Inge's *Picnic,* play and film, helps point the case. The play is basically about an interplay of sexual relationships in a small town, the picnic merely the focus for their clash and resolution. In the play the picnic is not staged, only alluded to, like the battles in *Henry V.* But when the play was made into a film the picnic itself took over. Here was what a film could do, actually show the town at play, the swarming kids, the games, the boating, the tired feet, the sly drinking, the progress of the sun into twilight and night. All this dwarfed the pallid Freudianism of the play—made, indeed, scenes taken directly from the play seem irrelevant by-play. Even in *Henry V* the battle's action dimmed the splendor of the lines.

Picnics and battles are natural film subjects. So are city streets, trains and planes, night and day, sun and shadow, dark halls and bright squares peopled with men, women and children, not as they are, but in their characteristic gesture. Dialogue and motive can only strengthen; the film lives by its pictures, not by its wits.

Whatever the stand one takes on this question, however, whether affirmation or denial of the film's capacity to create drama of character, one thing is abundantly clear: audiences the world over have decided in favor of the American viewpoint. American film production is the only constant in the world film industry because film audiences have liked the typical American product at home and abroad. Serious film artists in other countries have all come sorrowfully to know this; the foreign films most highly praised have seldom made any money at home. While the critical hosannahs mounted for the Italian naturalistic films of the post-World War II period, Italian audiences preferred *The Asphalt Jungle* or *Singin' in The Rain;* the superb Japanese films of the same period were frankly made for prestige and fared badly at the box-office, especially in Japan; the great German films of the twenties did little better. There are exceptions, of course, like *The Blue Angel* and the Guinness comedies, but these have among other and different virtues the action and satire of American films.

Not that the satire is a necessary ingredient. Arthur Mayer tells of a theater owner in the Gold Coast who has made a good living showing over and over again for years *King Kong* and *The Mark of Zorro*—perhaps the smallest repertory of any theater in history. Audiences in Bombay fail to exhaust the charms of *Maisie Goes to College* in twenty trips to the theater, and not to have seen a film four or five times brands one as a jaded cynic. Such audiences want simple action and simple laughter and lots of both; these the American film gives them. The esthetic question is whether the pattern dictated by the audience is not, on higher levels, the basic film standard.

A great many people have tried to tell the films what they should be. John Gould Fletcher, the American poet, writing in 1928, felt they could do well only symbolic fantasy, in the manner of the German films of the twenties. Jean Cocteau partially shares this view, as his interesting films demonstrate. Thomas Mann thought they had more in common with ballet and music than with the stage; his view is sympathetic to the many experiments with abstract films. The more popular view among college-bred people is that there is little difference between stage and screen, and two English writers, Raymond William and Michael Orrom, have recently published a defence of thinking them two sides of the same art form. This view is anathema to most serious film critics like Rudolf Arnheim and Paul Rotha, who imply that the worst cross the films have had to bear is confusing them with the stage.

In this respect the films are, of course, no different from any other art; the purposes of poetry and easel painting have been more hotly debated. Art's purposes are made by artists, not by critics or estheticians; the teleology is built into the creative acts. But declarations of purpose and the subsequent formation of schools shape most modern artists into coteries; one often feels that the commitment to a program, and the ideology of the program, are more important than creation. From this coterie mentality the films have been sharply yanked back again and again by popular response. The huge investments required for film making force producers to keep a wary eye on the money-changers at the temple doors. So much is obvious. The question is whether these repeated yanks back to close study of the box office returns have been good for the films.

American films have been highly sensitive to new developments at home and abroad. The big innovations have been ours: Thomas A. Edison invented the motion picture camera and David Wark Griffith developed the art. Edison seemed not to realize at first the possibilities of the film; he had to be persuaded by Thomas Armat into projection onto the screen, and by foreign competition into making story films. Their enormous success opened up the familiar avenues of production and distribution; enterprising independent producers and theater owners joined to set up new companies which successfully challenged Edison's attempt at early monopoly.

What Griffith did was develop the director's technique of making films. Making an average of two short films a week for the Biograph Company, Griffith began to develop the plastic use of the camera. Every film is an integration of camera shots; the word "motion" in motion pictures applies more to the camera than it does to reality. Griffith moved his camera up and down, far and near, left and right. He developed editing and cutting, the two basic creative film techniques.

Cutting refers to the film's abrupt switching from one locale to another. The simplest form is the rescue melodrama, the heroine tied inside the burning house, the hero riding to the rescue. The film cuts from inside the house to the hero thundering down the road, from the agonized face of the heroine to the foaming mouth and straining eyes of the horse, from the writhings of the lady to get free to the urgent body of her hero bent over his mount. This is, of course, what the stage can't do.

But to make these things work careful editing is necessary. The camera must not switch too abruptly; it must know how long to linger and when to move. The rhythm of the cuts must follow the pace of the story. This is the art of the film. If the old tag, *ars est celare artem*, has any merit it surely applies here, for most film goers are scarcely aware of cutting and editing. Yet the most superficial reflection will show that the film of the heroine inside the burning house is taken all at once, and the hero's ride shot another time all at once, and these two later edited into a unity. Moreover, this must be done with regard to the whole: all the other parts must be fitted in, transitions devised from one part to another, recurring shots re-inserted at effective moments.

Griffith denied being influenced by the longer Italian story films which came out before his. In any case his work during the years of the First World War, when he moved to long films, so developed film technique that only refinements have been added since. Even sound added only another editor's resource: cutting and editing still are the basic techniques. The new big screen has modified them toward more pageantry and less plasticity, perhaps for the worse.

Thanks to Griffith's genius, American film technique was miles ahead of Europe's by the end of the war. Thanks to permanent employment, Hollywood became a pool of experienced technicians and production became smooth and efficient. Thanks to American business methods the film industry prospered at home and dominated the world market. And, no thanks for this, all these developments owed most to the destruction and disruption of the war. Henceforth films would try many new paths. Griffith's stories shared the taste of the times for melodrama and sentiment; they smack of Belasco and Clyde Fitch rather than Ibsen or Shaw, and hundreds of films imitated his dismaying combination of melodrama and sentiment while missing his brilliant technique. Yet more sophisticated influences came soon; there is a touch of Shaw in the satiric films of the young Douglas Fairbanks, deftly scripted by John Emerson and Anita Loos, and the satire of American types developed in the Sennett comedies was matched by films with social messages. It is a fact not often noted that our films had a social conscience well before our poetry or drama.

American films turned readily to genre subjects. This helped them to absorb without being inundated by the influence of the German films after the First World War. The German films were a strange blend of fantasy and realism, often heavily stylized in acting and composition, and distinctly claustrophobic. Their influence took American film making indoors again, to some extent, emphasizing tricky lighting and camera angles as indoor photography tends to do. Hollywood imported German directors and actors by the boatload, and the native production learned much from German techniques. Yet the German heavy-handedness was rejected by audiences accustomed to the nimbler American pace, and the harsh expressionism of its emotional atmosphere never had a chance. German influence had a happier issue in comedy and musicals, badly in need of a touch of fantasy and playfulness, but this was given so distinctly American a flavor that it came to be thought of, in the thirties, as altogether native.

Nonetheless, German influences come second only to those of Griffith in American film history, and it is possible that a really international school of film making might have resulted from its graft on the Hollywood tree had not the coming of sound and the rise of Hitler ended the matter. Though Hollywood has been equally hospitable to other national influences, especially French directors and British and Scandinavian actors, none came with the power and thrust of the Germans; and by the same token only the Germans and the Italian naturalists have resisted weakly imitating American films in their own production.

Europeans, both intellectuals and masses, and the rest of the world as well, have lapped up American films voraciously since World War I. It is true that the intellectuals have repudiated our worst faults, but they are more tolerant than ours. Films quite ordinary by our standards are reviewed as serious art in Europe; and the art of the film, in which the United States is acknowledged as leader, has far more rank there than it does in this country. There are several reasons for this, one important one the simple fact that American films are exotica, like reports from the moon in science fiction. A deeper reason lies in the nature of European film production. Compared to ours it is sporadic, almost amateur in spirit. Periods of feverish activity are followed by periods of quiescence. Film business abroad is conducted on political levels; censorship is far more pervasive than ours. No European or Asiatic country could make films like *Mr. Smith Goes to Washington, I am a Fugitive from a Chain Gang, On the Waterfront,* or many others critical of government and justice. When serious social films are made they are propaganda for one side only, officially so in the U.S.S.R. and Nazi Germany, unofficially in Britain and France; while United States films have shown a wide variety of social message. And films in India or Ireland, among other places, have a more stringent sexual censorship than our code provides.

Taxes from film theaters are a far more important source of revenue in Europe than in the U.S.; moreover, a film made in a small country like Sweden cannot return its costs even with normal success in its own country. Hence negotiation about films is a regular part of government business and affects film making in unpredictable ways. The great German films of the twenties were made with government subsidies; so were the recent Japanese art films. But government subsidies may be withdrawn arbitrarily, and an industry dependent on them has no sense of continuity.

In the long run of nearly fifty years, despite short-lived import restrictions now and then, the rest of the world has had American films as its staple and the audiences have responded much as American audiences have. Films popular here have been popular abroad, by and large; trends in film making and film stars, more so.

Despite this the cultivated levels of American life have been ashamed of Hollywood and despise its typical product. This is a curious fact. In other countries intellectuals take part in films as a matter of course; British writers like Aldous Huxley and J. B. Priestley write for the films as readily as they do for magazines. But an American writer disappears into Hollywood as into darkest Africa, shamefacedly muttering about money. Unless he returns he is regarded as lost. The royal way to return is to write a book or a play satirizing and ridiculing the films. No such stigma attaches to film making elsewhere; foreign intellectuals are fascinated by films, write about them, talk about them, allude to them frequently. Film criticism abroad is on a much higher level than in the U.S.; film topics turn up in intellectual journals much more frequently than they do here; film writers and directors are part of the intellectual world.

No doubt the geographical isolation of Hollywood has something to do with this. Intellectual life in most other countries is centered around the capital; Italian films are made near Rome, British ones near London. Though Los Angeles may be the most typical American city, she may lay no claim to being a cultural center, even by the most rabid Angeleños. And often film people are cut off from native Californians by dissimilarities of background and approach. They live to themselves and by themselves, forming a colony in a vacuum which needs frequent infusions of fresh blood from the stage and literature to renew its vitality. Scott Fitzgerald alone among major American writers had a sympathetic attitude toward film making; far more typical was the attitude of his friend Edmund Wilson, whose outburst against the movies reprinted in his *The Shores of Light* represents the turned back of the intellectual American.

Of course the intellectuals have noted the pervasive influence of the films on American life, but only in passing. The bibliography on films in the average American college library is smaller than that on English country houses. Until very lately few universities except those in Los Angeles took any interest in films at all, and even now the only gesture many make is a program of filmed novels for English departments—a gesture which promotes misunderstanding of the films since it suggests literary and theatrical standards rather than film ones. Perhaps the most telling example lies in a comparison with the theater. A Broadway season, surely no less commercial than the yearly Hollywood production, causes among American intellectuals more interest, more talk, more expenditure, more critical estimate, more books than a decade of movies. The intellectuals don't patronize the very films they profess to like; art theaters accounted for less than three per cent of the movie theater seats in the U.S. in 1956.

This cleavage between the cultivated levels of American life and the films left the films, so sensitive to mass taste in any case, to go their own way, and it is possible that this has been a better way for the art of the film than the approving participation of the intellectuals would have provided. Manny Farber, one of the most discerning film critics the United States has produced, holds this view. He believes that the big-budget highly advertised films tend generally to become "stunning mixtures of mannerism, smooth construction and hot air," and that the better examples of good film art, catching the immediacy of some aspect of life, tend to turn up in small-budget films produced by young comers.

In such considerations the tenses waver. The day of the small-budget film is done; its audience is lost to television, and the

Hollywood studio space that produced them is now used for television serials. Many of the films Farber thought good were produced under the double feature system, which matched a big-budget "A" film with a small-budget "B" one, and distributed under the block-booking system, in which a theater owner was forced to contract for a group of films. Both these were violently attacked, the latter successfully in the courts. Double features survive, accounting for 50 per cent of United States movie programs, but the pairing is more often two "A" and two "B" films instead of the old block-booking combination. Farber's affection for "B" films was matched by that of a large group of real fans, adults who were not consciously intellectual but who loved the film medium and cherished the insights of such films as *Take Care of My Little Girl, The Great McGinty, He Walks By Night, When Strangers Meet, Easy Living, The Man Who Cheated Himself, Don't Bother to Knock, The Little Fugitive,* and many others— not the touted self-conscious arty films, overlighted, overacted, overscored, but the directness of life pinned wriggling to the wall, as Maritain said of Picasso. This audience has left the theater, leaving it to the kids and the bums. The family audience stays home round its television set. There is no one left to yank the films back to earth.

But though the theater audience is halved, the audience for film has enormously increased, not just through filmed television programs, but non-commercial films of all kinds. Films for instruction and propaganda are everywhere; around 7000 of them were produced last year. Forty universities belong to the University Film Producers' Association; many of them have staffs of twenty or more to make films for school use. Nearly every promotion venture, whether sales for a roofing manufacturer or funds for a new hospital, makes or rents a film. Home movies are omnipresent, and on-the-spot documentary has taken on new life.

The very first such documentary was French, but the U.S. produced the first art documentary in the work of Robert Flaherty, the only name in the film history fit to stand beside Griffith's. Flaherty's message to Hollywood, enormously influential, was to get out of the studios and film life. It was not a practical message for the mass entertainment business, for Flaherty's method meant spending two or three years on a single film, but it influenced not only our best films but those of Europe, the U.S.S.R. in particular. John Grierson in Britain and Canada, and Flaherty and Pare Lorentz in the U.S., fathered some extraordinary short films, some for propaganda, some not. Doctrinaire documentary makers forget the usefulness of the story; established studios overdo the story. Interaction of the two viewpoints has been healthy for films.

The true inheritor of the documentary tradition is television. In the hands especially of Edward R. Murrow and the Columbia Broadcasting System's men, this has become the most exciting use of the medium. The small screen is actually helpful to much documentary, giving it a sense of intimacy that minimizes its formlessness. Television documentary makes words nearly as important as pictures, but the pictures—the hospital ward, the faces at a farmer's meeting, soldiers at the barricades in Hungary or Lebanon, the instruments at a symphony rehearsal—vitalize the narrative and give the scene an immediacy that is more than reportorial, that touches art. Wider use of the new video tape recorder, especially when it becomes more portable, will make editing and cutting easier and launch the most wordy and pedestrian of newscasts, let alone more ambitious projects, into new realms.

The nettle of this development, as for all hopeful television developments, is sponsorship. The money-changers preside over the television scene no less than the movies, but in much less satisfactory ways. The box-office counts the popularity of a movie, but who counts the popularity of a television program? This problem lies at the center of everything television does today.

When television swept the United States it took over the structure of radio. In the United States radio paid its way by advertising, and despite many reservations it was a reasonably flexible system because program costs were small. Enterprising local stations, which make more money from programs of their own origination than they do from national ones, could experiment as they pleased. The medium itself was not very flexible, but anything within its range had a fair chance of being tried. But television is so costly as to make local sponsorship and local production extremely difficult. This turns programming over to the great corporations who can afford it, or, more accurately, to the advertising agencies who represent them.

Local radio and subsequently local television stations devised audience counting systems in order to sell time to sponsors. Nobody maintained any of these was more than a rough indication; thirty Boston families, no matter how carefully chosen, cannot stand surrogate for all Boston families, and no method has ever been devised to measure the degree of attention. The television set may be on, tuned to a certain program; the family may be round it, rapt with attention, or they may be eating supper. Even under radio the system became something of a halter round the necks of the stations; it became harder and harder to sell a program with a small rating. But in radio this could be borne; CBS once put out a promotion brochure about its highbrow "Invitation to Learning" program entitled "Our Sixty-Ninth Most Popular Program."

In sixty-ninth place "Invitation to Learning" could still do well enough to keep going; on television, it would be off the air after its original thirteen-week contract. An audience of a million is too slight for a television program, except the simplest local shows like newscasts. But even audiences of millions may not sell the sponsor's product, as Philip Morris, Inc., learned when its expensive show at the best time failed to arrest sagging sales. Yet television does sell, as many market surveys testify. The trouble lies in finding out how and why.

The increase in quiz shows and westerns in 1958 reflects the advertiser's conviction, based on experience, that these programs sell their sponsors' products. They are analogous to advertisements for sales in big department stores and classified advertising, direct and measurable. But there are other forms of advertising, based on good will over a long period of time, public relations and specialized audiences. The effect of such advertising is less measurable. If it is to continue, the great corporations interested in institutional good will have to disregard ratings to some degree and trust to intangibles.

These have provided the sponsorship for most of television's bravest adventures, most notably the series of dramas that featured the first five years of national television and has now declined in quality and quantity. The most original of these were written for television; others were adapted from plays and short stories. Most of them kept pretty close to the form of the play; the division into acts provided handy breaks for the commercials, thereby making the commercials actually welcome as a diversion from the tension of the play. Camera movement used screen technique; thus the form fell somewhere between stage and screen. The small screen makes the camera hampered in its movement, and this intimacy makes dialogue more important than in the films. At the present time it seems fairly safe to suggest that no new form will evolve. Television plays are like radio plays, whose promise was never fulfilled.

The staple of television drama is rather the continued serial, borrowed directly from radio. These are mostly genre comedy, "I Love Lucy," "Ozzie and Harriet," "Father Knows Best," and the westerns, following the models of Amos 'n Andy and Jack Benny on radio. This is something new in entertainment, bearing a slight resemblance to magazine serials and some light literature, like the "Lucia" books of E. F. Benson. Unlike the films and television drama, it is basically formless—indeed, the lack of form is its essence, for it is mainly an intimate glimpse into somebody's home. So slick and professional a show as Jack Benny's even is usually set in home surroundings. This intimacy is the hallmark of television, as it was of radio; about them there is the air of family fun, charades, impromptu games. The spirit carries over into the variety shows of Steve Allen and Perry Como, and above all the determinedly homey atmosphere of most of the quiz and contest programs.

Many of these programs remind one of early films—the genre themes, the children, the occasional social satire. But film editing insistently posed the problem of form, and live television as insistently denies it—its only form is its duration of so many minutes. Its strain of informal, often vulgar, intimacy runs oddly through American life at present—the tone is the same in *Reader's Digest*, Sunday School lessons, instruction manuals for new employees, Dr. Crane, Billy Graham, and many others. To this atmosphere of homey familiarity the quiz shows add competition. The mild sadism of seeing somebody made a fool while he is winning a prize has surely replaced card and parlor games; the laughter and chaffing ease the sense of competitive strain.

In such an atmosphere art and its twin, form, have no place, not even a spurious one. Consider the television personality; he is, as has been pleasantly remarked, more a domestic pet than an artist. Singers work in the cute boy or girl atmosphere rather than that of the rapt dedication of the artist. Musicals with artistic leanings have been resounding flops. Dancing, which filled the screens during the first years, has dwindled: ballet all but gone, informal dancing turned into acrobatics rather than patterns.

Many feel that only pay-as-you-go television can restore form, revive higher levels of programs and settle the sponsorship question. These are powerful arguments for it, and at the present it seems likely to be tried. The Federal Communications Commission bottled up television expansion for some years, from 1948 to 1952, in what seems now to have been a sensible move, to study channel permit procedures. Something similar may be in the offing for pay-as-you-go programs.

When the FCC did unfreeze television channels, it reserved a good many for educational use. Some cities, New York, Chicago, Cincinnati, San Francisco, Boston, Detroit and Miami among the larger ones, run several hours of programs a day, financed usually by private contributions; and some universities, Michigan State, Iowa State, North Carolina, and Missouri among them, run educational programs as training for students as well as service to the University and the community. The general effect of such television is summed up by William Y. Elliott, in *Television's Impact on America's Culture,* a study financed by the Ford Foundation published in 1956: "Despite [much good work here and there] the existing educational television stations are in a parlous condition. They have in only a few cases really safe prospects of adequate continuing financial support. . . . They are in grave straits to put enough good programming hours on the air to win and hold even a select audience." Since Mr. Elliott wrote this the revelation of the U.S.S.R.'s successes in science and the re-examination of the work of American education undoubtedly will mean some further experiment in education through television. It is fair to say, however, that most educators see the medium as at best a useful tool in large demonstration classes.

The public service area is a more encouraging one. From the beginning television networks have inaugurated programs, breaking from the radio pattern in which only advertising agencies or local stations did originations. Many of these perform valuable education in world affairs or cultural pursuits; the reports and the documentaries are very well done. On-the-spot coverage of special events like elections, congressional hearings, U.N. meetings, and such like have brought new awareness even to the best educated of the complications of the world we live in, and panels like "Meet the Press" and "Youth Wants to Know" raise hard questions for public administrators and their listeners.

Television has not, so far, incurred the disfavor of the intellectuals as much as Hollywood. Its public service programs have helped prevent this; so has the literate and tasteful criticism of John Crosby's syndicated column. On the whole, television has been better served by its press than either films or radio. Headquartering in New York, it has stayed closer to the center of things; and it is so varied and omnipresent that it has become as much a part of daily life as automobiles and refrigerators. Now that much of its production has moved to Hollywood the old complaints may arise once again, and since much of the vigor and charm of early television has already been lost to the clichés and conventions of audience participation programs, it may be hoped that this will be in its turn participation criticism which will force better and more varied programming aimed, occasionally at least, at special audiences.

Perhaps the real trouble with television is that there is no way for popular taste and response to guide it, as it has guided the films. There is no guarantee that pay-as-you-go television programming will perform this function; the best argument against it is its susceptibility to the same drive toward the least common denominator of taste which dominates free television. Free television seems certain, in the foreseeable future, to remain largely in the hands of the advertising agencies whose past performance indicates no great respect for their intellectual or artistic responsibilities.

There is no likelihood that the government will take over any segment of broadcasting. Nobody is really for it, and the examples of it from the rest of the world are not stimuli to imitation. It is possible that, short of totalitarian control, the media of mass communication do not have as much influence as is commonly supposed—or, to put it perhaps a little more accurately, that freely operating media check one another and dilute a potentially powerful influence. Operating in this fashion the American press is notorious for its lack of direct political influence; and broadcasting generally has refrained from trying to exert any at all. The "equal time" rule of thumb for political argument has on the whole worked well.

The study of indirect and sub-conscious influences has barely gotten under way, and bids fair to be no more conclusive than most other sociological studies. The frightening vistas raised by books like *The Hidden Persuaders* and films like *A Face in the Crowd* are about as realistic as science fiction and their prophetic power rather less acute.

The really troublesome problem in television and other media of communication in the United States is one shared by many other fields: how to retain and increase freedom in the face of giantism. And the answer to this, as to nearly everything else problematical in democracy, revolves around education. Intellectual and mature America turned its back on the films; it did not trouble to understand them and their vitality was a sort of peasant growth, rich but uneducated. But this was not an ideal situation. The films would have been a greater art, perhaps a truly great art, had they, like nineteenth century Italian opera, become truly national, engaging the support and interest of all levels of the population. Television has inherited some of the film's vitality. If no way is found to enrich it with cultivation and taste, it will remain a folkway, like basketball or knitting, no more interesting and no more significant.

chapter XII

The Religious Aspect

A. I. Abell

University of Notre Dame

▪▬

IN CONTEMPORARY America institutional religion—the great religious bodies, Protestant, Catholic, and Jewish—grows with a vigor equalled only in the early decades of the nineteenth century. In the last two decades church membership has increased at a ratio twice that of the rapidly accelerating population.[1] Nearly every American affirms that he is a Protestant, Catholic, or Jew while three out of every five is actually a member of one of the more than two hundred denominations which dot the religious landscape.[2] In a period marked by economic depression, global war, and efforts to contain communist totalitarianism, Americans look to religion as a major defense of democracy and the "American way of life."

Although the fear is often expressed that religion when consciously esteemed chiefly for patriotic ends must degenerate into "secular idolatry,"[3] the country's leadership is convinced that democracy rests upon a religious foundation and must fall unless the beliefs, attitudes, and virtues which religion inculcates are generally accepted. Shortly after his first election to the Presidency, Dwight D. Eisenhower stated: "Our government makes no sense unless it is founded in a deeply felt religious faith, and I don't care what it is."[4] In the same year, William O. Douglas,

---

1 Will Herberg, "Religion and Culture in Present-Day America," Notre Dame Symposium on Catholicism and the American Way of Life. In this same symposium, historian Francis X. Curran, S.J., speaking on "The Religious Revival and Organized Religion" contends that the importance of the current revival has been exaggerated, both quantitatively and qualitatively.

2 Frank S. Mead, *Handbook of Denominations in the United States* (New York, 1951), pp. 185–190.

3 William L. Sperry, *Religion in America* (New York, 1946), p. 19.

4 Quoted in Herberg, *op. cit.*

Associate Justice of the United States Supreme Court, speaking for a majority of his brethren in *Zorach v. Clauson,* a case involving religious instruction alongside public schools, affirmed: "We are a religious people whose institutions presuppose a Supreme Being." [5] In 1954 Congress inserted, "Under God," in the Pledge of Allegiance and two years later voted to make, "In God We Trust," used on the coinage since 1865, the official motto of the United States.[6]

In ways such as these the present-day American political and social order places its stamp of approval on religious effort in the absence of which the democratic venture must degenerate into anarchy and terminate in despotism. There is nothing exceptional in the American view that religion exerts a socially cohesive influence, save only that the *status quo* here upheld is democratic republicanism rather than historic forms of oligarchic rule. What is unique, historically, in the American system is that in seeking its social ends it imposes no legal restraints on the consciences of men. In America religious freedom—the liberty to believe what one wishes concerning God and the Universe—is a constitutionally guaranteed civil right. In America the political authority is wholly unconcerned with religious beliefs and practices so long as they seek a kingdom "in the other world," and acknowledge the existence of a "kingdom of this world," that is, "of an autonomous realm of natural reason, an expression of which is the Constitution and the allegiance of American citizenship." [7] During the Revolutionary and early National period, the new nation decided that, on the basis of the Colonial experience, both religion and civil society would the better prosper if the latter abandoned all attempts to prescribe and enforce religious beliefs. Accordingly, the existing state churches were disestablished and religious tests for voting and office-holding gradually abolished.[8] The federal government set up by the Constitution of 1787 was forbidden to require religious tests for federal office-holding and

5 343 U.S. 306, 313; 72 S. Ct. 679, 684; 96 Law. Ed. 954, 962 (1952).
6 Sydney E. Ahlstrom, *The Pieties of Usefulness: Religion in American Culture at Mid-Century* (Deland, Florida, 1957), pp. 1–5, reprinted from *Stetson University Bulletin,* LVII (July, 1957), 1–15.
7 Peter F. Drucker, "Organized Religion and the American Creed," *Review of Politics,* XVIII (July, 1956), 300.
8 E. B. Greene, *Religion and the State: The Making and Testing of an American Tradition* (New York, 1941).

in 1791 the First Amendment, one of ten amendments added to the Constitution as a bill of rights, stated that "Congress shall pass no law respecting an establishment of religion or prohibiting the free exercise thereof."

For its day this legislation was truly exceptional—indeed, unique. Even more remarkable was the spirit which motivated the new constitution-making. Only to a slight degree did hostility to religion enter into the picture. On the contrary, the church-state separation principle was approved, even demanded, by the great majority of religious people. The statement in the Virginia Constitution of 1776 voiced the convictions of many religious leaders as well as statesmen:

> That religion, or the duty we owe our Creator and the means of discharging it, can be directed only by reason and conviction, not by force or violence; and therefore all men are equally entitled to the free exercise of religion according to the dictates of conscience; and that it is the duty of all to practice Christian forbearance, love and charity towards each other.[9]

Practical considerations strengthened this attitude; many who favored union of church and state as the ideal realized that religious liberty was the only workable rule in a land of increasing religious diversity.

The whole Colonial experience had made for such diversity.[10] Into the American colonies were funneled the fragmentations caused by the English and Continental Reformations—Anglicans, Puritans, Dutch Reformed, Catholics, Quakers, and Huguenots in the seventeenth century, and Scotch-Irish Presbyterians, German Lutherans, Mennonites and various other sects in the eighteenth. Impressed by the religious no less than the economic successes of Spanish colonization, the English Crown expected the Anglican Church to be the exclusive agency of worship in the prospective colonies and to pursue an aggressive missionary policy—to instill into "the purged myndes" of the Indians "the

9 Kate Mason Rowland, *The Life of George Mason, 1725–1792* (New York, 1892), I, 435.
10 Colonial religious developments are considered in John Tracy Ellis, *Catholics in Colonial America* (Washington, 1957), esp. pp. 18–78, reprinted from *The American Ecclesiastical Review*, CXXXVI (January–May, 1957); W. W. Sweet, *Religion in Colonial America* (New York, 1942); Joseph Leiser, *American Judaism* (New York, 1925), pp. 7–91.

swete and lively liquor of the Gospell." But these hopes were
dashed by the violent religious and constitutional struggle which
coincided roughly with the great colonizing ventures of the
seventeenth century. In its weakness the Crown did not insist
on religious unity overseas; it was willing to tolerate, even to
encourage, religious diversity if and when this was the price of
successful colonization. The leaders and colonists were permitted
to do pretty much as they pleased in religious matters. Only in
the lower counties of New York and in the South, notably in
Virginia and South Carolina, was the Anglican Church strong
enough to get itself established. The non-Separatist Puritans,
who accepted the union-of-church-and-state principle, established
their version of Calvinist theocracy in Massachusetts, Connecticut, and New Hampshire. From the first, many in the Bay
Colony were at odds with its religious policy. Among these was
the celebrated Roger Williams who developed Rhode Island on
the principle of "soul liberty." Aware that in the light of the
Bellarmine theory Catholics owed only spiritual allegiance to the
Pope, Williams extended to them the guarantees of the colony.

Maryland was founded by Cecil Calvert, Lord Baltimore, in
large part, as a refuge for English Catholics. Baltimore wished all
his colonists, whatever their religious differences, to live in peace,
and for a time enforced full religious liberty among Trinitarian
Christians. But since the Catholics were from the beginning in
the minority, the Baltimores had to yield to the Protestants, first
to the Puritan and then to the Anglican element which applied
to Catholics the repressive penal laws of the Mother Country.
Had English Catholics been less obsessed with hopes of a Catholic Restoration and more alive to religious possibilities overseas,
they would have come to Maryland in greater numbers and
thereby strengthened Calvert's hand. William Penn was more
fortunate in his Quaker colony into which poured thousands upon
thousands of immigrants fleeing religious as well as economic
oppression in their home lands. Fed up with state churches,
Scotch-Irish Presbyterians, Mennonites and Lutheran pietists
found an earthly paradise in Pennsylvania. Jefferson and other
architects of religious freedom in the Revolutionary period never
tired of citing the Pennsylvania example. Certainly, religious

vitality in Pennsylvania compared favorably with that in the colonies having established churches.

This is not to imply that the situation in any region was satisfactory from the religious standpoint. In the colonies, taken as a whole, only one person in twelve was a church member in 1760. Inasmuch as religious commitment was broader than church membership, these figures exaggerate the degree of religious indifference. Yet it is true that as population increased and filled in the back country, a growing proportion of the people lost contact with the moralizing and civilizing influences of organized religion. Subsequent American history would exhibit a similar religious dearth—as the frontier advanced, as one immigrant wave after another reached our shores, as cities grew and industries relocated. And all religions were to be affected, not merely Protestantism but Catholicism and Judaism as well. It could scarcely be otherwise with the most mobile of the world's populations, with a people dedicated not only to the pursuit of happiness but also to the happiness of pursuit.

The religious situation in Colonial America would undoubtedly have been even less satisfactory had it not been for the Great Awakening which profoundly stirred the people, especially in the back country, during the second quarter of the eighteenth century. The Great Awakening was a religious revival which stressed the emotional aspects of the conversion process; it was the American counterpart, in a somewhat violent form, of German and other European versions of pietism. The Great Awakening was induced by lurid preaching of the fire-and-brimstone variety of which Jonathan Edwards' Enfield sermon, "Sinners in the Hands of an Angry God" is the classic example. To Edwards, the greatest of Colonial Calvinist theologians, not wealth, not social position, not learning, but a vivid religious experience signified one's election to eternal salvation. The democratizing influence of this attitude is easily visualized. The self-esteem of the poor and unlettered was enormously enhanced; with the Lord on their side, they were steeled to challenge the ruling classes, by revolution if necessary. The Great Awakening foreshadowed the camp meetings and other mass-conversion techniques of the next century. The four new colleges inspired by the Great Awakening—Presbyterian Princeton, Dutch Reformed Rutgers, Baptist Brown, and Congregationalist Dartmouth —were to find imitators in almost every newly peopled area of the country. But more immediately, the Great Awakening swelled the ranks of the dissenting bodies, notably the Baptists in New England and the Presbyterians and Quakers in the upland South. The spiritually awakened in all denominations took the patriot side in the American Revolution the success of which they expected to sound the death-knell of the established churches.[11]

It did not require a Great Awakening to put this idea into the heads of Colonial Catholics, less than twenty-five thousand in number. Charles Carroll of Carrollton entered into the Revolution in order to promote, as he said, the great cause of civil and religious liberty. His cousin, the Reverend John Carroll, soon to become the first Roman Catholic bishop in the new nation, was of like opinion. In his encyclopedic study of church-state relations, Anson Phelps Stokes lists Bishop Carroll among the twenty most distinguished founders of American religious liberty.[12] Of these founders, sixteen were Trinitarian Christians. Franklin, Jefferson, and possibly Madison were Christian Deists who sympathized with the rising Unitarian movement. Only Tom Paine rejected Christianity. With left-wing Protestants in the Anabaptist tradition religious liberty was a doctrinal tenet. Men under rationalizing influences (chiefly Deism) believed that religious freedom assuaged sectarian asperities and thereby promoted peace in the community. In religion the maxim of civil government was reversed, wrote Jefferson, to read, "divided we stand, united we fall."[13] Having discovered during the great Colonial revivals that they could thrive through persuasion alone, the powerful right-wing churches, mainly Anglican, Congregationalist, and Presbyterian, were easily reconciled to the triumph of the free-

---

11 W. W. Sweet, *Revivalism in America* (New York, 1944), summarizes and interprets this significant aspect of Protestant religious life.

12 *Church and State in the United States*, I, 355–356. For comments on this work, see Thomas T. McAvoy, C.S.C., "Critical Problems in American History," *Review of Politics*, XIII (April, 1951), 261–262, and John Tracy Ellis, "Church and State in the United States: A Critical Appraisal," *Catholic Historical Review*, XXXVIII (October, 1952), 285–316.

13 Letter to Dr. De La Motta, Savannah, Georgia, Synagogue, September 1, 1820, quoted in Stokes, *op. cit.*, I, 864.

dom principle.[14] The Congregationalist clergy of Connecticut put up no real fight against disestablishment, as Professor Charles Keller of Williams College brings out in his excellent monograph, *The Second Great Awakening in Connecticut*.[15]

The hopes of the founders were realized beyond their fondest expectations in the following generations.[16] Church membership increased more than three times as fast as the population during the whole of the nineteenth century. First of all, the Protestant Churches confronted and routed the speculative infidelity which stemmed from Deism and the secular outlooks of the Revolutionary generation. The main problem, however, was to overcome religious destitution on an ever-moving frontier, to impose restraints on vice, immorality, and crude behavior, to keep alive the ideals of civilization among a people engaged in the exhausting task of subduing a continent. Alexis de Tocqueville alluded to the political implications of the heightened religious emphasis. In his *Democracy in America*, he wrote:

> if you converse with these missionaries of Christian civilization you will be surprised to find how much value they set upon the goods of this world and that you meet with a politician where you expected to find a priest. They will tell you that all the American republics are collectively involved with each other; if the republics of the West were to fall into anarchy, or to be mastered by a despot, the republican institutions which now flourish upon the shore of the Atlantic Ocean would be in great peril. It is, therefore, our interest that the new States should be religious in order to maintain our liberties.[17]

It is true that some immorality and crime followed the emotional upheavals of the great protracted outdoor revivals—the camp meetings—which affected frontier people in great numbers after 1800. But predominantly, the frenzied revivals exerted a

14 For a brilliant analysis of this neglected aspect of the struggle for religious liberty, see Sidney E. Mead's article, "From Coercion to Persuasion: Another Look at the Rise of Religious Liberty and the Emergence of Denominationalism," *Church History*, XXIV (December, 1956), 317–337, and "American Protestantism During the Revolutionary Epoch," *Ibid.*, XXII (1953), 279–297.
15 (New Haven, Yale Historical Publications, XL, 1942), pp. 56–69.
16 See particularly Kenneth Scott Latourette, *A History of the Expansion of Christianity*, (vol. IV, *The Great Century*), pp. 175–516; W. W. Sweet, *Religion in the Development of American Culture, 1765–1840*; C. B. Goodykoontz, *Home Missions on the American Frontie*r (Caldwell, Idaho, 1939); and Stokes, *op. cit.*, I, 651–783.
17 (Trans. Reeve, rev. ed., 1900), I, 311–312.

morally constructive influence. From being "Rogue's Harbor," a refuge for escaped murderers, horse thieves, highway robbers and counterfeiters, Logan County in Kentucky as a result of the religious revivals became famed for its sobriety and rectitude. The pioneer Presbyterian minister in Kentucky, David Rice, wrote that "some neighborhoods, noted for their viciousness and profligate manners, are now as much noted for their piety and good order." [18] For the strength with which to establish a moral police force on the frontier, Protestantism relied mainly on the more conventional methods, notably church growth and auxiliary church organizations, for the systematic diffusion of religious knowledge. The Baptists, with their farmer preachers, and the Methodists, with their episcopally directed circuit riders and itinerant ministers, gained recruits by the hundreds of thousands. Also through various undenominational societies frontier religion was advanced— the American Sunday School Union, the American Bible Society, the American Tract Society and the American Home Missionary Society, all of which were established in the decade after 1816. More important perhaps were the foundations of higher education laid by the frontier colleges, most of which were Congregationalist or Presbyterian in origin, the fruits often of missionary zeal at Yale or Princeton.

Only as the Protestant ministry gave assurances that all men who truly sought salvation might attain it could they win recruits in impressive numbers. It was not that God was less sovereign, but that man was more important in relation to God. Into this democratized "new theology" entered both rational and humanitarian elements, the varying emphases of which were elaborated by a whole line of eminent theologians—from Jonathan Edwards through Samuel Hopkins and Nathaniel W. Taylor to William Ellery Channing, Charles G. Finney, and Horace Bushnell. The upshot was to lend theological sanction to sect-splitting and denominational proliferation—"fissiparous Protestantism" is Professor Latourette's term for it. Conspicuous examples are the Unitarian schism in Massachusetts and the division of Presbyterians into New School and Old School denominations. Fortunately, the upsurge in religious individualism

18 William Warren Sweet, *The Story of Religion in America*, (New York, 1939), p. 333.

was remarkably humane, benevolent, and reformist in character.[19] A late eighteenth century Connecticut law historian sounded the keynote of the new Protestantism—that the people were coming to believe that religion was not instituted for the purpose of rendering them miserable, but happy, that there is more merit in acting right than in thinking right, that the condition of men in a future state will not be dependent on the speculative opinions they may have adopted in the present.[20] Attitudes such as these inspired many pre-Civil War reforms—temperance, humane penology, decent treatment of the insane, and anti-slavery.

With some Protestants, reform took on a cooperative aspect—withdrawal from the "world" into frontier utopias where Christians might cultivate a sense of perfection and await the unfolding of the millennial promise.[21] The Shakers, officially the Millennial Church, or the United Society of True Believers, practicing celibacy and community of goods, numbered in their heyday around 1850, some six thousand members in twenty-two agricultural communities.[22] John Humphrey Noyes established the Oneida Community in the burnt-over revival district of central New York. It stressed community of goods, mutual criticism and complex marriage—combining disciplined sexual promiscuity and planned parenthood.[23] As economic enterprises, these communities were brilliantly successful, but failed religiously because they lost the power to win new recruits. This limitation did not apply to the Mormons—the Church of Jesus Christ of Latter Day Saints —who thrived in Utah and worked out techniques for the conquest of the semi-arid West.

Great as was Protestant success, especially on the frontier and among the well-to-do groups in the rising cities, Catholic growth

19 Sidney E. Mead, "Denominationalism: The Shape of Protestantism in America," *Church History*, XXIII (December, 1954), 291–320, the best short characterization of American Protestantism in its formative period, 1785–1850. See also Timothy L. Smith, *Revivalism and Social Reform in Mid-19th Century America* (New York, 1957), which brings out the social implications of Methodist and other types of perfectionist doctrine.

20 Keller, *op. cit.*, 227.

21 Whitney R. Cross, *The Burned-over District: The Social and Intellectual History of Enthusiastic Religion in Western New York, 1800–1850* (Ithaca, 1950).

22 Edward Deming Andrews, *The People Called Shakers: A Search for the Perfect Society* (New York, 1953).

23 Stow Persons, "Christian Communitarianism in America," in Donald Drew Egbert and Stow Persons, editors, *Socialism in American Life* (Princeton, 1952), I, 127–151.

was relatively even more phenomenal—from about a hundred thousand in 1800 to over four millions by 1860. Apart from natural increase, the Catholic membership derived from immigration—first from priests fleeing revolution in France and then from the Irish and German poor seeking homes and prosperity in the New World, a steadily enlarging stream until 1840 and thereafter an oceanic deluge. Nearly all the French refugees were Sulpicians whose contributions to the Catholic Church in the early National period are beyond calculation.[24] These priests were pioneer educators, establishing St. Mary's Seminary in Baltimore and the Theological Seminary of St. Thomas in Springfield, Kentucky, in the midst of the Maryland derived enclave of Catholics on the frontier. Besides aiding the Jesuits at Georgetown College, the Sulpicians founded St. Mary's College in Baltimore and Mt. St. Mary's College at Emmetsburg, Maryland. Nor did they neglect the missionary field. At Detroit, Father Gabriel Richard, the "greatest name in the missionary annals of the Sulpicians," helped lay the cultural foundations of Michigan and the Middle West. In the East, John Cheverus, the first bishop of Boston, made numerous converts, including Elizabeth Bayley Seton, a charming and saintly widow who founded the Daughters of Charity in 1812.

The French priests also proved to be excellent ecclesiastical administrators. Besides Cheverus in Boston, confreres David, Dubois, Dubourg, Flaget, Marechal, and Bruté were raised to the episcopacy where they lent firm support to their leaders, Bishop Carroll and his successors in building up an American clergy free of foreign influence save that of the Holy See. Carroll and his immediate successors warded off the internal and external dangers that beset the Church, namely, the attempt of lay trustees to control church property and clerical appointments, and the nativist drive to incite mob action and mass prejudice against Catholic advance.[25] Actually, the Church exercised some influence on society at large, especially through her schools, notably the academies whose number increased from fifty-one in 1840 to one hundred eighty-four two decades later. These schools were widely attended by Protestant youth. A "home" missionary in the West wrote that Catholics "have thoroughly

24 Charles G. Herbermann, *The Sulpicians in the United States* (New York, 1916).
25 John Tracy Ellis, *American Catholicism* (Chicago, 1956), pp. 40–81.

studied American character and institutions and are doing vastly more for their cause by their schools than by all their churches and cathedrals." Be this as it may, the Church mainly benefited Catholics on the social side through the growing number of charitable institutions which served as a refuge for a good part of the Catholic poor, keeping them out of almshouses and other public correctional institutions which long excluded all Catholic teaching and menaced the faith of Catholic inmates.[26]

The Jewish group grew slowly but steadily—from a few thousand in 1800 to fifty thousand in 1850 and a quarter million by 1881 when heavy immigration of Jews from Eastern Europe commenced. The first sizable Jewish accessions, mainly from Germany, elaborated a Reform Judaism which minimized ritualism and stressed ethics and social service. Their principal leader was the Cincinnati rabbi, Isaac Mayer Wise, who proved himself to be one of America's greatest religious organizers.[27]

In the great urban era which opened up after the Civil War, organized religion was brought face to face with urban industrial problems.[28] As the labor movement gained momentum during the 1870's and 1880's clergymen discovered that workers in alarming number had left the churches or planned to do so unless their grievances were speedily redressed. Workingmen were deserting the churches, labor leaders insisted, because ministers and church members worshipped wealth, sided with employers and frowned upon unions and labor legislation—the remedies or methods on which workers relied to raise their wages, shorten their hours and better their working conditions. The Reverend Washington Gladden, pastor of the First Congregational Church in Columbus, Ohio, summed up labor's attitude by an illustration.

26 John O'Grady, *Catholic Charities in the United States* (Washington, 1931); for the early story in capsule form, see A. I. Abell, "The Catholic Factor in Urban Welfare: The Early Period, 1850–1880," *Review of Politics*, XIV (July, 1952), 289–324.

27 Leiser, *op. cit.*, pp. 92–241; Nathan Glazer, *American Judaism* (Chicago, 1957), pp. 22–42.

28 The growth of social Christianity to World War I is traced in A. I. Abell, *The Urban Impact on American Protestantism, 1865–1900* (Harvard Historical Studies, LIV, 1943); Henry J. Browne, *The Catholic Church and the Knights of Labor* (Washington, 1949); James Dombrowski, *The Early Days of Christian Socialism in America* (New York, 1936); Mary Harrita Fox, *Peter E. Deitz, Labor Priest* (Notre Dame, 1953); C. Howard Hopkins, *The Rise of the Social Gospel in American Protestantism, 1865–1915* (New Haven, 1940); and Henry J. May, *Protestant Churches and Industrial America* (New York, 1949).

He cited the instance of a "tired looking shop girl" in Boston who in response to a query as to the reason for her failing to attend church, replied: "My employer goes. He is one of the pillars of the church. That's reason enough why I shouldn't go. I know how he treats his help." They were not opposed to Christianity, workers insisted; only to "churchianity"—their fancy word for pretense and pious fraud. By 1890 all informed Protestants recognized that labor alienation was widely prevalent, even if many were slow to admit that it stemmed from economic friction. Thus as late as 1892 the overwhelming majority of Congregational pastors in Massachusetts believed that industrial discontent had "little or no effect upon the attitude of the workingmen toward the churches."

Being predominantly workingmen in membership, the Catholic Church could less afford to antagonize the labor movement. But some priests and bishops did just that, opposing the Knights of Labor on the ground that the secrecy it practiced violated the moral law and endangered both Church and State. Disaster loomed when Rome itself forbade Quebec Catholics to remain in the Knights—a ruling which by implication told American Catholics to quit the organization. However, James Cardinal Gibbons, Archbishop of Baltimore, came personally to the defense of the Knights and persuaded the Holy See to suspend, in effect to lift, its condemnation. The unexpected publicity which accompanied his successful efforts reassured Catholic workingmen and encouraged reforming Catholics to redouble their efforts to secure labor's emancipation. They proceeded on the assumption that workers wanted reform, not revolution, that measures considerably this side of socialism, if honestly pushed, would satisfy wage-earning people and keep them loyally attached to the Church. They pointed out that labor organizations practiced secrecy for business, not evil, purposes, did not teach the destruction of property and believed "in settling their troubles by arbitration." Catholics friendly to labor believed that unions were striving primarily to secure fair labor contracts under the wage system; to aid them secure these as well as other improvements, many reforming Catholics favored compulsory arbitration in varying degrees, especially during and after the bloody Homestead and Pullman strikes of the early 1890's.

The Catholic attitude—most carefully stated by Pope Leo XIII in his encyclical on the condition of labor, May 15, 1891—did not differ essentially from that of progressive Protestants and Jews as formulated by their great leaders, notably Washington Gladden for the Protestants and Henry Berkowitz for the Jews. Berkowitz, a Philadelphia rabbi, in his book *Judaism and the Social Question* (1888), urged Jews in the spirit of the Mosaic legislation to "bring property into harmony with morality." Of all American clergymen Gladden was best informed on social questions, especially the labor problems. He favored industrial partnership in order that labor might share in the profits as well as the losses of industry. But until such time as this principle was fully accepted, he sanctioned labor's organization for effective combat. "If war is the order of the day," he said, "we must grant labor belligerent rights." Wishing the state to steer a course midway between individualism and socialism, Gladden would have government stop Sunday work, limit land ownership, own and operate telegraphs and railways, and prevent the accumulation of great fortunes.

Urban Protestantism was widely acclaimed after 1880 for its so-called institutional churches which to the spiritual added charitable, educational and recreational functions. Hundreds of these churches and missions were established from coast to coast; the bigger ones spent yearly hundreds of thousands of dollars on a varied philanthropy. The work of these churches, combined with that of the Salvation Army and religiously-led associations, was truly impressive. These churches were designed to retain congregations in down-town locations, to bring Protestantism into more intimate contact with the wage-earning population, and to encourage the poor to improve their condition through self-help. Some leaders believed that the churches should be social service laboratories, testing out new methods and agencies with a view to the adoption of the successful ones by the community at large.

Jews and Catholics launched comprehensive programs of social service, partly to counteract nativist feeling. A broad symposium, conducted by the weekly journal the *American Hebrew* in 1890, attributed the rapid growth of anti-Semitic feeling to repellent economic and social conditions in the Ghetto-like Jewish quarters in leading American cities. Consequently, all Jewish philanthropic and educational institutions, mostly controlled by the thoroughly Americanized Jews of German ancestry, redoubled their efforts to improve the lot of the newcomers from Russia and South-eastern Europe. They insisted that destitute paupers be kept in Europe and only refugees from persecution be sent to America. Educational programs stressed the idealistic as against the mate-rialistic content of American civilization. Jewish leaders estab-lished innumerable industrial training schools designed to divert the younger generation from trade into other forms of productive effort, not excluding agriculture.

In order to reestablish the church connections of the so-called "new immigration" from Southern and Eastern Europe, the Catholic Church after 1900 incorporated the whole corpus of the "new charity" into its working forces—the social settlement and its adjuncts, the professional social worker and the social service school. For a time, most of this work was done by lay women whose energy and ingenuity won the admiration of the whole country. They coordinated their efforts through the Na-tional Conference of Catholic Charities the first sessions of which they dominated.

Just as the frontier and cities challenged religion's effective-ness, so new philosophic and scientific currents challenged its authority. The followers of Ralph Waldo Emerson in the Trans-cendentalist movement denied the uniqueness of Christianity and sought to usher in an absolute natural religion. To this end, they tried after 1850 to popularize the Biblical criticism of the Tuebin-gen school and the findings of comparative religion. Octavus Brooks Frothingham and Thomas Wentworth Higginson of aboli-tionist and symphony orchestra fame were tireless propagandists through books and articles. Their effort bid fair not only to des-troy Christianity, but even, in conjunction with the Darwinian hypothesis which they uncritically accepted, to erase the very idea of God from the minds of men. That eventuality had its attractions for many who had visions of mankind's redemption and perpetual progress through science. In the years following the Civil War a "cult of science" arose, with its demigods in Charles Darwin and other great scientists, with its popularizers in John W. Draper, "Bob" Ingersoll, Lester F. Ward, E. L. Youmans and other bitter opponents of Christianity, and with its Appleton Scientific Series and various popular magazines of science.

The majority of the country's leading scientists favored the cult which also appealed to the educated middle classes and the old Yankee non-immigrant laboring classes. The Free Religious Association, formed in 1867 by erstwhile Christian transcendentalists, sought to weld these groups into a non-Christian, scientifically-orientated religion. On the side of practice, the Free Religious Association favored secularism, opposing the current drive for a Christian Amendment to mention God in the Federal Constitution, the exemption of church property from taxation, Bible-reading in the schools, public chaplains and the Puritan Sabbath. Under the leadership of Francis Ellingwood Abbot, the Association's chief spokesman, the National Liberal League was formed in the Centennial year to forward these objectives. The League soon went to pieces over the issue of obeying the recently-enacted Comstock anti-obscenity laws. The strait-laced Abbot frowned upon the willingness of some liberals to have the mails flooded with smutty, pornographic literature. Abbot subscribed to theism whereas some members of the Free Religious Association, notably Dr. Felix Adler, insisted that the findings of philosophy and science were inconclusive beyond the realms of morality and ethical culture. Leaders of the Association hoped that the study of comparative religion would in time disclose the essence of religion. The Parliament of Religions held at the Chicago World Fair in 1893 was one realization of the Association's aims. The leaders were annoyed, however, when Cardinal Gibbons contended that Catholicism was the only absolute religion, the result of an exclusive and special divine revelation; and they were exasperated beyond measure when other speakers made similar claims for their respective faiths.

In an effort to meet the challenge of science, the "progressive orthodox" among Protestant Christians shifted the center of authority in religion from scriptural and creedal infallibility to religious experience. Lyman Abbott, distinguished retired pastor of Plymouth Church, Brooklyn, and editor of *The Outlook*, explained in his *Reminiscences* (New York, 1915) that

> as the intellectual judgment is the final arbiter in science, so the spiritual consciousness is the final arbiter in religion. But no individual [he was

quick to point out] may take his own consciousness as an ultimate authority in religion, as no man takes his own observation and his conclusions thereon as an ultimate authority in science. He must reach the truth in the one case by a careful study of the observations and conclusions of scientifically minded men; in the other by a not less careful study of the spiritual experiences of spiritually minded men. The Bible and the Church are valuable to him as guides because they are the expressions of this spiritual consciousness, but they can never serve as substitutes.[29]

The "progressive orthodox" also conceded that science had discovered the true method of progress, namely that "the advance of society, like that of nature, is not sporadic, but gradual and consistent." But they denied that this upheld the "survival-of-the-fittest" philosophy currently used to justify neglect of the poor and the piling up of immense fortunes in the hands of the few. As against the Social Darwinism of Yale sociologist William Graham Sumner, and the "Gospel of Wealth" of steel magnate Andrew Carnegie, progressive Protestants insisted on the "Social Gospel" of charity, cooperation, and justice.

Now that science challenged the divine authority of the Scriptures, denominational rivalries seemed inappropriate and sinful. This conviction suggested the possibility of cooperation among Protestant groups for the more obvious common objectives. Building on local experiments around the turn of the century, the fraternal idea culminated in 1908 in the formation of the Federal Council of the Churches of Christ of America (the National Council since 1950), a consultative body representing thirty-three evangelical churches with communicants and adherents numbering over half the country's population. The Federal Council reflected the changing trends in American Protestantism: theological liberalism, denominational cooperation, and social reform. The famous "social creed" called not only for a living wage in every industry but also for "the highest wage that each industry can afford, and for the most equitable division of the products in industry that can ultimately be devised." Besides promoting "federalism" in religion, its main purpose, the Federal Council may well have encouraged the drive toward organic unity—a tendency that gained momentum in the present century, especially after World War I. In some towns and cities, neighboring congregations of different sects disbanded and then

29 Pp. 452–453.

re-formed into united or community churches. These churches dot the landscape of "suburbia," the phenomenal expansion of which since World War II has added a new dimension to American life. Mergers involving whole denominations took place: several large divisions of Lutherans formed in 1920 the United Lutheran Church of America, and nine years later the Christian Church, popular in the southern regions of the Middle West, joined with the older, more powerful Congregationalists to form the Congregationalist-Christian Church. In 1939 American Methodists, anxious to overcome historic schisms caused by the slavery contest and frontier individualism, reunited into one all-inclusive, though racially segregated denomination.

Coincident with the merger trend, intra-denominational wrangling increased, the result largely of contrasting evaluations of the scientific revolution. On the one hand, the conservatives who were "fundamentalist" or "literal" in belief, clung to the old-fashioned doctrines of seventeenth-century Protestantism with special emphasis on the virgin birth and bodily resurrection of Christ, the infallibility of the Bible and the literal truth of its statements regarding miracles. The Liberals, or Modernists, on the other hand, wished to "reconcile" Christianity with modern science by giving to the articles of Christian faith a symbolic rather than a literal meaning. Though this conflict had been brewing among Protestant leaders and intellectuals for many years, its issues did not greatly disturb the rank and file until the rapid spread of urban influences during the 1920's carried the conflict to the public and almost rent asunder the Baptist, Methodist, Presbyterian, United Brethren and other Protestant bodies.[30] The controversy between Fundamentalists and Modernists centered more and more around the theory of evolution. The Fundamentalists contended that this theory conflicted with the Biblical account of man's creation, and they insisted that state legislatures forbid the teaching of evolution in schools supported by public funds. In 1925 Tennessee made it unlawful for state schools "to teach any theory that denies the story of the Divine creation of man as taught in the Bible and to teach instead that man has descended from a lower order of animals." The law's constitutionality was soon tested when John T. Scopes, a biology

30 N. F. Furniss, *The Fundamentalist Controversy, 1918–1931* (New Haven, 1954).

teacher in a Dayton, Tennessee, high school, was arrested for disobeying the law. The case attracted nationwide attention. Clarence Darrow, the country's most famed criminal lawer, arrived to join the defense, while William Jennings Bryan, three times Democratic candidate for president and a leading Fundamentalist, aided the prosecution. The court upheld the law, although the Tennessee Supreme Court later reversed the lower court's decision and dismissed the case. The efforts of the Fundamentalists availed little; the Modernists by 1930 had the upper hand in nearly all leading Protestant denominations.

Catholic liberalism in America was social and nationalistic in content, the "phantom heresy" of late nineteenth-century "Americanism" failing to develop into anything resembling genuine Modernism.[31] Whereas Pope Pius X's encyclical *Pascendi Gregis* of 1907 denouncing Modernism as the denial of religion, had significance for Europe where Catholic Modernists were numerous and for the most part learned and highly articulate, the condemnation served mainly as a warning to American Catholics, few of whom had embraced Modernist doctrine. More feared than the higher criticism were the inroads of anti-Christian social philosophies, chiefly Marxian Socialism in its various forms. Against these the Catholic Church launched a crusade under leaders who were to devote decades to the task of organizing a Catholic social program. Most influential was the Reverend (Monsignor after 1933) John A. Ryan (1869–1945) who as academician, publicist, and administrator spent a half century promoting human welfare. Ryan published *A Living Wage: Its Ethical and Economic Aspects* (New York, 1906), a scholarly treatise which discussed the various methods through which the living-wage principle could be made a reality. Destined to have an even longer career, the journalist Frederick P. Kenkel headed the Central Bureau for the Promotion of Social Education established by the Central Verein in 1908.

The Central Verein was the most active group in the American Federation of Catholic Societies which was formed in 1901 to

31 On this question Thomas T. McAvoy, C.S.C., *The Great Crisis in American Catholic History, 1895–1900* (Chicago, 1957), is conclusive. See also Robert D. Cross, *The Emergence of Liberal Catholicism in America* (Cambridge, 1958).

defend Catholic interests and to promote the gradual Americanization of immigrants. This episcopally-approved and laymen-led
organization grew steadily, reaching the peak of its strength in
1912 with three million members affiliated through sixty colleges
and universities and twenty-four societies of nationwide scope.
In no small degree influenced by the Central Verein, the Federation elaborated a social program, conceding "that many of the
economic demands which Socialism makes are founded on right
and justice," and endorsing trade unionism and labor legislation
including social insurance. Both the Verein and the Federation
profited from the social zeal of the Reverend Peter E. Dietz who
for two decades after 1905 pioneered on the social-justice frontier.[32] He launched and edited for a short time the English section
of the *Central-Blatt and Social Justice* and initiated and served
as executive secretary of the Social Service Commission author-
ized in 1911 by the American Federation of Catholic Societies.
In 1910 Dietz organized the Militia of Christ which operating
chiefly through Catholic trade-union officials sought to increase
Catholic and to combat Socialist influence in the labor movement.
Five years later he established at Hot Springs, North Carolina,
a social service school for women which on its relocation in
Cincinnati became a Catholic labor school, the first in the Eng-
lish-speaking world. This school and the Militia of Christ were
prototypes of the many Catholic labor schools and of the Association of Catholic Trade Unionists which emerged in the late
1930's to fight Communist penetration into the newly formed
industrial unions.

In 1912 Father Dietz presented to Cardinal Gibbons a testi-
monial, signed by nearly all prominent Catholic trade unionists,
requesting the hierarchy to draw up an official "Catholic policy"
toward the labor movement. By the end of World War I the
hierarchy was ready to take this step. Early in 1919 the Administrative Committee of the National Catholic War Council (the
immediate precursor of the present National Catholic Welfare
Conference) issued the Bishop's Program of Social Reconstruction which listed and defended a dozen far-reaching proposals for
the reform, not the overthrow, of the existing order. The Program

32 Mary Harrita Fox, *op. cit.*

called for social insurance against unemployment, sickness, invalidism and old age; a Federal child labor law; the legal enforcement of labor's right to organize; public housing for the working classes; progressive taxation of inheritances, income and excess profits; stringent regulation of public utility rates; government competition with monopolies if necessary to secure effective control; worker participation in management; and cooperative productive societies and co-partnership arrangements in order to enable the majority of wage earners to "become owners, at least in part, of the instruments of production." All but the last of these proposed remedies were in some measure applied during the New Deal era of the 1930's.

The Bishops' Program of Social Reconstruction was obviously intended to promote the great ends of social justice.[33] The extensive programs of civic education and social service for immigrants launched by the National Catholic War Council and its peace-time successor professed the same objectives. "We hold," leaders emphasized, "that no plan short of complete social justice should be held as a goal in programs of good citizenship or Americanization." The men responsible for the Bishops' Program argued also that "the only safeguard of peace is social justice and a contented people"—a theory that was to be thoroughly explored by the Catholic Association for International Peace formed in 1927 by persons vitally interested in the Catholic social movement as well as in a juridically directed system of world organization.

More extensive and spectacular were the Protestant efforts in behalf of world peace. Shortly after the outbreak of World War I, a few British and American Churchmen meeting in London founded the World Alliance for International Friendship Through the Churches; out of this group grew the powerful Ecumenical movement within the non-Roman Catholic Christian Churches. Understanding and community of spirit, though not organic unity, were promoted through successive worldwide conferences on Life and Work or on Faith and Order, beginning

33 For later-day Catholicism, see Ellis, *American Catholicism*, pp. 122–159; Mc-Avoy, "The Catholic Church in the United States," in Waldemar Gurian and M. A. Fitzsimons, editors, *The Catholic Church in World Affairs* (Notre Dame, 1954), pp. 358–376; and Abell, The Catholic Church and the American Social Question,"*ibid.*, esp. pp. 384–399.

at Geneva in 1920 and culminating at Amsterdam in 1948 in the founding of the World Council of Churches.[34]

Although Ecumenicity laid foundations on which to erect a world peace structure, many of the men and women associated with the movement, especially in America, were uncompromising pacifists, opposed to all war as sinful, even if employed as a world police force. Relying on moral suasion alone, unaware of the need for a juridically-based international order, the pacifists powerfully reinforced all types of isolationism whether Protestant, Catholic, Jewish, or secularist.[35] Only with the coming of World War II did Protestants as a group urge the creation of a world security organization. Working under the authority of the Federal Council and led by John Foster Dulles, several hundred representative Protestants meeting at Delaware, Ohio, early in 1942 repudiated isolationism and recommended international cooperation along the lines of racial and social justice. The ultimate goal should be, they thought, "a duly constituted world government of delegated powers," with legislative, judicial and administrative agencies, "and adequate international police forces and provision for enforcing its worldwide economic authority." [36]

Inasmuch as similar views were vigorously defended by Pope Pius XII, isolationist sentiment among American Catholics noticeably softened. Partly because some dictatorial regimes, notably in Spain, favored their Church, many Catholics in this country were only mildly interested in proposals for world government. The problem was viewed in a different light by American Jews whose brethren were persecuted in many parts of the world and singled out for extermination in Hitlerian lands. These distressing trends could be reversed only through international action, an essential phase of which were the Zionist plans for a Jewish

34 Paul A. Carter, *The Decline and Revival of the Social Gospel: Social and Political Liberalism in American Protestant Churches, 1920–1940* (Ithaca, 1954), pp. 99–121, 183–200.

35 Devere Allen, *The Fight for Peace* (New York, 1930), pp. 51–54: Justin Wroe Nixon, *Protestantism's Hour of Decision* (Chicago, 1940), pp. 104–116; John A. Ryan, *Social Doctrine in Action: A Personal History* (New York, 1941), pp. 211–217.

36 "The Churches and a Just and Durable Peace," *Christian Century*, LIX (March 25, 1942), 390–397; "Protestants on Peace," *Newsweek*, XIX (March 16, 1942), 69; American Malvern," *Time*, XXXIX (March 16, 1942), 44–48. See also A. I. Abell, "La Situation Religieuse," in Yves Simon, with collaborators, *La Civilisation Americaine* (Paris, 1950), esp. pp. 231–236.

home in Palestine. With some notable exceptions, American Jewish leaders from every theological camp now embraced Zionism which formerly had been a religiously central doctrine for the strictly Orthodox only. Symbolic of Zionist growth was the changing attitude of Reform Judaism. After having repeatedly insisted that Judaism was a universal religion and not a rites-observing state or nation, Reform Jews in the late 1930's voiced neutrality on the Zionist issue, spoke highly of Talmudic Law and urged that some of it be observed in homes and temples.[37] More perhaps than religious or Judaic considerations, racial, national, and cultural desires and needs motivated the movement which terminated in the establishment of Israel in the aftermath of World War II.

In a sense, American Zionism was an aspect of American "Jewishness," a term widely used by Jewish scholars to suggest the preoccupation of the Jewish community with non-religious interests. As the Jewish immigrants from Eastern Europe underwent Americanization, mainly in the second generation, they abandoned Orthodox Judaism. Some joined Reform temples; a much larger number affiliated with Conservative synagogues. In the Jewish Theological Seminary started in 1891, and the United Synagogue of America organized in 1913, the Conservative group found its chief instruments of vigorous growth. But Jews, for the most part, refused to participate in organized public worship. Instead, they channeled their energies into a myriad of educational, charitable and cultural agencies. Many Jewish workingmen found a substitute for temple or synagogue in labor unions, some of which, as in the clothing trades, they controlled.

Only in its obvious magnitude did the Jewish religious problem differ from the situation Christians faced. While over-all church membership increased in the period between the two world wars, the gains were feeble compared to the number of souls garnered in previous decades or in the years since 1945. Religion was clearly unable to discipline the greed and secularism engendered by industrialism, strident nationalism, and international anarchy. Few could now seriously maintain that the world was growing morally better, that contemporary society, impelled by

37 Glazer, *op. cit.*, pp. 103–104.

Christian ethics, was in process of becoming the Kingdom of God on earth—as the earlier advocates of the Social Gospel had confidently assumed. Deceived by the surface manifestations of benevolence and good-will in secular society, religion had failed to perceive that as men and institutions rise to power and gain prestige they tend to become ethically autonomous and to a large extent impervious to outside influences. When Christian leaders began to sense this source of religious ineffectiveness, they drew sharply, in good Augustinian fashion, the distinction between the "church" and the "world" and sought to disentangle Christianity from contemporary liberal society and culture. The Ecumenicists intoned the exhortation, "Let the Church be the Church," meaning that organized Christianity must be in itself a transformed and transforming society and cease relying on its uncertain ability to give secular social forces a Christian direction. In the words of the historian of the later social gospel:

> The Church's social destiny was not simply to recruit leaders for trade unions and peace societies. In such matters as race relations within the Church, and above all the development of the Church as an international fellowship, Christians could accomplish tremendous social reforms simply by laboring to hold the Church up to its own ideals. To preach a sermon on race relations was good; to throw down the barriers between white and Negro at the communion was far better.[38]

This changing trend in Protestant effort was personally reinforced by the Reverend Reinhold Niebuhr, the most influential contemporary theologian among religious intellectuals.[39] Leaving a Detroit pastorate to become professor of applied Christianity in Union Theological Seminary, Niebuhr in a steady outpour of brilliantly written books and journalistic pieces expounded a theology which was neither Fundamentalist nor Modernist but "realist" or "neo-orthodox"—in essence an adaptation to American conditions of the crisis theology of Karl Barth, H. E. Brunner, and other Continental theologians. Early in his career an active pacifist and socialist, a self-styled Christian Marxist and open sympathizer with the aims of the Soviet Union, he urged

38 Carter, *op. cit.*, p. 120.
39 D. R. Davies, *Reinhold Niebuhr: Prophet from America* (New York, 1948); Hans Hofman, *The Theology of Reinhold Niebuhr* (New York, 1956); Holtan P. Odegard, *Sin and Science, Reinhold Niebuhr as Political Theologian* (Yellow Springs, Ohio, 1956).

Protestants to move theologically to the right while veering sociologically to the left. For Niebuhr was among the first to sense that, as men and institutions were prone to evil, cruelty and injustice inhered in the pacifist and socialist utopias no less than in capitalism and other current disorders. Niebuhr's thought and action persuaded many religiously inclined radicals to abandon revolutionary positions in favor of reform along New Deal lines as the only feasible program under existing circumstances. In the crisis of World War II he presided over the Union for Democratic Action, a group urging additional reform measures while vigorously combating totalitarian elements on both the right and the left. He was only less active in the Union's successor after the War, Americans for Democratic Action. He devoted his major energies, however, to creating "a means of expressing the whole of the traditional creed, from the Fall of Man to the Last Judgment, in a form that could not be dismissed as intellectually outdated." [40]

Protestant Christians under Niebuhr's influence well knew that religion should not be identified or too closely associated with secular programs, however good their professed intentions. This was essentially the attitude also of the Catholic leadership which in the period between the two wars stressed social justice, making use mainly of the social action department of the National Catholic Welfare Conference. Before as well as after the Great Depression, the department conducted a ceaseless propaganda for the Bishops' program of Social Reconstruction and other formulations of Catholic social doctrine. During the 1930's the crusade enlisted considerable lay support: from many of the followers of radio priest Charles E. Coughlin, more consistently from the Catholic League for Social Justice organized and directed by industrialist Michael O'Shaughnessy, and from the Catholic Worker group, which, with its houses of hospitality, gave a new slant and renewed vigor to the social settlement movement.[41] Most Catholics—some for religious, other for political reasons—supported the New Deal and the enlarging union labor movement.

But Catholic thinkers did not see in unionism and protective

40 Carter, *op. cit.*, p. 230.
41 A. I. Abell, "The Catholic Factor in the Social Justice Movement," in Notre Dame Symposium on Catholicism and the American Way of Life, 1957.

legislation the end-all of social reform, only the foundation on which to erect a modern guild system. As urged in 1931 by Pope Pius XI in the encyclical *Quadragesimo Anno* on the reconstruction of the social order, the direction of economic life should be assigned to occupational groups, "in a true sense autonomous," self-governing bodies, with power under government supervision to set prices, determine wage scales, and in general to control and regulate industrial conditions. United in the vocational group, employers and employees would forego class conflict and "join forces to produce goods and give service," thereby promoting social justice and the common good. Although neither employers nor employees favored the plan and the public generally confused it with Fascism, Catholic proponents of social justice sought steadily to steer current developments toward the eventual realization of a guild order. In this context was formed in 1937 the Association of Catholic Trade Unionists which participated in union organizational drives and fought Communism and racketeering in the labor movement in a manner reminiscent of Father Dietz's Militia of Christ a quarter-century earlier. More important, no doubt, were the Catholic labor schools, nearly a hundred by mid-century.

By this date, religious groups had shifted attention from social reform to education. The phenomenal increase in the birth rate after 1940 placed an almost unbearable burden on the nation's schools, public and private. Catholic parochial schools, which enrolled about half the Catholic population of school age, had always contended that the state should compensate them for the secular instruction they provided.[42] After 1930 these and other private schools received in several states various auxiliary aids such as bus service, lunch subsidies, and textbooks in secular subjects. In the allocation of funds for educational purposes the National Youth Administration and the GI Bill of Rights did not discriminate against students attending privately controlled institutions. But bills authorizing Federal aid to elementary and secondary schools on the same non-discriminatory basis failed to muster the necessary Congressional support.[43] Catholics re-

---

42 Richard J. Gabel, *Public Funds for Church and Private Schools* (Washington, 1937).
43 William A. Mitchell, "Religion and Federal Aid to Education," *Law and Contemporary Problems*, XIV (1949), 113–143.

taliated, helping to block passage of bills extending aid to public schools only.

Increasingly, the major faiths have cooperated to teach religion alongside the public schools in which are enrolled the vast majority of the nation's children. Beginning at Gary, Indiana, in 1914, arrangements were made whereby school authorities allotted time, generally a class period a week, for religious instruction. Only pupils whose parents granted permission in writing were "released" to the religious classes which were conducted in the school building or in some neighboring edifice by teachers selected and recompensed by the participating religious bodies. The plan spread rapidly after World War I, partly as a result of propaganda in its behalf by the International Committee for Religious Instruction which was formed in the early 1920's. As mid-century neared, nearly two million children, in more than a thousand communities, were attending religious classes under the plan. In released time the great faiths found a fairly satisfactory method of supplementing the work of their Sunday, Sabbath, and parochial schools.

Not all Americans approved public support of religious education; many in fact viewed with indignation the suggestion that the state by subsidy or otherwise should help the churches perform their educational function. They feared that public aid would breach the "wall" separating church and state and impair the guarantees of religious freedom as laid down in the First Amendment and enforced upon the various States through judicial applications of the Fourteenth.[44] These apprehensions have been powerfully portrayed by Protestants and Other Americans United for Separation of Church and State, an organization formed early in 1948 mainly to oppose plans to extend State and Federal aid to Catholic educational institutions. The religious education issue has been almost constantly before the courts in recent years. In *Everson v. Board of Education,* a New Jersey bus case decision, handed down in 1947, the United States Supreme Court insisted in the strongest terms that the wall separating church and state should remain unbreached, but denied by a 5–4 vote that the New Jersey statute reimbursing

44 Milton R. Konvitz, "Separation of Church and States: The First Freedom," *ibid.,* 44–60.

parents for bus fare of their children to and from private schools breached the wall. The law in Justice Black's majority opinion served a "public purpose" and did "no more than provide a general program to help parents get their children, regardless of their religion, safely and expeditiously to and from accredited schools." But the next year, in *McCullom v. Board of Education,* the Court, with only one Justice dissenting, ordered Champaign, Illinois, to discontinue its released time plan on the ground that it united church and state.

In defending its position, the Court noted that the Champaign plan used the "State's tax-supported public school buildings" for "the dissemination of religious doctrines" and helped sectarian groups "to provide pupils for their religious classes through use of the State compulsory public school machinery." [45] To many, in legal as well as in educational and religious circles, this reasoning was unconvincing.[46] While some school systems immediately dismantled their released time programs, others continued them in the expectation that the high Court would subsequently approve existing arrangements of a less ambitious and integral character than the Champaign plan. The desired result came in 1952 when in *Zorach v. Clauson* the Court approved released time as practiced in New York City where the religious instruction was given outside public school buildings. Speaking for the Court, Justice Douglas denied that the New York arrangement set up "an establishment of religion" or interfered with "the free exercise thereof." Concerning these prohibitions, the First Amendment required "complete and unequivocal" separation of church and state. But the First Amendment "does not say that in every and all respects there shall be separation of Church and State. Rather," Douglas explained, "it studiously defines the manner, the specific ways, in which there shall be no concert or union or dependency one on the other." Unless this "common sense of the matter" prevailed, "the state and religion would be aliens to each other—hostile, suspicious, and even unfriendly."

45 Quoted in Alpheus Thomas Mason and William M. Beaney, *American Constitutional Law* (New York, 1954), pp. 606–611.
46 Edward S. Corwin, "The Supreme Court as National School Board," *Law and Contemporary Problems,* XIV, 3–22; John Courtney Murray, "Law or Prepossessions," *ibid.,* 23–43; and more intemperately James M. O'Neill, *Religion and Education under the Constitution* (New York, 1949).

Justice Douglas elaborated the issues involved in the light of his felicitous sentence, "We are a religious people whose institutions presuppose a Supreme Being." The government could not finance religious groups, prefer one over another, or "force one or some religion on any person. But we find no constitutional requirement," he said, "which makes it necessary for government to be hostile to religion and to throw its weight against efforts to widen the effective scope of religious influence." The state followed "the best of our traditions" when it encouraged religious instruction "by adjusting the schedule of public events to sectarian needs. . . ." [47]

Released time was not the only means of utilizing the public schools for religious ends. School and church authorities in growing numbers believed that religion as fact and influence should be given its due place in the public school curriculum and be taught objectively by competent teachers like any other subject. This procedure aims not at religious commitment but at religious knowledge. The possibilities of objective religious instruction are being thoroughly explored by the American Council on Education whose special committees and study groups have published several reports, beginning in 1947 with the highly significant title *The Relation of Religion to Public Education—The Basic Principles.* Convinced that the Judaeo-Christian tradition is a basic factor in American democracy, the Council views as "sheer madness" the failure to emphasize the fact in public education. [48]

The American Council on Education embarked upon this phase of educational work at the behest of the National Conference of Christians and Jews. Formed in 1928 by Charles Evans Hughes, Newton D. Baker, S. Parkes Cadman, Roger W. Straus and Carlton J. H. Hayes, to counteract the religious bigotry and rancor evoked by Catholic Alfred E. Smith's campaign for the Presidency, the Conference resolved to "promote justice, amity, understanding and cooperation among Protestants, Catholics and Jews, and to analyze, moderate, and finally eliminate intergroup prejudices which disfigure and distort religious, business, social and political relations with a view to the establishment of a social order in which the religious ideals of brotherhood and justice shall become the standards of human relationships." Millions of Americans learned of these purposes through speaking tours (ministers, priests, and rabbis appearing on the same platform), a religious news service, and yearly brotherhood-week programs, all dating from the early days of the organization. By the end of its first quarter-century, the Conference, working through some sixty regional offices and five commissions (educational, religious, community, labor-management, and mass communications) was an active influence in three thousand villages, towns and cities.[49]

The programs sponsored by the National Conference of Christians and Jews synchronized with the renewed emphasis on religious and cultural pluralism by which America, in the opinion of some acute observers, is being steadily transformed from a one-religion into a three-religion country—from a predominantly Protestant into a more or less equally Protestant, Catholic, and Jewish country.[50] The conviction that these faiths equally serve to identify their adherents with democracy and the American way of life is stronger among the youth of the land than among older folks who continue to put a high value on sectarian rivalry and prestige. Tensions, even passions, have been generated by some issues, notably President Truman's proposal to enter into diplomatic relations with the Vatican. The current religious revival tends to accentuate tensions in that each religious body is apprehensive about the future, fearing that it may not be able to retain its relative position in the struggle for souls.[51]

In some degree, however, tension and conflict truly mirror the American religious scene. In the land preeminently of religious freedom, if not of "free religion," many divergent paths are trod in man's search for God. The religious nonconformist, be he prophet or heretic, has always been able to recruit a following— as if this was the most natural way to gain spiritual enrichment. It is this attitude which encourages the multiplicity of religious

49 Carlton J. H. Hayes, "A Symbol—And a Promise," Nat. Conf. of Christians and Jews, *Building for Brotherhood* (New York, 1956), pp. 1–6; Nat. Conf. of Christians and Jews, *How the National Conference of Christians and Jews Strengthens. . . .* (New York, 1956).

50 Will Herberg, *op. cit.* and his *Protestant-Catholic-Jew: An Essay in American Religious Sociology* (New York, 1955).

51 See "Religious Conflict in the United States," *Journal of Social Issues*, XII (1956), 3–66, for a keen analysis by six experts.

bodies in America. Aside from the need to objectify theocratic and faith-healing beliefs (as in the Church of Christ Scientist), sect-making in America aims mainly at the renewal of old faiths: as once-vital churches grow cold and formal new ones are formed to reproduce the old life and fervor.[52] But religious individualism has not obscured the social vision of the many churches. Most of them have made a continuing contribution to education on all levels, to understanding among the diverse racial and immigrant strains in the population, and to social service and social reform. Undeniably, religion in America has strengthened the foundations of democracy and measurably advanced, often in a pioneering manner, the great cause of reform, both personal and social.

[52] Charles Samuel Braden, *These Also Believe* (New York, 1949); Elmer T. Clark, *The Small Sects in America* (New York, 1949).

chapter **XIII**

American Civilization: the Universal and the Unique

M. A. Fitzsimons
University of Notre Dame

THE QUESTION "What does America stand for?" ultimately asks "What is American Civilization?" Americans have usually replied with a confidence and optimism that did not wholly mask uneasiness. In the American Republic's early days its citizens felt an urgent necessity to identify their new nation in the international community. A later history of uprooting and rapid change kept the sense of newness and the question of identity alive and quick.

Today, this almost perennial question is asked more demandingly and, oddly enough, Americans have raised it for others to answer. This anxiety and doubt arise from the recent experiences of the United States in international affairs. We see that a large part of the world is in ferment, fusing in nationalist movements aspirations for self-government and ambitions for the fruits and tools of Western industrialism and science. We know that in providing a model we have been an important cause of this global restlessness. As a result we have been concerned with the means and ways of helping other nations from our spiritual and material resources.

Anxiety and doubt are sometimes compounded when we recognize that we are engaged in a world struggle with the Soviet Union, a regime which offers a simple explanation of history, a philosophy, and a program of promises expediently adapted to the demands of the people of the world.

Those who in response to this challenge call for or propound an all-embracing "American ideology for our side" are untrue to our greatest traditions as well as to the pluralism of contemporary America. Our inability to blueprint humanity's future does not stem primarily from our differences but from our respect for the dignity of man and his political communities. Human dignity and freedom are inseparable, and in affirming them we directly meet their difficult consequences. These are that we cannot manufacture a simple global faith to rival communism and that we must soberly remind the restless people of the world that ultimately each nation makes itself to its own flourishing or undoing. This may be lukewarm or even cold comfort to the ardent nationalism which mingles beyond all capacity for distinction demands for independence with desires to compress decades and centuries of economic change into a single generation. But we are not limited to sober words of caution. The American outlook is quick, indeed over-quick, to favor independence movements and envisages a great body of independent nations, each largely responsible for its own affairs. Within this great republic of the world it is prepared for a generous sharing of experience and skills.

What, then, is American civilization? What are its unique elements, its general elements and its points of universal significance?

American civilization has developed from the responses of European colonists and immigrants to the unique opportunities of a sparsely settled continent. The mainly English founders of our first settlements came from a Europe which had experienced the Renaissance, an important source of our optimistic humanism, and the Reformation, the source of the pervasive Protestanism of our society, its secular dynamism, and its religious diversity. From the beginning there was pluralism rather than unity and many of the settlers, especially in New England, came from English and European religious minorities. As a rule, except perhaps in Virginia, the elements of European culture were reproduced here in different proportions from Europe. Colonial New England was culturally more akin to Cromwellian England than to Laud's or Walpole's England. The new American combinations developed in special ways in the New World. When the American colonies and Britain quarrelled over conflicting interests, a conflict sharpened by the clamorous demands of the American back-country, the colonists based their Declaration of

Independence from Britain on a universal statement, the rights of all men.

This eloquent apology for a revolution is the foundation document of our political belief. And the liveliness of this belief, supported by the apparently endless opportunities of the American continent, has been proof against the regular and often disturbing discovery that these simple statements of the natural law tradition are never assured social realities but are aspirations which present challenges to every generation.

The American experience has been expressed in a social faith, and this faith, historically of Protestant origin, has generally been limited enough not to become a substitute religion and yet broad enough to allow Jew, Protestant, and Catholic to share it and to acquire a very pronounced American character. This social faith, "the substance of things hoped for," is the central force of American civilization.

American civilization, then, is not something already wrought out and achieved—it is something aspired to, the promise of American life.

> Such as we were we gave ourselves outright.
> (The deed of gift was many deeds of war).
> To the land vaguely realizing westward,
> But still unstoried, artless, unenhanced,
> Such as she was, such as she would become.[1]

America may be the land of our fathers, but far more is it the land of our children. The promise has its vague features, even though it has been spelled out with drab literalness in a multitude of utopias. The content of demands based on man's unalienable rights have differed with the years. At one time it involved a vision of a simple agrarian democracy, at another it evoked the ardor of those who sought the Kingdom of God on earth. The human and especially the American imagination is earthbound and only too often in aspiring to familiarity uses material images. Thus, the American future is too often presented in materalistic terms of comforts and horsepower abounding. But adversity on occasion helps to sketch the vision more sharply. Thus, at the Populist Party convention in October, 1892, the

1 Robert Frost, "The Gift Outright."

farmers, aroused by their sufferings from railroads, trusts, commission merchants, and banks, echoed the words of the Southern Populist, Tom Watson. Monopoly was the enemy: "Monopoly of power, of place, of privilege, of wealth, of progress." "Keep the avenues of honor free. Close no entrance to the poorest, the weakest, the humblest." "Recreate an America that said to ambition: 'The field is clear, the contest fair, come, and win your share if you can.'" [2]

These words make clear that the American hope for the future does not mean economic levelling. Moreover, the dream is constantly belied. At times, the frustration derives from political and economic arrangements, and becomes the basis for an agrarian crusade or a New Deal. The dream of a progressively better future cannot be the pattern for all families, particularly those born to wealth. But the hope and faith persist, and the public expression of doubt about the continued validity of the dream is a quite efficient way to commit political suicide. This is not the naive optimism with which some European critics have charged us. As faith in the future, it is as much a striving and dutiful hopefulness as it is a matter of temperament. Arnold Toynbee has suggested that those who came to America often thought they had sloughed off the burdens of Original Sin as well as of the Old World by their migration. This would have been startling news to the seventeenth century puritans, to John Adams and the authors of *The Federalist*—and still seems perverse to the numerous American Christians whose religion goes beyond emotionalism to include theology.

When an American says that man and society can be made better, he may intend to indicate many things, from a simple reform position to a genuine belief in perfectibility. But he is likely to act in support of his belief. The habit began early and with a puritan conscience. An open continent and, later, an expanding economy, have strengthened the habit.

Elsewhere, except in Canada and Africa, populous societies or people of advanced culture confronted an expanding Europe. This expansion of Europe, which marks America's beginning, is also

2 Quoted in Eric F. Goldman, *Rendezvous with Destiny* (New York, 1956), p. 42. Watson expresses American contradictions and the American ordeal very well, for the man who in the quotation above spoke so universally, also, proved to be severely anti-Negro and anti-Catholic.

the beginning of the modern age, that is, the creation of the modern world community through the dominance of Europe in the world, once so securely supported by European science and industry. This dominance is over and in the crisis that attends the passing of the European and modern age, the United States, the formidable offspring of Europe and the New World, finds itself torn between its ties with Europe and the sympathies promoted by its universal political affirmations.

America was a New World to Europe but it had its inhabitants, the Indians. As a rule, they were provided for so casually and dealt with so fiercely that in this encounter we cannot escape a verdict of ruthlessness. Colonial American Protestants were not much concerned with the Christianization of the Indian. But the ruthlessness derived even more from their land hunger. The land hunger possessed Europeans and Englishmen, but America imposed few of the restraints within which Europeans lived. The colonists acted as though

> The World was all before them, where to choose
> Their place of rest, and Providence their guide.

How many times, I wonder, did early Americans see themselves in this passage from *Genesis:*

"Now the Lord had said unto Abram, Get thee out of thy country, and from thy kindred, and from thy father's house, unto a land that I will show thee: And I will make of thee a great nation, and I will bless thee, and make thy name great; and thou shalt be a blessing." [3]

It was a new world, where men thought that they could start anew. Here men could even act out the social contract in the Mayflower Compact, thus making a historical reality of a European theory. Historical developments—for example, the transformation of New England theology into a more secular and optimistic creed, paralleled the opportunities in fostering the vision of a better world. Ultimately, when American conditions were bad, as they frequently were, perhaps the most severe criticism was expressed in the charge that the United States was reproducing the inequalities and injustices of the Old World.

Only Canada, Australia, and New Zealand have had a compar-

3 King James Version, 12, 1–2.

able opportunity. The American continent provided something unique, and this uniqueness suggests the greatest caution in offering the American experience as a model for other nations. This experience has wearied, exhausted, and inspired generations of men, who in the intensity of their domestic preoccupations have professed political principles for all men but given little thought to the world impact of those principles. The material abundance, which rewarded the labors of those who professed these principles, gave the American way of life an attractive force that has disturbed the whole world. But this abundance has been maintained by a continuous uprooting of the American people, by a disruption of the settlement, accumulation, and continuity that in the past has fostered culture, and finally by the general acceptance of the immediately convenient and the standardized.

Each of these four points requires considerable elaboration.

The first, the contrast between American political universalism and American preoccupation with domestic tasks, appears with the independence of the Colonies. To this day the American is overwhelmingly inclined to devote himself to his pursuits in society and society is the great overlord of the state and the person.

In becoming an independent nation the American people preferred to withdraw into the gigantic tasks of their domestic life. But the American Revolution and the new American nation, though turned in upon itself, had a remarkable effect on world history. The American War for Independence was won in the course of fighting that raged around the globe. The spectacle of a new nation coming into political existence stirred the nationalist sentiments of a number of European people, notably the French, Irish, and Poles, and heralded the age of national revolutions, which has not yet ended in Asia and Africa.

This anti-imperialist struggle is the foundation legend of the American people, and it explains their general readiness to respond sympathetically to the struggles of other people which are presented as risings against imperial powers. Indeed, the very demands of justifying the Declaration of Independence have caused Americans to underrate their long colonial training in governing themselves, a source of the political wisdom of the Constitution and *The Federalist*.

Such an unhistorical approach, which readily becomes a kind

of cosmic Jacksonianism, suggesting that people can begin at once to govern themselves, is greatly strengthened by the terms in which the Americans proclaimed their independence to the world.

These terms were universal. Thus, we have one of the major paradoxes of American history—the establishment of a nation, largely preoccupied with its own affairs, on the basis of principles which are stated to be universal.

"We hold these truths to be self-evident; that all men are created equal, that they are endowed by their Creator with certain unalienable rights, that among these are life, liberty and the pursuit of happiness."

This Declaration explicitly mentions all men, even though some of its authors were slaveowners. Their affirmations would eventually be upheld in a Civil War, only to raise other problems that are with us yet. The generations of immigrants claimed the rights, only to find that the pursuit of happiness often meant back-breaking labors, a pursuit which seemed without end. Willa Cather wrote: "A pioneer should have imagination, should be able to enjoy the idea of things more than the things themselves." [4]

The American political tradition, then, consists of the affirmations of principles and the giving of example—a kind of preaching universalism. This tradition and American isolation help to explain the moralizing strain which is so prominent in American statements on foreign policy, and the legalistic strain is partly explicable in terms of our experience under the Constitution.

This paradox was frequently expressed in claims about the historic mission of the United States. Lincoln said in 1858: "Our defense is in the preservation of the spirit which prizes liberty as the heritage of all men, in all lands everywhere. Destroy this spirit and you have planted the seeds of despotism around your doors." In his eulogy of Henry Clay Lincoln said that the Whig politician loved his country, because it was his own, but mostly because he saw in the advancement of a free country "the advancement . . . and glory of human liberty, human right, and human nature." [5]

The introversion and sense of uniqueness often took a more

4 Willa Cather, *O Pioneers!* (New York: Houghton Mifflin, 1948), p. 59.
5 Bosler (ed.), *Collected Works of Abraham Lincoln* (Rutgers, 1953), II, p. 126.

arrogant form. In 1850 Governor B. Gratz Brown of Missouri reached this height, which did not long remain a record. "With the past we have literally nothing to do, save to dream of it. Its lessons are lost and its tongue is silent. We are ourselves at the head and front of all political experience—precedents have lost their virtue and all their authority is gone . . . experience . . . can profit us only to guard from antiquated delusions."

This sense of uniqueness, however, is usually coupled with a universal vision. "We are the mediating nation of the World," said Woodrow Wilson; "we are compounded of the nations of the world; we mediate their blood, we mediate their traditions, we mediate their sentiments, their tastes,—their passions; we are ourselves compounded of those things. We are, therefore, able to understand all nations." [6]

The sense of uniqueness and concern about our identity were supported by the constant uprooting of people and undermining of regional ways of life that accompanied the rapid settlement of a continent. This, my second point, wrought an obliteration of history and the sense of continuity. In the promise of American life each person should have his opportunities. But this was made possible only by the dynamism that so frequently meant a starting from scratch or near it. The process was marked by a terrible wastefulness of soil, resources, and men. In Willa Cather's *O Pioneers!*, Mrs. Bergson objected: "I don't want to move again, out to some raw place, maybe, where we'd be worse off than we are here, and all to do over again." [7]

Our historical memories grope through few monuments marking the handwork of the early settlers, the revolutionary leaders, and founding fathers. The vast transformations of a continent, later more rapidly transformed by industry and the automobile, require a great effort of the imagination to picture the early scenes as vibrant with a life different from but related to our own. Henry James noted: "History, as yet, has left in the United States but so thin and impalpable a deposit that we very soon touch the hard substratum of nature." This absence of a sure historical sense of continuity has contributed to American self-consciousness. Critical visitors to the new republic abounded, and Amer-

6 August Heckscher (ed.), *The Politics of Woodrow Wilson* (New York, 1956), p. 251.
7 Cather, *op. cit.*, p. 59.

icans eagerly persisted in inquiring about the foreigners' judgments. Henry James thought that his countrymen's excessive self-consciousness was explained by their awareness that "the experimental element" had not "dropped out of their great political undertaking." [8] For "experimental" we may substitute "the promise of American life."

In our own land we have been *conquistadores* of the soil and its resources. Region after region advanced toward distinctive local cultures only to undergo challenges from new-settled areas or economic changes that in turn cut off the regional development. The very sweep of this movement, which so wholly changed the character of old towns and cities, created multitudes of new ones, and ruthlessly proliferated ghost towns as well as boom towns, reveals American dynamism at its purest, and this process meant the constant uprooting of people.

No one has adequately described the massive uprooting of people which industrial changes caused in Europe. These changes met fewer obstacles and inhibitions in the United States. The promise of American life was the sustaining faith but many Americans found the process of change painful and on occasion turned against the immigrant as the cause of change. Actually, American and immigrant were suffering the same ordeal. These nativist movements sought to limit the numbers and influence of the newcomers. But, as a rule, they met with little success, because it was impossible to formulate a narrow and acceptable definition of Americanism.

The United States, then, shared most intimately in another European experience, the nineteenth and twentieth centuries wandering of people. Between 1820 and 1930, 38,000,000 people migrated to the United States, about sixty per cent of the European movement. [9]

The immigrant often enough found himself lonely, poor, and toil-weary. For a time he might be very conscious of his foreign background and inevitably assertive of it, at least in congenial circles. Rarely, however, did he know much about the history of his native country and his new nationalism was usually rather romantic and fantastic.

But even the national societies founded by the foreign-born

8 Henry James, *Hawthorne* (New York, 1880), pp. 12, 148.
9 D. F. Bowers, *Foreign Influence in American Life* (Princeton, 1944), p. 3.

became a regular part of the American scene and a force in politics. Even where the societies may not have been concerned with politics, they were sought out by politicians, for the immigrant could vote. Thus the observation of the eighteenth century French-American, de Crevecoeur was confirmed: "We know, properly speaking, no stranger. This is every person's country." And Walt Whitman in his preface to *Leaves of Grass* wrote: "The American poets are to enclose old and new, for America is the race of races."

The immigrants Americanized rapidly. Their children or grandchildren found that they were Americans and, unfortunately, lost their forebears' language. The process of Americanization went on in schools, churches, mills, labor gangs, and shops. In all this there was considerable social pressure, but the greatest pressure of all came from the opportunity of becoming an American. Where other countries put obstacles in the way of naturalization, the United States made it easy—and there was the constant pressure of neighbors puzzled at any failure to seize the opportunity.

The immigrant was Americanized by being drawn into the swirling life of the country and the process was so efficient because it was not planned and deliberate. Thus the United States became composed of a great variety of racial stocks. Sentimental and affectionate ties were maintained with the homeland—but, as has already been suggested, this did not mean that the new Americans were familiar with the ways of Europe. In accepting America as the land of opportunity, the new Americans took over the American image of Europe as a land of ancient burdens and venerable inequities. They became Americans by choice and in becoming Americans they also compounded American pluralism.

No modern state, even such spacious countries as Canada, Brazil, and Australia, has admitted immigrants so freely as the United States did until the period after the First World War. The wide-open American door has been almost closed, and under conditions that have been not at all generous. Here nativist suspicions played their part. But the growing concern for economic and social security, far more than questions of political security, was bound to raise barriers against unrestricted immigration.

Uprooting, of course, means mobility and the rapid growth which creates opportunities exacts mobility and dislocation as its price. Transportation has been almost an obsession with Americans. Indeed, in its early days the American Republic's survival appeared to depend upon the establishment of a road and canal system. The Federal government subsidized road-building and, later, lavished public lands to secure the building of railroads. The concern for mobility persists and the young American is likely to regard the possession of a car as the seal of independent manhood.

In American business a young man may change his employment a number of times, and, if ambition has dictated the changes, a prospective employer welcomes the diversity of experience. In England a record of several employers is more likely to be considered as evidence of a restless and possibly undesirable character.

This mobility inclines Americans to look on things with the eyes of transients and to settle for the convenient and comfortable. Homes are bought on credit and often resold within two or three years. Now, while considerable care is taken of the homes, the thought that they may soon be sold inhibits individual and aesthetic developments. A house must be a recognizably standard one to attract purchasers and the writers of the mortgage.

So, the subject of uprooting and mobility has led to my third point, the general acceptance of the immediately convenient and the standardized, the uniform. This criticism has been made very frequently and without qualification or understanding. A nearly venerable tradition of commentary pictures our country as a society of mechanized humanity consisting of drab and uniform robots. The criticism has never had much effect on us because we know how much diversity it ignored.

There are three principal sources of the uniformity which characterizes much of our way of life. The first is the process of Americanization of the immigrant and the ceaseless process of uprooting which the American and the immigrant alike experienced. On both, the active demands of America's promise have imposed a certain common character, a concern with becoming rather than with being.

The second source has been the desire for material abundance and comforts. The search for quick returns drove farmers to the cultivation of one crop, tobacco, or cotton, or wheat. Apart from the early history of tobacco cultivation, these crops were destined for industrial Europe and there was little demand for special qualities and refinement. Later the industrial system developed the capacity for abundance and flourished in a growing continental market. Adam Smith wrote of the wonders to be achieved from the division of labor. In our country this division, which means standardization and interchangeable parts, was carried out most fully. There were few solid traditions of craftsmanship and craft privileges to delay the triumph of industrialism. Moreover, American industrialism was initially conceived as a national system and thus served a market that did not make demands for high quality.

Paradoxically, the abundant productive records of this national industrial system have helped to stir the world, and in the twentieth century American business has found a world market. Agriculture and shipping, which once worked for world markets and free trade, have now turned to protectionist policies and subsidies. But a number of American industrialists, while still directed to the domestic market as the major field, have become sensitive to the requirements of international trade, and are proponents of lower tariffs and reciprocity agreements.

The third source is the consideration of the same mass market applied to cultural matters—newspapers, entertainment, radio, and television. Here effectiveness in reaching the largest audience is so important because the problem of financial support nakedly stalks all these enterprises. Britain and other countries with more definite traditions of culture may establish state systems of broadcasting and of artistic patronage. Here, partly in consequence of American pluralism and partly out of mistrust of concentrated political power, the same policy has been unacceptable. As a result, these activities generally must be commercial. This is not wholly and, perhaps, not even primarily a regrettable situation. What is regrettable is that the concern to have the largest possible audience is often the occasion for seeking the lowest common denominator.

But there are various checks against making the common man too common and too uniform. Publishers and other businessmen have recognized that there are many markets to cultivate and that there is a willingness to support endeavors of high quality. Contributions from the radio audience help to support the Metropolitan Opera Company and the New York Philharmonic. Our tax laws give exemptions and encourage gifts to foundations and educational institutions, which, therefore, have a special opportunity and responsibility to put brakes on commercially reckless vulgarity and unnecessary uniformity.

Business has also learned more than a little to think of man in terms other than those of employee and purchaser, to consider purpose and community, and these developments have slowed down American dynamism.

Politics reveals American diversity very clearly. The politician seeks a position which may reconcile conflicting interests. But our federal system, the separation of powers, and majority rule, all encourage the expression of diverse interests. The failure of many critics of American uniformity to see this diversity, when we ourselves are so aware of the great differences even in the politics of such neighbor states as Indiana, Michigan and Ohio, may tempt us to dismiss their judgments as wholly uninformed.

There is a striking irony in the contrast between our suspicion of concentrated political and economic power and our acceptance of the pervasive influence of the mass media of entertainment and communications. Our history abounds in crusades against the use big business has made of its power, and big business, as a result, has developed in responsibility. Here again, business with its privilege of generous spending for advertising and consequently for sponsorship, has a responsibility. It is understandable that a highly competitive business should be concerned with programs calculated to reach wide audiences. Thus, a considerable responsibility falls on the relatively non-competitive businesses.

Mechanization and the acceptance of uniformity produce comforts and abundance but they involve perils to the person and spirit. The prevalence of uniformity in goods leads us to look for uniformity in people. The regularity of machines induces us to look for an extra-human regularity in people. In dealing with large numbers of men we are driven to mechanical classifications of them and we may yield to the temptation of thinking that people should conform to them, as though the classifications represented the true idea of man. Abundance of material things may also make men oblivious of the spirit.

In short, man can only be in precarious balance in this life. An inability to appreciate this is responsible for some of the manifestations of the life-adjustment program that has been so zealously adopted in our high schools. With some people life-adjustment seems to mean the promotion of self-contentment, the stern enemy of all ambition and the spirit. The success of these teachers is evidenced by large numbers of dutiful American young people who are prepared to be docile and unlively members of our society. These youth are quite content to be alike and can not even understand how wasteful and pointless it is for people to be so much alike. A generation of such finished clods would mean the total end of American dynamism. This came from a vibrant faith that drove men on to hardship and sacrifice. The faith presumed religion, and humanism and religion presuppose man, a spirit and person, not human material to be uniformly stamped.

The spirit cannot be measured but, if it is therefore ignored, it takes its own revenge in perverse and demonic ways. Man's unquiet heart, his spirit, makes him a pilgrim to eternal life. I have suggested that Americans tend to look on things with the eyes of transients, who seek more things. When this quest misleads them into forgetting the person and spirit, they are lost pilgrims who in aspiring to become have neglected to live.

The swirling American way of life is currently in a conspiracy against the solitude in which man may find himself, and, thus, learn to prize the parts of man's nature that may be sacrificed in the complete acceptance of abundance and uniformity.

American activism, moreover, has generally tended to oppose cultivation and refinement. In 1779 John Adams wrote of his impressions of Paris: "I cannot help suspecting that the more elegance, the less virtue, in all times and countries." [10] Adams may be considered a puritan but even Jefferson expressed American self-consciousness about art. Our third president said that he was an enthusiast and patron of the arts in order to further the fame and reputation of his countrymen.

10 Quoted by D. W. Brogan, *American Themes* (New York, 1948), p. 14.

This is the self-consciousness of people who, thinking in national terms, were less interested in the past than in the future. But the culture of the West is ours, and only the parochial outlook of nationalism causes us to neglect that heritage and some Europeans to think that it is their special achievement. The study of the cultural sources of the West is a necessary preliminary to discerning the spiritual dangers with which part of our civilization may threaten us. And this knowledge of our own spiritual resources is the only basis for responding meaningfully to the diverse cultural traditions of our world that meet today.

Here our universities have a great opportunity for the conservation and advancement of our society and civilization. The university may best serve society not by catering to all its technical and service demands but by helping the development of students as persons, as men discovering and unfolding their full capabilities, as spirits, as thinkers, as inquirers, as lovers of beauty.

The tradition of the liberal arts must be strengthened and vitalized, and this is a more urgent task than answering the demands for scientists and engineers. The universities will render their greatest service to our society by helping to educate a group of men whose outlook may permeate society and enable it to make our humanity the master of our power and dynamism.

This task is necessary for ourselves and the world because of our impact upon it. With cultivation we may learn to make distinctions, to accept uniformity where it serves us and, at the same time, to rejoice in the diversity of nature and people. We cannot deny our universal political affirmations, but we can learn that they are not only abstractions which can be universally, immediately, and mechanically applied. Are we, for example, promoting the rights of man to life, liberty and the pursuit of happiness, when we urge the transference of authority from a colonial government to a partly detribalized people, who will at once be ruled by an oligarchy?

Today, our universal affirmations and our industrially and scientifically produced abundance, the latter the result of a unique development, have contributed powerfully to the modern international crisis. People of diverse heritages seek to borrow Western science and industrialism. Our world has been brought together as in a community but a community without a moral consensus other than a fear of war and a desire for independence and economic improvement. The ultimate resolution of this crisis involving the meeting of several civilizations and many cultures attempting to share in some common political ideas and industrial and scientific techniques is surely a long way off.

But in this work we have certain advantages: our own experience as well as our few traditions may permit us to improvise imaginatively and creatively in an unprecedented situation. Our response to the needs of other people, shallow as it has sometimes been, should also help us. The pluralism of American society can also assist us, first in that we can draw on Jews, Protestants, Catholics, Negroes, Chinese, and Japanese—in short, on the diversity of American society, for special work, where their origins or understanding may serve, but, above all, in formulating the terms of the solution, which must be pluralist. Finally, American optimism chastened enough to have lost impatience will be the necessary sustainer of this long labor.

The promise of American life, our civilization, now confronts two almost contradictory demands. We must recognize the universal influence it has and maintain with flexibility and responsibility our universal affirmations. In the past many American spokesmen insisted, as Woodrow Wilson did, that "America must have this consciousness, that on all sides it touches elbows and touches hearts with all the nations of mankind." [11]

Here our dilemma is that America cannot become an empire, and yet cannot content itself with a preaching universalism, preoccupied with domestic affairs. The world's peace and future probably depend on our solution of the dilemma. We cannot escape the dilemma, because the very influence of Western ideas and techniques throughout the world today reveals a general sentiment in Asia and Africa that their traditional civilizations and cultures have failed or are inadequate.

This source of global restlessness makes the second demand upon our civilization all the more urgent. The demand is to strengthen our universalism with spiritual depth, and the richness and understanding of the human person. Here our experience suggests that rapid industrialization and transformation are paid for heavily in human cost. Indeed this caution clearly points to

11 Heckscher, *op. cit.*, p. 253.

the conclusion that the United States itself faces many of the problems of Western civilization, and some of those problems, materialism, mechanization, and mass culture, are now also world problems. But the world may learn from our optimism and the promise of American life that men often rise to their opportunities and in the common life inspired by this pursuit may create a new society as firm and as pluralist as our own.

The two demands made on us are heavy, and the voice of the European past may seem to suggest that, as only one can be fulfilled, a choice must be made. André Siegfried apparently believes this, for he considers American optimism to be the now near dead creed of Liberal Europe of one hundred years ago.[12] But he fails to see that we have lived and flourished by putting together what were thought to be conflicting—the Hamiltonian vision of society and the values of Jeffersonian individualism. What the past seems to suggest is a contradiction may not be so for the future. The recognition that heavy but not impossible demands are made of us should be assurance enough to draw from us the whole energies and resources of American society and American man. The task will be all the harder because the material abundance, the pace of change, and the complexity of American life are a constant temptation to superficiality. Moreover, those in American society who would so change it are weighted down and sometimes deterred by the obvious power of the social forces that must be redirected. The individual's relation to society has inevitably been the theme of much of American literature and thought. Awareness of that society's extraordinary power, in considerable measure undirected, is something new. But American man in each of their persons may hearten himself with the thought that the historian and sociologist are not likely to solve the problem of how social change occurs in any way that excludes the creative role of individuals.

12 André Siegfried, *Nations Have Souls*, (New York, 1952).